Mircea Eliade's Vision for a New Humanism

Mircea Eliade's
Vision for a
New Humanism

DAVID CAVE

New York   Oxford
OXFORD UNIVERSITY PRESS
1993

Oxford University Press

Oxford   New York   Toronto
Delhi   Bombay   Calcutta   Madras   Karachi
Kuala Lumpur   Singapore   Hong Kong   Tokyo
Nairobi   Dar es Salaam   Cape Town
Melbourne   Auckland   Madrid

and associated companies in
Berlin   Ibadan

Published by Oxford University Press, Inc.
200 Madison Avenue, New York, NY 10016

Oxford is a registered trademark of Oxford University Press

Library of Congress Cataloging-in-Publication Data
Cave, David.
Mircea Eliade's vision for a new humanism / David Cave.
p. cm.   Includes bibliographical references and index.
ISBN 0-19-507434-3
1. Eliade, Mircea, 1907–
2. Humanism—20th century,
3. Religion.
4. Man.   I. Title.
BL43.E4C38 1993
291'.092—dc20
91–39810

1 3 5 7 9 8 6 4 2

Printed in the United States of America
on acid-free paper

To Peggy,
faithful companion, wonderful friend,
and loving wife

PREFACE

I first became acquainted with Eliade through his autobiography. What amazed me was how driven he was in his need to create, which for him meant to write from the enormous range of his readings and his multiform experiences. Eliade wrote broadly. He had an obsessive need to create an oeuvre. From the journalistic and apologetic to the literary and the scholarly, Eliade wrote in all genres for all audiences.

Yet behind this body of work an interpretive schema and visionary impulse cohered, stabilized, and directed his life. Eliade interpreted his life, as he would all human life, as being mythological in structure. Humans undergo repeated initiations in the pursuit of meaning. This mythological thrust to human life interested me. But what interested me more was the nature of the vision and impulse that inspired and drove him as a humanist. This study is a prolegomenon to the visionary impulse behind Eliade's prolix life. It also looks at how Eliade foresaw this impulse for culture at large, the audience to whom Eliade ultimately directed his writings.

In helping me refine and sober my initial readings of Eliade and initiate me into the complexities and controversies surrounding him, I am grateful to a number of people. Now at Baylor University, John Jonsson encouraged me to consider researching the thought of Eliade. Glen Stassen and E. Glenn Hinson, at Southern Seminary, commented on the initial drafts of each chapter and on the final manuscript. At the University of Chicago, Jerald Brauer, Joseph Kitagawa, Wendy Doniger O'Flaherty, and Paul Wheatley provided helpful perspectives on the life and thought of Eliade. The late Ioan Culianu confirmed my research direction at a time when I needed it, read the entire manuscript, and encouraged its publication. I am grateful for what he did and am grieved that such an eminent scholar and warm human being should have been so tragically taken from us.

Special thanks goes to Lawrence Sullivan at Harvard University. From when he first instructed me when I was a visiting student at the University of Chicago to when he read the entire text, Sullivan's comments were indispensable for giving me and others confidence in the manuscript.

At Indiana University, Matei Calinescu taught me how to appreciate and read Eliade's fantastic literature. He also alerted me to upcoming and existing studies on Eliade.

Mac Linscott Ricketts, at Louisburg College, carefully read and edited the entire manuscript. He offered helpful suggestions and criticisms. When I wrote to him for information on Eliade's Romanian years, he promptly responded with valuable material.

To Ed Linenthal at the University of Wisconsin, Oshkosh, I owe a word of thanks. He urged me to follow through with my revisions and affirmed my labors when I was feeling guilty for giving too much attention to the book at the expense of other obligations. Also at Oshkosh, I am grateful to Betty Dickinson for helping me in the mechanics of computer operation and in the use of new software. Indeed, the entire Religious Studies department at Oshkosh was a timely support group during the year I taught there and went through the lonely ordeal of the work of writing and revising.

Lastly, but always firstly and faithfully, I am grateful to my wife, Peggy. She has put up with many sacrifices, always, though, with devoted patience and understanding. And to Jonathan, our two-year-old, I am also grateful. His presence reminds me of what is finally most important.

Fort Mitchell, Ky.   D.C.
April 1992

CONTENTS

Mircea Eliade's Vision for a New Humanism

1

Introduction

Despite the great number of works on the late historian of religion and writer Mircea Eliade, there is the need for another book. For no book that I have seen has adequately dealt with the visionary impulse behind the totality of Eliade's prolific and manifold life work, as both a scholar and writer. This visionary impulse I identify as his hope for a new humanism. Certainly many studies devoted to Eliade have scrutinized his theoretical assumptions, have dug for his elusive methodology, have highlighted his contributions to the already large corpus on myth and religious symbolism, explored the existential implications to his sacred/profane cosmology, and—perhaps most consistently—have responded to his interpretation of history. And to Eliade the writer of novels, short stories, and plays, the above themes and intentions have been equally applied as well. Literary critics have analyzed Eliade's style, content, plot and character development, use of genre and paralleled these to other writers. In short, Eliade has been approached from many directions.

Left to themselves, these studies hardly offer a cohesive picture of Eliade. Moreover, some of the criticisms brought against him are misaligned because they fail to take Eliade for what he was trying to do. So if we are to find any cohesion to this diversity and realign many of the criticisms, it is essential to position Eliade around that which motivated his life work: a hope for a new humanity. I do not claim this is his only impulse. But I do believe it is the most encompassing and persistent.

Not only is a book necessary to reposition Eliade, but there is also room for demonstrating the relevance of his thought and methodological orientation to issues circulating today in and outside the academy of religion. Certainly pluralism in all its varieties—religious, cultural and ethnic, socio-political, linguistic, disciplinary, methodological—with relativism and fragmentation as its side effects, is a stimulating, creative, yet often divisive problem in the academy and in popular culture. Canon formation, the reading and use of other

peoples' texts and myths—be it from feminists, deconstructionists, funda-
mentalists—the soundness of one methodology or assumption over another,
conversations (or lack of) between disparate fields, moral and cultural relativism, these and other dynamics interpenetrate the problematics of pluralism. To
the creative yet problematic opportunities of pluralism, Eliade has something
to say.

To another contemporary issue, Eliade's interpretation of symbols as tied to
cosmic structures and rhythms is appropriate to current and ongoing ecological
concerns. Less concerned with the physical threat to human surival, Eliade's
understanding of symbols addresses the importance of ecology as a paradigm
within which humans define themselves as human beings and orient their
existential sense of place. For, at least for the present, there is only one
habitable world, and all humans live on it, regardless of whether they consciously see it as having meaning for them or not. Ecology or landscape affects
our hermeneutics. There is the need, then, to take seriously a "hermeneutics
of landscape."[1]

Yet this "hermeneutics of landscape" is today less defined by the natural
world as by the modern city and the electronic world of communications and
its array of artifical images. However beneficial and destructive the modern
city and electronic communications are, it cannot be denied that humans rely
less on the natural landscape to interpret their place in the world and center
themselves accordingly. Today telecommunications trespass national, social,
geographic, and private boundaries with little obstruction. It nullifies the
influence of topography in the imagination's construction of meaning. The
artificialness and aerial travel of telecommunications simply bypasses the
earthly eccentricities of individual and changing topographies. The imagination is passively shaped by horizons beamed from afar. As such, world culture
is being homogenized at an alarming pace. All boundaries have become permeable. And all space is anyone's and everyone's space. As the Romanian
poet Andrei Codrescu has observed, "the inside is the outside and the outside
is the inside; the self is the other and the other is the self."[2] On the need for
establishing individual centers of meaning and of the influence of the natural
landscape in shaping the metaphysical and religious imagination, Eliade gives
much attention.

A study on Eliade is also appropriate for reevaluating his place in the history
of religions. It is no longer as easy to determine how important Eliade is to the
history of religions. During the sixties and seventies the history of religions
largely rotated around his insights, orientations, and terminology. Today, and
during the latter part of his career, his views have been less dominant and his
place has been less secure. Critical reconsiderations of his views, use of facts,
and suppositions have sobered many of the previously wholesale appropria-

tions of his ideas. There has also been mounting inquiry into his earlier right-wing political associations and espousals while in Romania during the 1930s. Combined, criticisms of his thought and investigations into his years in Romania have set Eliade out of the center to be one center among many or ignored altogether. As this study attests and proposes, Eliade cannot be so sidelined, nor should he be. In Romania, where for many years his works were kept from public distribution, there is an active promotion of the Eliadean corpus. Though not directly or solely attributable to Eliade, there are occuring in the history of religions and in the larger academy interdisciplinary discussions and collaborations, continued attention to myth and mythologies, applications of the history of religions to modern culture, and sharings between the scholarly and literary modes of inquiry. All these are practices and interests that Eliade never ceased to encourage and write about. Directly or indirectly, for good or for ill, the thought, work, and life of Eliade continue to be relevant and deserving of attention.

At this point I wish to say a few words regarding the increasing interest into Eliade's earlier ideological positions. Due in part to today's interest in uncovering the hidden or secret lives of public figures, being politically and ideologically correct, sensitive, and tolerant, and to the fact that theory cannot be divorced from biography and context, attention has been given to Eliade's right-wing positions, statements, and associations. Charges of anti-Semitism, anti-Judaism, and fascism have been made of him. But on what basis should we make inquiries into his past? Central to Eliade's own methodological position, and mentioned on many ocassions in his writings, is what Eliade spoke to as the futility of the search for origins, of what *actually* happened at the beginning. Origins are frequently impossible to trace, much less around which to find consensus. To the mythic mind, origins are of the realm of myth anyway. Despite Eliade's aversion to origins and his own taciturnity in filling in many of the details to his own life—even if he is one of the most self-documenting scholars of this century—it is fair to say, on the whole, that Eliade would think such inquiries were consistent with his own mode of interpretation. His hermeneutics built up erudition (the historical facts) and then, based on that erudition, interpreted the facts. So to reconstruct the Romanian context during the 1920s and the 1930s and Eliade's own place in it, can serve not only to understand Eliade the person and thinker, it can also be a fruitful sociological and historical enterprise and a contribution to the history of ideas. Nevertheless, insofar as a work, a person, a phenomenon, an idea is seen from only one angle of vision and not placed within the totality of its ouevre, life, context, and history, is it inappropriately understood. To cover over incriminating material or to focus solely on it is to give a partial and distorted representation of the subject. And to be content with one-sided representations encourages inaccurate appraisals and ill-used and ill-motivated scholarship.

With that being said, investigations into Eliade's past are needed, but under the motivation that they serve in furthering our understanding of the person and his ideas.[3] All facts should come into interpreting the whole Eliade. The historical facts need to be weighed against, and in dialogue with, the theoretical sides of the person, and vice versa. In my study I make no pretense of having settled the debate as to *how* right-wing Eliade was. That he was is uncontested. It is possible the debate will never be settled, for again one has the problem of origins and the obstacles to getting at the origins. I have had to rely on those who have given the time to studying Eliade's earlier life and so do not speak from the primary archival materials, which, in any regard, have only become fully accessible in the past few years. Even with what has come to light, there are strong discrepancies among those looking into Eliade's past. From what has appeard so far, Mac Linscott Rickett's two-volume *Mircea Eliade: Romanian Roots, 1907–1945*,[4] is the most comprehensive, detailed, and impartial source of documents I have found. I have greatly relied on this work for material on Eliade's Romanian years. Whatever its faults and limitations, it at least has tried to present in as raw form as possible (as much as edited and translated works can be) what Eliade wrote during his years in Romania. As other documents get exposure[5] and more come to light, there will then be new modifications or confirmations to the best interpretations that can now be made.

Biography of Eliade

To give a biographical overview is to reiterate Eliade's autobiography and journals and Rickett's *Romanian Roots*. Those wanting a full history should refer to these. Some of what is only minimally touched on in the biography below is referred to in greater detail in the following chapters. So only a cursory treatment will be given here of Eliade's life so as to orient readers unfamiliar with him. The biography is divided into four sections: Pre-India, 1907–28; India, 1928–31; Post-India, 1931–45; Exile, 1945 and onward.

Pre-India, 1907–28

Born in 1907 to Captain Gheorghe Eliade and Ioana Stoenesco, Eliade was a precocious and adventurous boy with a lively imagination. He became aware of his desire to be a writer early. In 1921 he published his first article, "The Enemy of the Silkworm," an entymological fantasy, in the science newspaper

Ziarul Ştiinţelor Populare (The Newspaper of Popular Sciences). In the same year, for a prize offered by the same periodical, he submitted his essay, ''How I Found the Philosopher's Stone,'' for which he won first prize. Regarded by a Romanian literary critic as a work evincing genius, the essay merged well Eliade's early interests of wedding science and fantasy with philosophy. From this period to the time when he graduated from lycée, he wrote profusely on a variety of subjects—zoology, entymology, alchemy, the history of religions, personal adventures, historical works, and biography—with the breadth of reading to match. His love for Romania and its language and culture were already quite pronounced; and writers such as Balzac, Dostoevsky, Papini, Hasedu, Iorga, and Voltaire were read with great interest and admired as much for their prolificness and encyclopedic knowledge as for what they wrote. In 1925, in an article discussing the Romanian archeologist and historian Vasile Parvan, we get a foreshadowing of Eliade's desire to decipher the creative impulse and meaning of historical facts. Says he:

> The historian ordinarily either lets himself be overwhelmed by the weight and number of events—and then he no longer sees reality; or else he plunges into the world of his imagination and creates explanations and arguments whose ideological value is completely alien to ours. But there are also historians who, in addition to assimilating facts, also understand the spirit of the era they are studying, the local color—and at the same time a marvelous intuition makes them capable of understanding the key to many events about which the documents say nothing.[6]

In 1925 Eliade graduated from lycée and enrolled in the literature and philosophy department of the University of Bucharest. His readings and writings would continue at the same alarming pace, obsessed as he was in his desire to learn, to swallow, and to synthesize almost everything that came his way. His voraciousness was motivated as much by an insecurity to prove himself to his teachers as by a desire to meet up to the destiny to which he was already sensing himself ''called.'' In the university he came to admire his long-to-be mentor, Nae Ionescu, from whom he would learn of the importance of structures, intuition, and broad experiences for understanding religious and historical phenomena. During his university years he also acquired an interest in the Anthroposophy of Rudolf Steiner for its combination of the spiritual and the logical in its approach to religious material. It was from Steiner that Eliade became exposed to Goethe and his morphology of plants. By this time Eliade had decided to become an historian of religions. He had read Raffaelle Pettazoni's *I Misteri*, which, Eliade would later remark, influenced him more than any other book into becoming an historian of religion.

In college Eliade wrote for the periodical *Cuvântul* (The Word), edited by

Ionescu. Eliade wrote literary criticism, travelogues, cultural and biographical pieces, and views on his own philosophy. His writings in the history of religions showed a distaste for reductionism and a desire for synthesis. He wrote on initiation, mystery religions, Buddhism, Taoism, the Oriental approach to science, the conflict between the flesh and the spirit in Christianity; and he accepted Vittorio Macchioro's thesis that religion is not a matter of knowledge but of experience. He would also praise the Italian church historian Ernesto Buonaiuti for being a historian who *knew* mystical experience.

Eliade was always a writer who wrote his ideas for the public. Between 1927 and 1928 he challenged the young generation to pursue creativity, asceticism, masculinity, virility, and authentic experience. He had no patience for sentimentalism and wasted energies. It was invested upon the generation growing up between the wars to shape Romania's future, and there was no time to waste. Eliade argued for a positive dillentantism of critical insights, of syntheses, and for a philosophy of history. As models, Eliade cited Montesquieu, Vico, Gobineau, Marx, Chamberlain, and Spengler, among others, as men who "have *seen* over and above matter, certain concepts: race, class, culture," calling the young generation to accept their method but not their vision.[7]

It was in 1927 that Eliade read the American historian of science George Sarton and his "new humanism," from whom Eliade would get the term for his own distinct usage. Eliade was impressed with Sarton's humanistic approach to science and history and with his humanistic ideals.

Once in 1927, and again in 1928, Eliade travelled to Italy to do research for his master's thesis on "Italian Philosophy from Marsilio Ficino to Giordano Bruno." It was while in Rome in 1928 that Eliade came across the name of Maharajah Manindra Chandra Nandy of Kassimbazar, former patron of the Indian philosopher Surendranath Dasgupta. Learning that Dasgupta had once been subsidized and that the Maharajah had promoted cultural and educational works, Eliade wrote to the Maharajah to secure a stipend to study in India with Dasgupta at the University of Calcutta. The stipend was granted and Eliade would leave for India in November 1928.

During this stage of Eliade's life Romania was in great political conflict. In 1907, the year of Eliade's birth, a massive peasant revolt claimed the lives of approximately eleven thousand. In 1916 Romania entered the war against Austria-Hungary, and between 1910 and 1921 a series of political parties arose, from the National Democratic Party in 1910, the Peasant Party in 1918, and the Romanian Communist Party in 1921. In 1920 the Democratic Party split with one branch founding the National Democratic Christian Party. And in 1919 we have the beginnings of the Legion of the Archangel Michael, officially founded in 1927. Political turbulences disassociating the peasant class from the bourgeoisie government, with parties preserving the divide and others attempting to lessen or overturn it, caused a highly ideologically volitile period to arise, into which many leading intellectuals of the day were drawn.

India, 1928–31

Arriving in India in December of 1928, after visting Egypt and Sri Lanka, Eliade embarked on an intense scholarly yet romantic plunge into the dizzing, tumultuous, and visceral world of India. He came to study first-hand the Oriental culture with which he was well familiar through books. He also came to make his own cultural creations, and, in his own way through authentic experiences, to seek the absolute.

Intellectually, India did not contribute any new theoretical perspectives from what he had already begun to seed and turn over in Romania. His ideas on the cosmicization of the individual, symbols, myth, and the irreducibility of religious experience were already grounded. India would simply deepen and fill out these persuasions with experiential and factual data. In line with other Romanians coming out of German traditionalism, Eliade paralled Goethe's own desire to go to India. Goethe wrote from Italy to Knebel in 1787:

> After what I have seen of plants and fishes in the region of Naples, in Sicily, I should be sorely tempted, if I were ten years younger, to make a journey to India—not for the purpose of discovering something new, but in order to view in my own way what has been discovered.[8]

Though no new theoretical orientations were added from his trip to India, Eliade, nevertheless, learned of the continuing viability of religious symbols. He became persuaded of their significance to the religious believer and to culture at large, even if they were only unconsciously understood and appropriated. India would also sober Eliade to his own personal limits and inadequacies as a European. He found that he was not called to the religious life nor could he be an Oriental. Moreover, India persuaded him of the relativities of the absolute and of the absolute's "presence" in history and through culture.

Eliade became proficient in Sanskrit and Indian philosophy and, among journalistic pieces sent back to Bucharest and a few articles on the history of religions, gathered material for his doctoral dissertation on yoga and Indian spirituality. From his articles, "Philology and Culture" (1929) and "Botanical Knowledge and Ancient India" (1931), we get articulations of Eliade's philosophy of history and his later, to be more elaborated, "creative hermeneutics."

As would be the case throughout Eliade's life, Eliade could not refrain from writing literature. In India he wrote *Isabel și Apele Diavolului* (Isabel and the

Devil's Waters), published in Bucharest in 1930. It received from the womens' literary society "Femina" the prize for the best novel of 1930, the first time a male author had ever won the award.

In India Eliade was exposed to the brutalities and oppression of British rule. Writing of a 1930 riot but published in 1932 after he had already left India, Eliade wrote, "Cracked skulls and fractured limbs—these can be seen in any country. But this was something else, something one can only see in British India: children trampled underfoot by horses, children bleeding from hooves and billy clubs."[9] In a 1977 interview Eliade said, "I became politically aware in India. . . . I was one hundred percent anti-British. The British repression of the *swaraj* militants infuriated me, disgusted me. . . . I was ashamed of my race."[10]

More research is needed of Eliade's Indian years, but there is no doubt that it left an indelible mark on him. He left India the more earnest in his cultural "mission" and persuaded of the viability of archaic and Oriental spirituality for the Western world.

In Romania during this time, the National Peasant Party had risen in power, floundered, brought back King Carol after he had been exiled by the Liberal Party in 1925, and was broken up by Carol himself in 1930 when he abolished all political parties. The loss of the peasants' political position gave new steam to the Legionary, headed by Corneliu Zelea Codreanu. Moreover, Nae Ionescu, shunned by the monarchy, now threw his support behind the Legionary, though never joining it as a member. Romania was internally polarized between the Romanian pesantry, making up 80 percent of the population, and the monarchy. It was into this scenario that Eliade returned.

Post-India, 1931–45

After a year of obligatory military service, Eliade went back to his unrelenting literary and scholarly productions. In 1933 he published *Maitreyi*, a novel based on his romance with Maitreyi, Dasgupta's daughter. The novel won Eliade a literary prize and brought him instant popular success. He completed his doctoral thesis, "The Psychology of Indian Meditation," in 1932, later published in French in 1936 and in English as *Yoga: Immortality and Freedom*, in 1954 and 1956 editions. At the University of Bucharest, Eliade was appointed assistant to Ionescu and lectured on Indian metaphysics. In 1934 he married Nina Mares. In 1937 he published "Cosmologie și Alchimie Babiloniană," an important work that carried forward his alchemical interests and expressed themes in the history of religions that would prevail throughout his later scholarly works. Eliade also founded *Zalmoxis: A Review of Religious Studies*, soliciting international contributions; it lasted for only three editions.

Between 1932 and 1933 he participated in the cultural symposium Criterion, an important forum in his mind for the type of collaborative effort needed for transforming Romanian culture.

Much outspoken during the 1930s, Eliade became the uncontested spokesperson for the young generation, evidenced especially in *Soliloquii* (1932), a series of articles expressing his personal philosophy for his generation. Eliade challenged them to make culture and to emphasize the primacy of the spiritual for creating a new Romania. Eliade's nationalism was especially strong. He denounced the Romanian government and called for the restoration of Romania's autochthonous roots at the level of government and higher culture. Though nationalistic and engaged in journalistic pieces, he remained conversant with the European and American intellectual currents of the day and he continued to write literature.

Eliade's latter years in Romania were especially tumultuous, consonant with the political polarizations and violence in the country. Democracy was foundering; social and economic inequalities prevailed; ultrarightist, communist, and democratic groups, and the monarchy vied for power; violent ethnic atrocities were committed; and Carol, seeing Romania weakened by international tensions and threatened by the rising power of Germany, made overtures to Hitler to avoid being invaded. Eliade became disillusioned with democracy, and felt that a dictatorship was the best route for Romania. He gave moral support to Legionary ideals and saw many of his friends suffer for these ideals. He himself was detained for his associations with the Iron Guard (the Legionary) and with Nae Ionescu.

To take Eliade from these pressures, Prime Minister G. Tattaresco appointed him a cultural attaché to London. Eliade remained in London from 1940 to 1941, doing research in his spare time on what would be his morphology of symbols. In 1941 he was sent as cultural advisor to Lisbon, where he remained until 1945, and where his wife, Nina Mares, would die of cancer in 1944. Eliade returned one more time to Romania before leaving indefinitely in 1945 to take up residence in Paris.

Exile: 1945 and Onward

It was while in Paris as an exile from 1945 to 1955 that Eliade became internationally known for his work as a historian of religions. Working against poverty and having to write in a new language, he wrote in French such works as *Patterns in Comparative Religion; Cosmos and History: The Myth of the Eternal Return; Yoga: Immortality and Freedom;* and *Shamanism: Archaic Techniques of Ecstasy,* which were quick to establish his reputation. Between 1949 and 1954 he wrote in Romanian (the language of his dreams and literary imagination) his literary masterpiece, *Noaptea de Sânziene* (*The Forbidden Forest*). His Parisian years were also marked by his meeting some of the great intellectuals of the day, Dumézil, Pettazzoni, Jung, Lévi-Strauss, Corbin, van der Leeuw, Tucci, and reunion with friends from Romania, similarly notable, E. M. Cioran and Eugène Ionesco. Under the invitation of Dumézil, Eliade taught at l'Ecole des Hautes Etudes in 1946. In 1950, Eliade would marry his second wife, Christinel Cottesco. In 1955, after meeting the historian of religion Joachim Wach from the University of Chicago, Eliade was invited by Wach to give the Haskell Lectures at Chicago. After a two-year try-out period, Eliade and Christinel decided to stay on at Chicago. Already famous and with his path-breaking books behind him, Eliade made Chicago, nevertheless, a highly productive period. He kept up his consummate journal-keeping, wrote novellas and short stories (largely for private audiences) and composed shorter works in the history of religions. He colaunched in 1960 with Joseph M. Kitagawa and Charles Long the journal *History of Religions*, in which he would present his "A New Humanism" article. Capping his career as a historian of religions, between 1976 and 1983 he wrote his three-volume *A History of Religious Ideas* in its French version. His finale was being editor-in-chief of the sixteen-volume *Encyclopedia of Religion*, begun in 1979 and completed by others in 1986, only a few months after his death in April of that year.

Nature of This Book

Readers will note that I am largely sympathetic to Eliade's cultural and pluralistic vision and that I consider informative, insightful, and valid many of his interpretations of religious experience. I have tried to read Eliade as much as possible on his own terms and to place him within the frame of reference he himself was trying to construct, which I contend is the new humanism. As such my book is phenomenological in orientation, in the broad meaning of the term: I look at the phenomenon of Eliade and describe what he is doing. The whole Eliade is included. I resort to his journals, autobiography, literature, scholarly works, and writings from newspaper and review articles. The work is also hermeneutical. Based on what I understand him to say and on what is available on him, I have interpreted Eliade's thought in dialogue with his life and his life in dialogue with his thought, in a sort of biographical exegesis. From the interpretations gained, I see what they can illumine for those in the academic study of religion, for those who are not, and for those largely receptive to the world of myths and symbols; though I hope those not so disposed can still gain from my treatment. While my treatment is largely sympathetic and descriptive, I try to lay bare some of the weaknesses of and limits to Eliade's thought and work. From what is exposed criticisms and judgments can then be made.

Notes

1. I am grateful for my discussion with Phil Arnold in which, if I recall, he mentioned this phrase.

2. Andrei Codrescu, *The Disappearance of the Outside* (Reading, MA: Addison-Wesley Publishing, 1990).

3. Norman Manea, along with other Romanian intellectuals, calls for an objective inquiry into Eliade's past, now that more Romanian documents of Eliade's earlier years are becoming available and can be openly discussed. Manea respects Eliade and is sincere in his queries. While he does put the onus of proof on Eliade's right-wingedness on Eliade, Manea is the type of critic who will best uncover and interpret the whole Eliade. See Manea, "Happy Guilt: Mircea Eliade, fascism, and the unhappy fate of Romania," *The New Republic* (August 5, 1991), 35–37.

4. Mac Linscott Ricketts, *Mircea Eliade: The Romanian Roots, 1907–1945*, 2 vols. (New York: Columbia University Press, East European Monographs, Boulder, CO, 1988).

5. I refer to the documents in London of what Eliade wrote while there as cultural attaché for the Romanian government from 1940 to 1941. While the Romanian Adriana Berger is said to have read them and found strong pro-Nazi statements by Eliade, she has not presented them to the public to the degree that Ricketts has done with Eliade's Romanian writings. Because of this, and until these documents can be set against the Romanian corpus, I must at this time be more cautious in accepting her interpretations of Eliade's ideological statements over what Ricketts presents. See Adriana Berger's review essay, "Facism and Religion in Romania," *Annals of Scholarship* 6,4 (1989), 455–65; and the paper "Anti-Judaism and Anti-Historicism in Eliade's Writings," read by another at the American Academy of Religion Meeting in 1990.

6. Ricketts, *Romanian Roots*, p. 81.

7. Ricketts, *Romanian Roots*, pp. 250–51.

8. Rudolf Steiner, *Goethe the Scientist,* trans. Olin D. Wannamaker (New York: Anthroposophic Press, 1950), p. 1.

9. Ricketts, *Romanian Roots*, p. 395. When this was published Eliade was told he would never be allowed to return to India. Ricketts does not say who told Eliade. Ibid., p. 1288 n. 55.

10. Mircea Eliade, *Ordeal by Labyrinth*, trans. Derek Coltman (Chicago: University of Chicago Press, 1982), p. 392.

2

The New Humanism as a Hermeneutics of a "Participatory Morphology" and as a Spiritual Vision

> If one can see the seed of religious creativity that sprouts and grows in sundry ways, it would be fitting to think rather along the lines of Goethe. —JAN DE VRIES[1]

> Eliade explicitly conceives the study of the history of religions as part of the struggle for regaining a new and adequate spirituality.
> —ZWI WERBLOWSKY[2]

Eliade's new humanism is a hermeneutical program of what I call a "participatory morphology." However implicitly or explicitly he articulated a methodology, Eliade lived out the full implications of his hermeneutical discoveries. He lived in a constant dialogue between experience and method. The importance of this relationship between experience and method is understood when placed within the context of the hermeneutical tradition. Out of this tradition Eliade contributed his own transformative and universal hermeneutics of a distinctive style and vision.

A Hermeneutics of a "Participatory Morphology"

From the Greek word *hermeneuein* (to interpret), hermeneutics has etymological association with the name of the Greek god Hermes, messenger of the gods and deity of boundaries. As messenger, Hermes mediates between a source and an audience forming a triadic relationship. The message conveyed to, and received by, the audience relies upon the accuracy with which the mediator received and understood the message and on the ability and receptivity of the audience to receive the message. If the actual or imaginative distance is great between source and audience or if the audience has a prejudice against the source, then the message will be misconstrued, regardless of the mediator's fidelity to the text.[3]

The Hermeneutical Tradition in the History of Religions

It was during the nineteenth century, when evolutionary theories and rationalistic interpretations were in vogue, that we find a great imaginative distance between the primitive cultures then being discovered and the modern student of religion. Those pioneers in the scientific study of religion, Max Müller, E. B. Tylor, R. R. Marrett, Andrew Lang, and Wilhelm Schmidt, reflected the zeitgeist that existentially distanced the universe of the primitive from the modern's own universe of meaning. For the modern the spirituality of the primitive had no categorical continuity with modern culture. On an evolutionary scale, the primitive's perception of the sacred and subsequent construction of meaning is only a stage in the history of culture, an inferior stage out of which the scientific, empirical period forseen by August Comte would evolve.

So long as moderns considered their religious ancestors "not like us," did the spirituality of the ancestors remain incomprehensible, or at least irrelevant, to the modern student.[4] In time, as major challenges upset the modern's smug methodological position, those once on the periphery entered the modern's realm of acceptable forms of religiosity. Challenges to the modern's methodological center came from the phenomenology of religion in Nathan Söderblom, Rudolf Otto, and Gerardus van der Leeuw; from advances in archeology and ethnology; from the depth psychology studies of Sigmund Freud and C. G. Jung; and, of course, from the world-upsetting implications of the First and Second World Wars.[5] These intellectual, cultural, and political challenges forced the modern student of religion to rethink traditional definitions of religion and the way in which the West should interpret the religious-cultural "other." The problem of understanding became indeed a *problem,* a problem requiring systematic study through the newly developing science of hermeneutics.

The hermeneutical tradition, founded by the father of hermeneutics, Schleiermacher, arose in Schleiermacher's native country, Germany. It proceeded through Wilhelm Dilthey, Eric Auerbach, Martin Heidegger, and Hans-Georg Gadamer, with today the French in deconstruction providing the next phase. Applied to the humanistic sciences, hermeneutics redefined the parameters and asked new questions on the relation of the "other" to one's own world-view. No longer relegated to an inferior and less-than-parity position, these "others"—principally defined as the archaic and the Oriental—were now termed "they are like us." And if they were like us, the next step became, "why should we want to know about them."[6] Acknowledging interconnection and answering why moderns should know about the others, Dilthey said:

> In the human order . . . man knows man; however alien another man may be to us, he is not alien in the sense of an unknowable physical thing.

> Universal history thus becomes the field of hermeneutics. To understand myself is to make the greatest detour, via the memory which retains what has become meaningful for all mankind. Hermeneutics is the rise of the individual to the knowledge of the universal history, the universalisation of the individual.[7]

Individuals (and cultures) know themselves better and more fully when their network of meaning is placed within the context of a universal history. Although hermeneutics supposes interconnectedness, phenomenology does not. When Rudolf Otto said in his opening chapter to his study of the holy, *Das Heilige* (1917), that those who cannot "direct" their "mind to a moment of deeply-felt religious experience" are "requested to read no farther," he limited the phenomenon to only a select group, those who had experienced such religious experience.[8] Otto established no historical grounding for those outside of such experience seeking to interpret it.[9] Similarly, the phenomenologist of religion Gerardus van der Leeuw, in his *Religion in Essence and Manifestation,* failed to establish a hermeneutical interconnectedness with the phenomenon. The observer of a phenomenon is to "withdraw to one side, and endeavour to observe what appears while adopting the attitude of intellectual suspense," said van der Leeuw.[10] Van der Leeuw, however, did forsee hermeneutics playing a larger role in phenomenology. In the history of religions it would be Joachim Wach and later Mircea Eliade who positioned hermeneutics at the center of the phenomenological enterprise.

Influenced by Schleiermacher, Dilthey, Leopold von Ranke, and especially August Boeckh, Wach used the tools of phenomenology, history, psychology, and sociology to interpret religious experience; and he encouraged a strong empathy with, and logical approach to, the phenomenon under study and articulated an explicit methodology and theology in his hermeneutics.[11] Following Wach at Chicago in 1956, Eliade's hermeneutics was more closely tied to the data, to the actual "texts" of the religion.[12] His methodology was less clear than Wach's, and he refrained from theological intentions. Eliade's hermeneutics was rooted not in the line of Schleiermacher and Dilthey but in his own experience.[13] His methodology included an existential engagement with the texts informed by a broad erudition in religious symbols. Only as a symbol is placed within the purview of universal culture could the text approach its truest meaning. From such hermeneutical discoveries Eliade believed a philosophical anthropology for modern culture would emerge.

Eliade's Distinct Hermeneutics

In *L'Hermeneutique de Mircea Eliade,* Adrian Marino says that all of Eliade's central ideas and themes found their expression in his Romanian oeuvre prior to 1940.[14] But it would be their universal ambitions that would most distinguish Eliade's hermeneutics. Similar to Dilthey's hermeneutics, Eliade's opens the interpeter to universal culture. In the broad comparative line of Max Müller and George Dumézil, Eliade seeks a common religious heritage among humans based on the universal presence of symbols.[15] But to have a universal hermeneutics a theory of human nature is needed to draw the different cultures together. This unity of the human spirit Eliade found in the anthropological concept of *homo religiosus,* an irreducible construct wherein the person encounters the sacred through symbols. Symbols reveal for Eliade an ontology. They are the most pure medium through which the sacred is communicated. Since no symbolic form is pure but exists as a dialectic between the sacred (eternal, cosmic structures) and the profane (temporal, historical forms), hermeneutics is required to decipher the structural meanings covered over by historical accretions. Futhermore, since symbols are temporally and spatially multivalent, it is only by placing them within a religious morphology of symbols that their particular and universal meanings are apprehended. By resorting to a morphology, instead of aligning symbols along a chronological, evolutionary line, Eliade could compare religious facts across space and time even when the cultures involved had had no known historical or geographical contact. Thus, for instance, Eliade interpreted the regenerative meanings attached to lunar symbolism by comparing fertility myths among the Eskimos, Australians, Indians, Greeks, Romans, Persians, Algerians, French, Germans, and Portuguese—in only three paragraphs![16] Symbols universalize. They cohere. They express the unity of humankind. And all local/provincial phenomena find their true and more complete meaning in the larger, global meaning of symbols.[17]

This procedure of placing a local symbol within a global morphology of symbols puts the interpreter amongst a whole range of historical meanings that have come to define the human person. Through successive existential encounters with these other worlds of meaning, the interpreter will enlarge what it means to be a human being. As this knowledge increases, new creative expressions of being human will arise, thus a new humanism. Eliade saw hermeneutics as creative in three ways: 1) it enriches the mind and the life of the hermeneute, 2) it reveals certain values not apparent on the level of immediate experience, and 3) it leads the hermeneute into a discovery of the whole of life and into larger panoramas of symbols.[18]

The creative nature of Eliade's hermeneutics has the often dubious distinction of making tremendous use of the imagination in the interpretive process. Aside from his scholarship, Eliade was also a professional writer, and was gifted with the ability to create imaginary universes of meaning. His imaginative powers provided him with an intuitive power to understand esoteric texts and mystical and even barborous cultural practices. He could bring any world, created or real, from the reaches of the unconscious or human history and make it readily present. But as Adriana Berger clarifies, Eliade's use of the imagination is "far from being the mere fantasy we usually take it to be; [it] is the active and creative scene of encounters with other worlds through which understanding is achieved."[19] The imagination, she continues:

> appears as both a means of knowledge and a modality of being, and in that sense it bears a philosophical (existential) dimension. The imagination is thus a mediation, an intermediary world, which objectivizes itself in the physical one.[20]

In the manner that it mediates meaning from "other worlds" of meaning, the imagination has, for Eliade, a metaphysical function; that is, it defines and establishes meaningful existence. The imagination can create meaning for present, concrete experience even if there is no meaning to be found in the texts. By "no meaning to be found" is meant that historical gaps, cultural blinders, inadequate methodological tools, and the "opacity" of modern consciousness temporarily preclude present meaning from being found.[21] As the literary critic Matei Calinescu notes, for Eliade to find meaning *even if it is not there* makes sense if we realize Eliade's "metaphysics of meaning."[22] This metaphysic hinges on the notions of "imagination" and "creativity." The imagination enables one to discover (to uncover, reveal what was unrecognizable, hidden, invisible), and to discover is to create, and to create is to discover (or uncover) reality. *True* history of religions by definition becomes an "authentic and imaginative hermeneutic."[23] The world is not without meaning. Its meaning is merely unrecognizable for the reason that the sacred is hidden or "camouflaged" in the profane. It is precisely because meaning is *unrecognizable* that the hermeneute is to decipher the latent meanings for present and universal culture. Such a task summarizes the hermeneutical ambitions Eliade holds for the history of religions.

In as much as Eliade's hermeneutics held so central a place in his own life and in his vision for the history of religions and for universal culture, it is not suprising that he saw it possess a salvific function. Marino describes Eliade's hermeneutics as "l'hermeneutique militante," not merely for exegetical or religious purposes but for "political" one's as well, to the extent that it sought to address social and cultural ideologies.[24] Never, perhaps, in the hermeneutical tradition has a hermeneutics been invested with a greater theoretical capacity for effectiveness and direct influence on present reality, says Marino.[25] But to have such an ambition for hermeneutics in the history of religions made Eliade subject to the criticisms of many historians of religions.[26]

We can note several points to Eliade's distinctive hermeneutical program at this stage. First, it exploits the existential interconnectedness between the subject and object of study. Other places and other times have a bearing on who we are, and we are not unattached from, and incapable of, experiencing their worlds of meaning. Second, it recognizes that meaning must be uncovered and proposed; meaning is not readily apparent or achievable, but must, at times, be created. Third, meaning is an ontological and existential construct: it establishes being and affirms existence.

The New Humanism as a Morphology

Eliade's morphology of symbols falls within the general science of the phenomenology of religion. It shares in the phenomenological principles of *epoché* (''bracketing'') and the eidetic vision.[27] Though a morphology respects the givenness of a religious fact, as does phenomenology, a morphology sets up comparisons; it holds in tandem competing forms and orders them into a harmonious but tension-laden whole.

Jonathan Z. Smith identifies four ''modes'' or ''styles'' in the comparative practice, one of these being the morphological. The other three are the ethnographic, the encyclopedic, and the evolutionary.[28] Of the four, only the morphological synthesizes a wide range of data, maintains plurality, and proffers an interpretive scheme.[29]

The morphological pattern comes from Wolfgang von Goethe (1749–1832), the great German poet and philosopher.[30] It was from Goethe that Eliade got his inspiration.[31]

The Goethian morphology postulates a once ''existent'' primordial plant (*Urpflanze*) that orders in an integrating fashion all variant plants spawned throughout time. The primordial plant itself is an archetypal, metaphorical, symbolic concept having no historical actuality, except as it is manifested through the wide diversity of its variants in and throughout history. The primordial plant is beyond the vicissitudes of time and so, however much the variations on the plant might be and become, the structure of the primordial plant stays true within each variant.[32] As an archetype, the primordial plant is older in structure but not in chronology to all its derived plants. That is, X is simpler than Y, logically and formerly prior, but not necessarily prior in time.[33] Hierarchically, the order is from the simpler to the complex, with the simpler being no less inferior to the complex. Similarly, as an archetype, the plant is universal: it traverses both space and time; yet, at all times, it holds in

a dialectical tension its particular and universal expressions. The particular—
the many historical manifestations—is always found in the universal—the
Urpflanze—and the universal always submits to the particular.[34]

One constructs a morphology on four principal activities: 1) recognizing the
living forms of what is being studied, 2) seeing in context the forms' tangible
and visible parts, 3) perceiving within their manifestations an inner essence
which ties the variants together and to the archetype, and, finally, 4) mastering
the forms by seeing their concrete expressions as a whole.[35]

While a morphology preserves the irreducible quality of a phenomenon and
reaches across space and time, it suffers at not being historically grounded
enough. It does not attempt "thick descriptions" of a culture, nor are its forms
necessarily defined in relation to their historical and social structures; a morphology decontextualizes and deinstitutionalizes its expressions. The institution of the priesthood or of the cult, for instance, would be interpreted according to its structural continuity with other similar institutions and cults, but the
particular priesthood or cult itself would not be studied as an institution per se
in all its sociological and political dynamics within its own particular tradition
and context. A morphology fades the lines between traditions and institutions.
In addition, it minimizes the historical development (diachronicity) of a form
within a tradition, prefering instead structural connections (synchronicity)
between traditions. And lastly, a morphology is governed by the concept or
paradigm that defines the structure.[36]

Eliade was not unaware of these problems. He knew that in the end a
creative tension between the "structural" and the "historical," or developmental and contextual, study of religion must remain.[37] Julien Ries places the
historical dimension as one of the three prongs to Eliade's methodology,[38] and
in his own writings Eliade made a shift from the systematic to a more historical
approach.[39] And in regards to Eliade's morphology of symbols, as I will
show, symbols, as Eliade interprets them, have their own contextual rooted-
ness. Nevertheless, despite the flexibility of Eliade's method or "system,"
not being historically grounded enough remains a problem for Eliade's
method.

If the new humanism is to be characterized as morphological in structure, it
must in some way address the morphological and historical tension. In other
words, how is history to be expressed in the new humanism? It is precisely
because there is a tension between the historical and the structural that I
believe a morphology is the most adequate arrangement for conceptualizing
the new humanism. For in being able to manage simultaneously diverse and
even contrary religious phenomena, a morphology balances the manifold ways
in which Eliade understood history. There is circular time, dream time, linear
time, imaginary time, among other forms of time, that are found in the human
religious experience. No single type of history or time defines the new human-

ism. The morphological-historical tension remains, but it is placed in a much larger framework, that of the new humanism. It is through this framework that we are to understand what Eliade's scholarly and literary oeuvre were trying to do.

From what has been said so far it is possible to describe in three ways why the new humanism is to be morphological in form. First, like the primordial *Urpflanze* plant, the new humanism is atemporal. It exists as a perennial structure throughout the variants of Eliade's scholarly and literary life. In defining the new humanism as the "primordial plant" I do what Eliade recommended for the historian of religions, that he or she "would do well to search for the 'original plant' in his [or her] own field, for the primal image."[40] In other words, the new humanism is itself a symbol. As an archetype, the new humanism has its history. It arose at a particular time in Eliade's intellectual development, around 1927 after having read of the term in the writings of George Sarton.[41] But as an archetype, the new humanism is old in structure and not in chronology. Its elements and variants are found throughout Eliade's life, from his *Memoirs of a Lead Soldier* in 1923 to his *History of Religious Ideas* in the 1970s and 1980s. It is misleading and fruitless, therefore, to establish the genesis of any of Eliade's ideas at a precise period. Eliade's thought and life unfolded more than they evolved.

Second, a morphology complements the variegated and paradoxical quality of Eliade's own writings and thought, and, third, it suits his ontology. From his earliest tempestuous years as an adolescent and young leader to his later serenity as professor at the University of Chicago, Eliade explored through the imagination and sometimes experientially a boggling range of subjects, from rape, suicide, and the demonic, to mysticism and beatific creativity. His writings shifted from frank confessions on matters of religious faith and rallying cries for nationalistic renewal to an enigmatic taciturnity on the very same subjects. Not suprisingly, Eliade has been labeled many things: an agnostic, a cryptotheologian, an Orthodox believer, "the most influential student of religion today," a right-wing xenophobic, a defender of the Jews, the leading spokesman for women, a male chauvinist, and other labels. Eliade, in a way, is all of these. His fertility for fertility's sake sprouted the wheat along with the tares.

The many-sidedness of Eliade is a natural extension of his religious, aesthetic ontology.[42] In an article published in 1927 in the newspaper *Cuvântul* (The Word), Eliade speaks about aesthetic and religious experiences having a unity, however diverse their expressions:

> [T]he pure aesthetic emotion remains the *same,* whether it is produced through contemplation of a Greek statue, a Florentine canvas, or a Byzantine icon. *Forms* of art can and do vary, because they take rise from varied mentalities and sensibilities. But these forms are only *pretexts,* infinite in number, for arriving at

a single plane—just as a religious experience, leading to a single transcendent plane, can be actualized through meditation on an endless series of dogmas. The thousands of mystical confessions collected from the Catholic world can all be reduced to the same confession: the divine presence of the deity, through love.[43]

Whether in life or in thought, Eliade's "radical pluralism"[44] in all its variety and frequent contradictions, was never without a coherence of its own. If there is any norm to Eliade it comes in the totality of his thought, with this totality defined as his new humanism. The whole is the norm.[45]

A "Participatory Morphology"

Commenting on what shapes a scholar's methodology toward the subject, Walter Capps says that the field of study is indubitably defined by the orientation of the scholar's perspective. Says he:

> [W]hat the scholar does within the subject-field depends upon where he is standing. Where he stands influences what he discovers. Furthermore, where he stands and what he discovers are implicit in what he is trying to do. All of these factors, in turn, form his conception of the field and help set the operational definition he gives to religion.[46]

What Eliade was "trying to do" for the history of religions was to consolidate it around a vision for a new humanism. He stood on the boundary of all cultures and religions[47] and discovered the universal harmony of *homo religiosus*. *Homo religiosus* is not confined to religion proper but transcends all structural and doctrinal distinctions associated with religion. The history of religions becomes not a mere academic discipline for studying religion and religions. Instead, it is conceived as a humanistic enterprise whereby what was fundamental to human religiosity can be extricated for deepening and enlarging the human experience.

In the sense that the new humanism encourages, through a hermeneutics of engagement, a broad assimilation of religio-cultural experiences from across space and time, the new humanism can be termed a "participatory morphology." Charles Long says that "Eliade moves from his morphology of symbols to the level of comparison, criticism, and dialogue."[48] Eliade, though, did not mean for the interpreter simply to move *from* a morphology of symbols in the act of interpretation. The interpreter should remain *within* and *participate in* the morphology of symbols itself. Marino refers to the existential quality of Eliade's universal hermeneutics:

> The hermeneutics of Eliade—in the totality of his oeuvres and of his extra-European hypotheses—has an existential base. It is here that he confers the

tension and the vitality which characterizes [his hermeneutics]. One does not only find here the aspect of an inert construction of the intelligence: Eliade is totally "engaged" in his system of thought.[49]

Eliade himself wrote on 1 January 1960 that the symbolic world is a lived "text," a "text" in need of interpretation so as to provide meaning to one's existence:

> Every exile is a Ulysses traveling toward Ithaca. Every real existence reproduces the *Odyssey*. The path toward Ithaca, toward the center [sic]. I had known that for a long time. What I have just discovered is that the change to become a new Ulysses is given to *any* exile *whatsoever* (precisely because he has been condemned by the gods, that is, by the "powers" which decide historical, earthly destinies.) But to realize this, the exile must be capable of penetrating the hidden meaning of his wanderings, and of understanding them as a long series of initiation trials (willed by the gods) and so many obstacles on the path which brings him back to the hearth (toward the center). That means: seeing signs, hidden meanings, symbols, in the sufferings, the depressions, the dry periods in everyday life. Seeing them and reading them even *if they aren't there;* if one sees them, one can build a structure and read a message in the formless flow of things and the monotonous flux of historical facts.[50]

This journal entry demonstrates the existential engagement of Eliade's hermeneutics. A person interprets his or her existence as a series of messages in route toward his or her center.

The hermeneutics of the new humanism is characterized as a "participatory morphology" in four ways. First, as a hermeneutical program the new humanism aims to provide meaning to one's existence. A person participates in meaning, and meaning informs and gives values to one's place. Second, the hermeneutical and comparative enterprise is naturally participatory. It is impossible to understand the "other" unless some degree of interconnection between subject and subject is assumed. Third, *homo religiosus* is *homo symbolicus;* humans live and understand their life through symbols, and, being symbol-making beings, humans hold, express, and participate in a plurality of symbolic forms; hence, they participate in a morphology of symbols. And lastly, the new humanism, taken as the Goethian primordial plant, is the archetype for all the variants throughout Eliade's life work.

Such an intensely "lived-in" hermeneutics draws immediately to mind the prolonged debate on how neutral can and should a methodology be. As for being methodologically neutral, in the sense of being objectively detached from the material, Eliade is not. The new humanism advocates the transformation of humans to creatively new potentials, and his methodology is intensely dialogical with his life and with the religious and cultural experiences of other peoples. What Eliade did as a historian of religions was not something he "left at the office." I agree, therefore, with Keith Yandell that Eliade is not religiously neutral; he is not the cold scientist.[51]

This lack of methodological neutrality does not, however, imply a confessional bias. To posit the "sacred" as a structure of human consciousness, which includes the interpreter, does not mean one assumes a devotional posture towards any particular religious belief. What positing the "sacred" does suggest is that one is willing to accept the reality of other symbolic worlds of meaning. I would agree, then, with Robert Segal that Eliade is a "believer" when Segal defines a "believer" as one who believes in the "reality of the sacred," however defined.[52] A morphology allows for and accepts the coexistence of a diversity of religious beliefs with no single belief favored over another. To accept the irreducibility of the sacred and the givenness of another's symbolic expression only makes the historian of religions a great pluralist, not an evangelist for any given belief or set of beliefs. Nevertheless, with the above qualifiers, a morphology's particular–universal, historical–ahistorical dialectic does not preclude a confessional posture. As long as a confessional posture avoids universalizing itself over other religious expressions and belief systems, one can be a pluralist and be methodologically neutral. Ninian Smart's assertion, therefore, that methodologies should be "agnostic"—i.e., that the objects of religious experience and belief ought to remain autonomous from whether they "exist/are true"—is acceptable.[53] A morphology abstains from reducing another's belief to one's own conceptual belief system.

One last point should be addressed. A morphology does not presume an uncritical moral and ontological relativism, as Keith Yandell assumes from Eliade's non-normative methodology.[54] Eliade's dispassionate phenomenological-morphological appraisal of other religious forms does not mean his system is without internal checks against accepting wholeheartedly the religious or cultural expression under study, however barbarous or sublime that expression might be. Symbols are validated or rejected by whether or not they can surive repeated valuations and devaluations in history and by whether they can integrate a plurality of symbols.[55]

To use Yandell's point of departure in his critique of Eliade's apparent indifference to evil behavior, Eliade's morphology of symbols would not treat Hitler's "religion" and views of human nature indifferently, uncritically, and relatively. Hitler's symbolic universe was, and proved in time to be, on a large scale, inadequate, restrictive, provisional, and empty for suceeding generations and cultures. His universe of symbols obstructed and publically disqualified the symbolic experiences of others, notably the Jews, and his myth of an Aryan race could not approach a totality of plural symbols from many cultures and religions. Hitler's totality included only a single cultural group to the exclusion of others. Within Eliade's framework, Hitler failed to recognize or accept the dialectical nature of a symbol as it moves between the part and the whole; Hitler prioritized and ranked the part over the whole.[56]

The New Humanism as a Spiritual Vision

To define the new humanism as the "primordial plant" to Eliade's scholarly and aesthetic oeuvre, we would expect his vision of a new humanism to permeate and unite his work as an historian of religions and as a writer. That the new humanism informed his scholarship is clear.[57] The new humanism was not so clearly expressed by him in his literature. But insofar as both fields came from the same head, that literature for Eliade constituted an instrument of knowledge in its own right, and that Eliade insisted upon being understood in his totality, does his literature complement and supplement his history of religions' goal for a broader and deeper understanding of human consciousness. And in the same manner that Eliade encountered strange and distant religious and cultural worlds, he created his own foreign and exotic worlds of the imagination for similar experiential encounters for himself and for others. Whether through the history of religions or through his literary creations, Eliade believed that the total human experience as we know it could be endlessly enriched.

The Vision

Eliade's article entitled "A New Humanism" first appeared in 1961 to inagurate and set the direction for the newly founded journal, *The History of Religions*. Both the journal and the article also announced new directions for the history of religions. The journal was to bring together historians of religion in a dialogical way as a means for integrating the works of specialists and generalists for elucidating the worlds of religion for contemporary culture. With Eliade providing the flagship article, he stated his own methodological and philosophical orientation and vision for the discipline of the history of religions. Eliade would revise, expand, and reprint the article in his *The Quest: History and Meaning in Religion* (1969).[58] *The Quest,* in effect, is a historical and thematic elaboration upon the central propositions of the new humanism article.

A basic contention of the article is that Western society and its values— cultural and religious—are no longer in a position of predominance in the world. With the East entering "history" and with the "active" resurgence of archaic traditions, Westerners are having to reorient themselves to a new, more global consciousness. No longer are Westerners the only ones to "make history." Oriental values are challenging those of the West, forcing the West to take seriously the spiritualities of Asia and of archaic peoples, past and present. Because of these global changes and because the West is now more willing than ever to meet the "others" on the same spiritual level, there is a need for true dialogue. And dialogue must occur, says Eliade, on each culture's respective plane of reference; in other words, do not measure the cultural "progress" of the Dogon of Sudan with the technological "advancements" of the United States. The aim is to understand, compare, and, as much as possible, experience the cultural creations of each for what they contribute toward helping humans live and create in the world. This encounter with the "others" will help eliminate cultural provincialism as well as create existential moments for mutual transformation. As the West meets the archaic and the Oriental worlds, and all other worlds for that matter, the West will arrive at a deeper and broader knowledge of what it means to be human. More than any other humanistic discipline, Eliade feels it is the history of religions, through a "creative hermeneutics," that can best bring about such transformations to human consciousness.

The spiritual dimension that Eliade brings to his hermeneutics sets him apart from other humanistic and social scientists and from many historians of religions. Eliade sees no ultimate value in erudition alone. It is not enough to have merely reconstructed the religious phenomenon and its cultural context, however precise and comprehensive. Nor does one arrive at the total meaning of a phenomenon when it is reduced to its social, political, or economic expressions. Rather, religious acts, rites, ceremonies, movements, beliefs, etc. achieve their total and transformative potential when they are taken on their own plane of reference, that is, as *religious* phenomena. The religious dimension is as intrinsic to religious phenomena as art is to artistic creations. Both deal with individual experiences and transpersonal realites and, hence, cannot be reduced to and explained away by their historical causes. Taken on their own plane of reference, then, the religious and the artistic possess an irreducible essential nature.

The irreducibility of the phenomenon does not mean that the historical element can be ignored or that historical reconstruction is unfruitful. No religious phenomenon exists apart from history. Religious data can only be understood as historical data, and their interpretation for culture can only arise from a historical context. But, in the last analysis—and here Eliade is accused for being a-contextual—the religious phenomenon acquires its most complete meaning when set within the totality of a symbol's morphology. To situate within totality is the methodological key. Totality is also the paradigm for the history of religions as a "total discipline." It creatively holds in tension both phenomenology and history.

A Spiritual Vision

If we are to extrapolate and formulate the new humanism's morphology, we must draw up a working definition of the new humanism. Eliade did the same for the sacred with he "defined" it as that which is opposite of the profane.[59] The new humanism, similarly and unavoidably, must be "defined" as ambiguously if we are to do justice to the breadth of the term.

For now the new humanism is "defined" as a spiritual, humanistic orientation toward totality capable of modifying the quality of human existence itself. The term "spiritual"[60] was often used by Eliade in reference to the individual and to culture in general. In Romania he often spoke of the "primacy of the spiritual" over the political, the economic, and all other "materialistic" goals. In a series of articles between 1927 and 1928 to the Romanian young generation—those growing up between the two world wars—Eliade challenged them to develop their inner person, their individual personality, and their intellectual and religious life. It is this intellectual and inner sense which Eliade meant by spiritual. Mac Linscott Ricketts, Eliade's biographer, clarifies:

> [W]ith regard to the word "spiritual," be it said immediately, English-speaking readers should not be misled into thinking something purely *religious* is intended. In Romanian, the word "spiritual," while it may refer to the religious, has also more generally the value of the German *geistig*: that is, it denotes the *mental,* the *intellectual,* that which is not material or physical. It is in this larger sense that both Ionescu and Eliade mean the term when they speak of the "primacy of the spiritual." This is not to imply that the religious is excluded, but only that it is not the *primary* sense intended.[61]

By "spiritual" in the new humanism, then, I mean a quality of being, a way of thought, and a world of meaning not subject to the transitoriness of politics, economics, and historicism. It is that world of meaning to which myths and symbols are addressed.[62]

As for being "humanistic," the new humanism is concerned with the religious, philosophical, and practical concerns of humans. Eliade's phenomenology may be criticized for being too detached from concrete life; but his new humanism, we find, is capable of being particularly concrete. In contrast to the humanism of the Renaissance, Eliade's new humanism goes beyond Plato and the recovery of classical Greek texts. It stretches, instead, to the mind and spirituality of the primitive and their "classical" "texts" (their myths and symbols). Eliade seeks not a classical science, but a philosophy of science and culture based on a synthesis of reason and intuition and on the viability of myth and symbols for existential meaning.

The "orientation toward totality" implies that one be cognizant of the plurality of religious forms and worldviews and, subsequently, that one adopt a hermeneutical position that actively engages in a dialogical encounter with these forms and worldviews in arriving at syntheses. Finally, the new humanism involves a continual modification of the human condition; it seeks to improve upon that which is provincial and sterile.

Notes

1. Jan de Vries, *The Study of Religion: A Historical Approach,* trans. Kees W. Bolle (New York: Harcourt, Brace & World, 1967), p. 222.

2. R. J. Zwi Werblowsky, review of *The History of Religious Ideas: From the Stone Age to the Eleusinian Mysteries,* by Mircea Eliade, *History of Religions* 23 (November 1983), 181.

3. Charles Long, *Significations* (Philadelphia: Fortress Press, 1986), pp. 21–22. Friedrich Schleiermacher (1768–1834), the "father" of modern hermeneutics, sought a universal hermeneutics from the need to overcome misunderstanding among peoples.

4. Jonathan Z. Smith, *Map Is Not Territory* (Leiden: E.J. Brill, 1978), pp. 241–44.

5. One could also add the development of the human sciences, the World Parliament of Religions of 1893, and the growth of liberalism in American religious studies, as other factors in redefining the modern's approach to prior and distant cultures.See Joseph Kitagawa, "The History of Religions in America," in *The History of Religions: Essays in Methodology,* ed. Joseph M. Kitagawa and Mircea Eliade (Chicago: University of Chicago Press, 1959), pp. 3–5.

6. Smith, *Map Is Not Territory,* p. 242.

7. Cited in Paul Ricoeur, *Hermeneutics and the Human Sciences,* trans. and ed. John B. Thompson (Cambridge: Cambridge University Press, 1981), pp. 49 and 52.

8. Rudolf Otto, *The Idea of the Holy,* trans. John W. Harvey (New York: Oxford University Press, 1958), p. 8.

9. Long, *Significations,* pp. 38–43.

10. Gerardus van der Leeuw, *Religion in Essence and Manifestation,* vol. 2, trans. J. E. Turner (New York: Harper & Row, 1963), pp. 688.

11. Joachim Wach, *Introduction to the History of Religions,* ed. Joseph M. Kitagawa and Gregory D. Alles, (New York: Macmillan Publishing, 1988), pp. xv–xvi.

12. Charles Long, "A Look at the Chicago Tradition in the History of Religions: Retrospect and Future," in *The History of Religions: Retrospect and Prospect,* ed. Joseph M. Kitagawa (New York: Macmillan Publishing, 1985), p. 95.

13. Adrian Marino, "Mircea Eliade's Hermeneutics," in *Imagination and Meaning: The Scholarly and Literary Worlds of Mircea Eliade,* ed. Norman J. Girardot and Mac Linscott Ricketts (New York: Seabury Press, 1982), p. 19.

14. Adrian Marino, *L'Hermeneutique de Mircea Eliade,* trans. Jean Gouillard (Paris: Gallimard, 1981), p. 15.

15. Julien Ries, "Histoire des religions, phenomenologie et hermeneutique," in *L'Herne: Mircea Eliade,* ed. Constantin Tacou (Paris: Editions de L'Herne, No. 33, 1978), p. 87.

16. Mircea Eliade, *Patterns in Comparative Religion,* trans. Rosemary Sheed (London: Sheed & Ward, 1958), pp. 1–38, 156.

17. Marino, *L'Hermeneutique,* pp. 306–9; and in *Imagination,* p. 62.

18. Eliade, *Ordeal by Labyrinth,* pp. 128–9.

19. Adriana Berger, "Cultural Hermeneutics: The Concept of Imagination in the Phenomenological Approaches of Henry Corbin and Mircea Eliade," *The Journal of Religion* 2 (April 1986), 141. Berger also says this in relation to Henry Corbin.

20. Ibid., p. 142.

21. Marino, *Imagination,* p. 28.

22. Matei Calinescu, "Mircea Eliade's Journals," *The Denver Quarterly* 12,1 (1977), 315.

23. Ibid.

24. Marino, *L'Hermeneutique,* pp. 285ff.

25. Ibid., p. 293.

26. See C. J. Bleeker in *Science of Religion, Studies in Methodology,* ed. Lauri Honko (The Hague: Mouton Publishers, 1979), p. 175. W. G. Oxtoby cautions against the subjectivism in phenomenology and the particular "missions" it can generate. See "Religionswissenschaft Revisited," in *Religions in Antiquity,* ed. Leroy S. Rouner (Leiden: E.J. Brill, 1968), p. 594 et. passim. On the matter of seeing a creative role for the history of religions see Ugo Bianchi in "The History of Religions," *Encyclopedia of Religion,* 6:399f.; and in "Current Methodological Issues in the History of Religions," in Kitagawa, *Retrospect and Prospect,* Bianchi is uneasy with the word "hermeneutics." He prefers finding "structural similarities." See Kitagawa, p. 64.

27. Douglas Allen, *Structure and Creativity in Religion: Hermeneutics in Mircea Eliade's Phenomenology and New Directions* (The Hague: Mouton Publishers, 1978), p. 58.

28. Smith, *Map Is Not Territory,* p. 244.

29. The philosopher David Rasmussen labels Eliade's phenomenology of a morphological hermeneutics as an "eidetic reintegration." When the essense of a religious creation is apprehended, it is "reintegrated" into a structure where its meaning can then be understood. The value of a morphology within the phenomenological framework is its ability to suit both the subject and the object by not reducing the phenomenon and by its ability to interpret the phenomeon in its particular and universal meaning. See David Rasmussen, "Mircea Eliade: Structural Hermeneutics and Philosophy," *Philosophy Today* 12 (1968), 143.

30. See Goethe's comment on the character of a morphology, coming nearly four years before his *Versuch, die Metamorphose der Pflanzen zur erklaren* in 1790. Goethe, *Italian Journey, 1786–1788,* trans. W. H. Auden and Elizabeth Mayer (San Francisco: North Point Press, 1982), p. 55.

31. Ioan P. Culianu, *Mircea Eliade* (Assisi: Cittadella Editrice, 1977), p. 5; and Eliade, *Ordeal,* p. 142. And see Eliade's early comments (5 April 1951) on the value of

Goethe's morphology for the natural sciences and, especially, for the "classification, analysis, and interpretation of spiritual creations" in Eliade, *Journal I, 1945–1955,* trans. from the Romanian by Mac Linscott Ricketts (Chicago: University of Chicago Press, 1990), pp. 125–26.

32. For what follows see Smith, *Map Is Not Territory,* pp. 253–59.

33. Ibid.

34. Ibid.

35. Ibid.

36. Ibid.

37. Mircea Eliade, *The Quest: History and Meaning In Religion* (Chicago: The University of Chicago Press, 1969), pp. 8–9.

38. Ries, *L'Herne,* pp. 82–84.

39. In conversation with me (12/9/87), Joseph Kitagawa said that if Eliade made any "transformations" in his method since arriving at the University of Chicago in 1957, it was his shift in emphasis from the systematic to the historical method.

40. Eliade, *Ordeal,* p. 142.

41. Ricketts, *Romanian Roots,* pp. 316–17.

42. Matei Calinescu terms Eliade's metaphysics as an "aesthetic ontology." But Eliade's ontology is also religious in the sense that Eliade believed humans needed to be continuously transformed to a more complete mode of human existence. Calinescu, "Imagination and Meaning: Aesthetic Attitudes and Ideas in Mircea Eliade's Thought," *The Journal of Religion* 57,1 (January 1977), 15

43. Cited in Ricketts, *Romanian Roots,* p. 255.

44. Jerald Brauer said to me (12/9/87) that the Eliadean period at the University of Chicago can be typologized as of "radical pluralism." Two previous periods at the Divinity School at the University of Chicago were, first, the "socio-economic" headed by Shirley Jackson Case and Shailer Matthews, and, second, the "process" period headed by Charles Hartshorne.

45. Marino, *L'Hermeneutique,* p. 321.

46. Walter H. Capps in Honko, *Science of Religion,* p. 180.

47. E. M. Cioran, "Beginnings of a Friendship," in *Myths and Symbols: Studies in Honor of Mircea Eliade,* ed. Joseph M. Kitagawa and Charles M. Long (Chicago: University of Chicago Press, 1969), p. 414.

48. Long, *Significations,* p. 50.

49. Marino, *L'Hermeneutique,* p. 298.

50. Mircea Eliade, *No Souvenirs,* pp. 84–85.

51. Keith E. Yandell, "Can There be a Science of Religion?" *Christian Scholars Review* 15,1 (1986), 28–41.

52. Segal's follow up article, "Robert Segal's Reply" to Eric Sharpe in *Religious Traditions,* 11 (1988), p. 14ff. Eliade's theory does not mean, though, that Eliade need endorse the composition of any particular believer's point of view.

53. Smart, "Beyond Eliade," p. 183.

54. Yandell, "Can There Be a Science of Religion?", p. 32.

55. I will speak more on this later. But the totality refered to here is not that of which

Gregory Alles speaks when he writes of "totality as an instrument of Western colonial domination and cultural imperialism." See Alles, "Wach, Eliade, and the Critique from Totality," *Numen* 35,1 (1988), 117. For Eliade we can never presume to have reached or conceptualized totality; it remains an unreachable "transcendent" limit adjudicating all relative positions. So Eliade's view of totality also differs from Kant's rule "Act as if the maxim of your action were to become by your will a general law of nature." Immanuel Kant, "Metaphysical Foundations of Morals," in *The Philosophy of Kant,* ed. Carl J. Friedrich (New York: Random House, 1977), p. 170.

56. See Eliade's statements on idolatry in *Patterns,* pp. 25–26.

57. With the new humanism as the "primordial plant," I am establishing it as the method by which Eliade sought to interpret and transform universal culture. The following quote from his journal on 25 April 1951 anticipates the new humanism for what he refers to as the "method" behind his "scientific-philosophical production." Eliade says, "Someday I ought to write a 'rational history' of my entire scientific-philosophical production, showing the hidden relation that exists among all these works, apparently disparate, and explaining why I wrote them, and to what extend they contribute *not* to a 'system' but to the foundation of a method." Eliade, *Journal I: 1945–1955,* p. 129.

58. Eliade, *The Quest,* pp. 1–11.

59. See Eliade's *Patterns;* and *The Sacred and the Profane* (New York: Harper & Row, 1957).

60. While I agree with Ioan Culianu that "spiritual" raises all kinds of red flags, it is nevertheless an important term to Eliade's own creative program and one which he frequently used, always, though, in its Romanian sense. Culianu, *Mircea Eliade,* p. 88.

61. Ricketts, *Romanian Roots,* p. 115.

62. See Eliade's *Images and Symbols: Studies in Religious Symbolism,* trans. Philip Mairet (New York: Sheed & Ward, 1969) and his *Sacred and the Profane.*

3

The Nature of the Human Condition: Humans as Symbolic

In the wonderful novel *The Guide,* by R. K. Narayan, the protagonist Raju learns of the power of the symbol. Just out of prison and needing to reflect on the direction his life must now take, Raju takes refuge in an abandoned Hindu temple. He is discovered here one day by Velan, a devout but troubled Hindu. Being a courteous and inquisitive man, Raju inquires into Velan's life. As they discuss Velan's pressing problems, Velan begins to mistake Raju for a holy man. Though no more than a rehabilitated travel guide and entrepreneur, Raju, by his association with a sacred place, takes on the power of a sacred symbol. The stone slab upon which he sits assumes *ex cathedra* status for Velan and for the gathering devout. Regardless of what Raju tells Velan about Raju's former ''profane'' life and of his present hypocrisy, Velan continues to regard Raju as a holy man, so much so that he and the gathering worshippers expect Raju to pray down rain upon their drought-stricken land. In Eliadean terms, Raju has become a ''hierophany,'' a dialectical symbol of the sacred capable of mediating the powers of the cosmos.[1]

This story indicates how the sacred can be found in ordinary life, people, and things, and how in the symbol others are capable of acquiring meaning and hope. The power of a symbol lies in its ability to reflect different levels of reality and to transform the world for those who choose and are able to see the sacred in the symbol.

The dialectical, multivocal, and transformative qualities of the symbol are key to Eliade's theory of symbols. These qualities are central to his hermeneutics,[2] ontology, and to the manner by which a hierophany is able to express the sacred in everyday reality. Symbols, therefore, are foundational to the character of Eliade's new humanism and to the way it is to articulate itself in culture. Based on Eliade's theory of symbols, we can begin to define the new humanism as a dialectical, incarnational, and cosmic spirituality wherein every person and culture is understood in relation to the whole. Before I elaborate on this thesis, however, I will look at the character of life as symbolic.

The Character of Symbolic Existence

Symbols are consubstantial with the human condition. As cultural beings, humans create symbols.[3] They have a "symbol-forming power," says Eliade.[4] All that humans produce is symbolic, from language, to rites, myths, art, and science. Even prior to language and discursive reasoning the world revealed itself as a symbol. If symbols are "consubstantial with human existence itself" and precede all language and discursive reasoning, then symbolic thought cannot be the privileged condition of certain people or be sidelined to some retrograde, outdated mentality. For Eliade, symbolic thinking is the only way humans orient themselves and acquire meaning in the universe.

In the opening of his three-volume *The History of Religious Ideas,* in an insightful hermeneutical claim, Eliade says that primordial humans overcame their initial existential disequilibrium of "being in the world" by positing symbolic space. Says he:

> It is sufficient to recall that the vertical posture already marks a transcending of the condition typical of the primates. Uprightness cannot be maintained except in a state of wakefulness. It is because of man's vertical posture that space is organized in a structure inaccessible to the prehominians: in four horizontal directions radiating from an "up"–"down" central axis. In other words, space can be organized around the human body as extending forward, backward, to right, to left, upward, and downward. It is from this original and originating experience—feeling oneself "thrown" into the middle of an apparently limitless, unknown, and threatening extension—that the different methods of *orientatio* are developed; for it is impossible to survive for any length of time in the vertigo brought on by disorientation. This experience of space oriented around a "center" explains the importance of the paradigmatic divisions and distributions of territories, agglomerations, and habitations and their cosmological symbolism.[5]

It is difficult if not impossible to know how existentially "anxious" were the primal people. But in Eliade's existentialism the earliest humans required meaning, belonging, and a sense of the real as much as do people of the modern age. All of humanity is part of a human–cosmic homology. The human, as upright *homo erectus,* constitutes a "center," a symbolic mode of being spatially oriented in the world. Centered between the expanse of the heavens and the outlay of the earth humans discovered symbolic, sacred space. As qualitatively different from all other surrounding profane space, sacred space provides humans with meaning and order. Profane space, in contrast, is meaningless and chaotic, the realm yet to be made hospitable. To construct symbolic sacred space is itself a religious act, since, for Eliade, religion is that which deals with meaning, being, and truth. The human, therefore, as a symbol-making being (*homo symbolicus*) is, at the same time, *homo religiosus*.

With the human person refered to, in Eliade's quote above, as a cosmic symbol, the new humanism is decidedly humanistic. It is not that humans are the end and measure of all things, as naturalists and positivist-existentialists would hold. Rather, Eliade's human subject is of a Goethian quality wherein humans are regarded as a creative and malleable work of art. Humans are to make of their lives a work of art. Anthropology, as the meaning of being human, is of endless creations.[6]

The interpretations that Eliade brings to symbols, and the transformative power he invests in them, developed as he studied the religious and cultural world of the "primitives."[7] For the primitive all symbols are religious. Symbols, says Eliade, "point to something *real* or to a *structure of the world*. For on the archaic levels of culture, the *real*—that is, the powerful, the meaningful, the living—is equivalent to the *sacred*."[8] Insofar as primitives consciously lived their symbols, everyday life held the potential to manifest the real and give meaning to a person's actions. To a primitive agriculturalist, for instance, the spade represents more than an implement for cultivation. It is at the same time symbolically homologous to the phallus impregnating the fertile womb. The act of sowing assumes greater metaphysical significance than what the simple act itself suggests.

It was during Eliade's four-year period of study and travel in India between 1928 and 1931 that he was awakened to the power symbols hold on both the conscious and unconscious planes. He saw how the symbolic lingam, the phallic-shaped stone representing the god Shiva, could evoke such strong devotion from its worshippers. Upon his return to Romania, Eliade proceded to speak for how symbols are indeed modes of knowledge and vehicles of meaning. Contrary to the intellectuals of the day, Eliade saw how symbolic thought continued to operate in modern culture, even if in degraded form and incomprehensible to the intelligentsia. Writing in 1937, Eliade was pleased to hear of scholars such as Ananda Coomaraswamy, René Guénon, J. Evola, and others restoring the spiritual value of the symbol. Modern society may have abolished the vitality of Christianity at the higher cultural levels, but it cannot completely snuff out the structural capacity of the human as *homo religiosus*, holds Eliade. Regardless of how "realistic," this-worldly, and secular humans may become, symbols will never disappear from the human psyche. The aspect of symbols might change, but their continued functioning in human life will not. The nostalgia for paradise, of that time of first beginnings, unity, sacrality, and bliss is one of humans' most basic longings, and the symbols for that nostalgia persist in people's unconscious aspirations, in their dreams, ideals, and in their literary and artistic creations. That these nostalgias were driven into the unconscious is, itself, an indictment of the spiritual condition of modern society. So, for Eliade, as the symbols and archetypes of humans' fundamental longings as *homines religiosi* are restored, humans will regain a more intimate attachment to cosmic sacrality and instill everyday existence with meaning.

The New Humanism as Dialectical and Incarnational

By their very nature, symbols constitute a dialectic. Coming from the Greek verb *sumbolum,* a symbol means a token, an insignia whereby those of two parties can identify each other. A symbol reveals and conceals its meanings, says Paul Ricoeur, and so its meanings are only apparent to the initiated, to those "trained" to see and interpret them.[9] In Eliade's theory of symbols the disclosed–concealed character of a symbol occurs in the modern psyche between what the symbol means (discloses) to the conscious mind and what it means (conceals) beyond the immediate plane of reality, subsumed to the unconscious. For the primitive both the symbol's hidden and revealed meanings occur at the conscious level. Eliade's fond usage of the cosmic tree is a good example of this two-fold quality of symbols.

To the modern nonreligious person a tree may have various meanings: stability, growth, beauty, etc. At this level the tree serves several purposes, much in the same way Jung understood symbols to function in directing the psyche toward "individuation."[10] Left at this level, however, the symbol remains only at the stage of immediate experience; it has yet to be universalized, cosmicized.

For those, however, who visualize the full significance of the symbol, the tree as symbol is associated with the cosmic tree. A whole cosmology of birth and rebirth, regeneration, and perpetual fertility is revealed. Nature itself is seen as a symbolic living reality. Assuredly, the tree functions for both the symbol-numbed and the symbol-attuned individual. But for the person who perceives the *religious* symbolism of the tree, the symbol holds deeper, broader, and more universal messages. The interpreter in the end broadens his or her own isolated existential position to a more universal one.

When associated with the sacred, the symbol as a dialectic becomes a *hierophany,* that manifestation of the sacred whereby meaning and a perception of the cosmos breaks into everyday existence. As I will later show, this breakage into the everyday is less in *contrast* to the ordinary (the profane) as it is a *contact* with the ordinary. The sacred is very much in, and often indistinguishable from, the profane.[11] This idea of the rupturing of planes came to Eliade in the late 1930s, but the term "hierophany" was not coined until his post-Romanian 1949 *Traité d'histoire des religions (Patterns in Comparative Religion)*.[12]

In the same way that anything can conceivably become a symbol, so can anything serve to manifest the sacred, from a stone, a tree, a mountain, a person, to a particular space or conception of time, as in history being the domain of Yahweh's activity. The following quotation suffices to tie together the symbol and a hierophany:

> Since man is *homo symbolicus,* and all his activities involve symbolism, it follows that all religious facts have a symbolic character. This is certainly true if we realize that every religious act and every cult object aims at a metaempiricial reality. When a tree becomes a cult object, it is not as a *Tree* that it is venerated, but as a *hierophany,* that is, a manifestation of the sacred. And every religious act, by the simple fact that it is *religious,* is endowed with a meaning which, in the last instance, is "symbolic," since it refers to supernatural values or beings.[13]

It is important to restate that a hierophany does not lose its material essence and function. An Indian's spade and his tilling of the soil maintain their material, economic, and alimentary functions even as the Indian takes what he is doing as a cosmic symbol of fertility. Similarly, a stone remains a stone even though it is invested with sacred meaning. For Christians, the person Jesus Christ manifests God, but Jesus remains a human being who still eats, gets dirty, suffers, and weeps. Both the religious and the nonreligious person will acknowledge the facticity of the tilling process and the reality of the stone and of the historical Jesus and see "something" in them. But only insofar as a person acknowledges the act, the object, or the person as a hierophany susceptible of "awakening" or "bursting" open lived reality, does the hierophany truly become a religious symbol. So it is more than understanding the "fact" of a hierophany. Any skilled interpreter of the symbols can come to that much. It is, rather, when one's consciousness and approach to reality is affected as a result of the hierophany that this defines the person as religious. She or he is opened to an ontological, epistemological, and soteriological difference between ordinary space and time and sacred space and time. The symbol discloses and changes one to another cosmological orientation. If not previously disposed to such a posture, a person can be initiated into it, and this by a hierophany. For every hierophany is an "ontophany," an existential awakening to Being.[14]

In his book *The Two and The One,* Eliade provides an example of such an awakening. In the chapter, "Experiences of Mystical Light," Eliade cites the case of the psychologist, Dr. R. M. Bucke who, one evening, encountered a bright, firelike light which engulfed him and, according to his acount, penetrated him. From that experience Bucke came to a "cosmic consciousness." Eliade says this experience can be explained from a shamanic, Hindu, Buddhist, Catholic, or Jungian point of view, among others. "But the fundamental point," says Eliade, "is that thanks to this experience of the inner light, Dr. Bucke had access to a spiritual world the existence of which he had not even suspected until then, and that the access to this trancendental world constituted for him an *incipit vita nova.*"[15]

Dr. Bucke mentions a case under his own observation of a woman who encountered a similarly strange but confirming light. She recounts that "the mental experinces following the light . . . are always essentially the same—namely an intense desire to reveal man to himself and to aid those who are trying to find something worth living for in what they call this 'life.' "[16] Eliade notes how this woman's experience had no trancendental message except that of having a "humanitarian" character. Her "new life," "second birth," "were confined to the level of human activities."[17] Both for Dr. Bucke and the women, their encounter with a "mystical light" became for them a symbol of the sacred, of something powerfully different from this world. They acknowledged and were empowered by a hierophany, the inbreaking of the sacred into everyday existence.

As I stated earlier, a person does not have to defend a particular faith to acknowledge the existence of a mythic and symbolic metaphysic. One is simply willing to accept the fact that myths and symbols can point to other universes of meaning, however these universes of meaning may be defined or expressed. The sacred, and what Eliade means by the spiritual and by religion, does not necessarily involve a belief in a God or gods.[18] There is no need for any mediating concept or deity between ordinary, profane experience and extraordinary, sacred experience.[19] It is left to theology to supply the content of the sacred. For Eliade the sacred is simply, but fundamentally, a qualitative and limiting distinction from the profane, involving distinctions of orientation in time and space and in the human's self-understanding in relation to the two orientations. Though Eliade assumes the irreducibility of the sacred, the sacred is not dualistically separable from the profane, for the sacred is at once contained in and qualifies the profane. The sacred and the profane interact and interrelate dialectically, similar in function to the mutual complementarity of the Chinese polarity yin/yang.[20] It is in Eliade's literature, specifically his literature of the fantastic (*littérature fantastique*), that we see the close and ambiguous interrelationship between the sacred and the profane. Through this genre Eliade explores the ways in which the sacred can be camouflaged in everyday activity and how ordinary life becomes replete with meaning.

One work of this genre which, for Eliade, attests to the paradoxical relationship of the sacred camouflaged within the profane was Şarpele (The Snake), a novel written in two weeks in 1937 and regarded by Eliade as a "product purely of the imagination." Relying on no outside sources and writing by night in installments without referring to what he had written the night before (since he had already passed on the former night's material to the copy boy), Eliade was startled upon completing the work at how coherent and consistent the plot and the symbols remained throughout. Reflecting later on this experience, Eliade realized he had succeeded in demonstrating "that the 'sacred' *apparently* is not different from the 'profane,' that the 'fantastic' is camouflaged in the 'real,' that the world is what it shows itself to be, and is at the same time a cipher."[21] Eliade had experienced the presence of the fantastic expressing itself through the unconscious. He had discovered what he terms in his literature the "unrecognizability of miracle."

The above comments regarding the dialectic of the sacred in hierophanies and in the "unrecognizability of miracle," speak to how concrete in ordinary life Eliade's use and understanding of symbols can be. According to the historian of religion, Ioan Culianu, Eliade's view of symbols does indeed take into consideration social involvement and social communication, much in the same way as the anthropologist Clifford Geertz understands symbols.[22] Eliade cannot be dismissed as being Platonic, as in given to ideal forms and in belittling present and historical existence. For Eliade the meaning of the symbol is found through historical structures. In the same way, universal archetypes filter through their variant symbols throughout time. It is in the sense that the idea lives in the concrete that Eliade is Aristotelian, and such an orientation is elemental to a morphology.[23] So while Eliade emphasizes universals and syntheses, his thought has, nevertheless, the potential to illuminate the concrete and the contextual.[24] To emphasize further the concrete and incarnational aspect of Eliade's interpretation of symbols, one need only mention the inherent limits to a hierophany. Every hierophany belongs to a specific time and place, to a history. The Indian *asvattha* tree, for example, has meaning only for a particular Indian group. The Baal cult of ancient Canaan was limited to a particular period until the Yahweh cult superseded it (or absorbed it). In each case the symbol was confined to a particular context. One culture, subsequently, may not necessarily understand the hierophany of another culture: a South Asian Hindu may not grasp the symbol of Jesus Christ as a Western Christian would. That there would be a lack of connection between symbols of different cultures is obvious, but it is an aspect of symbols that is not appreciated enough in Eliade's thought. Interpreters instead focus on

Eliade's emphasis on the transspatial and transtemporal quality of symbols. But it is because there is such disconnectedness among certain symbols that the new humanism must interpret other people's cultural symbols in the hope of broadening and transforming one's own world of meaning.

Another way symbols as hierophany are contextually limited is that hierophanies undergo cycles of devaluation and revaluation. To the Yahwists, the cult of Baal proved too provincial, too limited to context, too local, and, therefore, restrictive. Similarly, for Christians, Jesus and the kingdom of God idea prevailed over the motifs of the Deuteronomic law and the nation of Israel. In each case a symbol was devalued, absorbed, or altered by a community in favor of another symbol that proved more universal and efficacious for manifesting the sacred. It is as symbols move toward totality that they undergo various valuations and devaluations over time.

This notion of the valuation and devaluation of hierophanies, however, leads Eliade's morphology of symbols to assume a particular religious slant. Commenting on Eliade's "progressional view of hierophanies," Stephen J. Reno notes that for Eliade this devaluation and revaluation of hierophanies leads Eliade to speak of Christ as the "supreme hierophany."[25] Reno quotes from *Patterns in Comparative Religion*. Here Eliade says that all hierophanies are "prefigurations" of the "Incarnation" and as such the "pagan religious ways (fetishes, idols and such)" were but "desperate attempts to prefigure the mystery of the incarnation."[26] And why would Jesus Christ be regarded as the *supreme* hierophany up to which all others build? Reno quotes from Eliade's *Myth, Dreams and Mysteries* where, in contrasting the way in which the sacred manifests itself in a stone and in Jesus Christ, Eliade says that the sacred "limits," "historicises," itself more in the person of Jesus than it does in a stone.[27] This assertion, says Reno, of Jesus being a greater limitation of the sacred in history, attests to a "methodological principle whereby hierophanies might be differentiated and arranged in some ascending sequence" based on the "degree of the paradox of the incarnation."[28]

For Reno this perceived "methodological principle" in Eliade poses a problem of methodology, though Reno does not say exactly why it is a problem. One might suppose that it makes a hierarchical value judgment, or to say that God was incarnated in history oversteps the line between describing a belief objectively and in taking the belief as fact. But if there is a limitation and qualification to be found in Eliade's progression of hierophanies, the limitation is founded upon a more fundamental assumption than on which Reno bases his argument.

As I have shown, hierophanies are manifestations of the sacred that break into temporal, profane existence. The more a hierophany is said to limit itself in history, the more complex is its dialectic of holding together the temporal and the eternal. Consequently, according to Eliade, Jesus Christ, as a hierophany, is "superior" to a stone. As hierophanies, they have the same structure, but the Christ symbol, as a limitation of the sacred (*kenosis*), more completely and more radically lodges itself in history. And were we to take history, or the problem of history, as the central theme to Eliade's thought—be it in his literary or scholarly work[29]—we find that Eliade is led by necessity to value most Jesus Christ as a hierophany over all other hierophanies, since history is the governing criteria for defining the nature and function of a hierophany. From among all the manifestations of the sacred, therefore, we find in Eliade's method a preponderance toward the Christian symbol.

With this preponderance in mind we can next ask, how does Eliade's valorization of the Christian hierophany figure in with his phenomenological morphology? In chapter 2 I stated that a morphology handles a complexity of religious and cultural forms. These forms progress from the simple to the complex,[30] where, in an interacting relationship, the simple is contained in the complex and the complex has no more elements than what the simple can provide: the seed prefigures the tree but all aspects of the tree are contained in the seed. When Eliade ranks Jesus Christ above the stone he is simply being true to the morphological process: stones (our seed) antecede logically Jesus Christ (our tree) but coexist in the Incarnation symbol.

But just as there is no single kind of tree, there is equally no single religion. For Eliade to say that all hierophanies lead to Christ (which is one tree among many trees—Judaism, Islam, Buddhism, Hinduism, etc.) is, to return to our analogy, to select one tree for its preferred characteristic (in this case "history") from all other trees and their particular characteristics. It is to select a redwood, for instance, over a maple because the redwood best accents the prized characteristic, "stability," as determinative of "treeness." *A fortiori*, to return to Eliade, it is the element of "history" in the nature of hierophanies which gives Eliade's morphology, and thus his new humanism, a decidedly Christian slant.[31] For it is Christianity that most completely historicizes the sacred. A morphology, therefore, is found to be limited to its governing paradigm;[32] in Eliade's case it is the paradigm of "history." So in contrast to many of Eliade's interpreters who say he is ahistorical or antihistory, the above argument demonstrates that Eliade has a strong historical regard. In fact, Eliade's method is ruled by history. In a sense, it is restricted by the historical problem. In order to be open to the strengths of other religions, therefore, students of religion operating through an Eliadean paradigm, must bracket the historical standard. Even when Eliade focuses on the archaic and Oriental interpretations of history, it is still the historical problem that concerns Eliade.[33] Eliade's theory of history and of hierophanies remains, in the end, provincial to Christianity.

As a Cosmic Spirituality

By looking fore and aft and up and down, the early humans oriented themselves in the cosmos and overcame the existential anxieties of disequilibrium of being in the world. The cosmos—the vast heavens, the rhythms of the moon, of the sun, and of the plants—and human life coexisted in an athropo–cosmic relationship of an I–Thou nature. Insofar as the universe held an inner meaning, the individual's life equally could have meaning and power.

Eliade's idea of the cosmicization of the individual through symbols first appears in 1932 in *Soliloquii,* a "work in progress" begun during his period in India.[34] "Man's first duty," said Eliade, "is God's first example: his cosmicization."[35] To cosmicize the individual means to elevate the human to a plane beyond the dualisms—good/bad, night/dark, self/other—tensions, and anxieties of ordinary life.[36] One does not, though, become detached from the historical plane of the everyday. Cosmicization, rather, ranks the planes of human life—material, psychological, political, metaphysical, religious—in a hierarchical order, with a cosmic, universal consciousness as the pinnacle.[37] Says Eliade, "A philosophy which starts with man means one that takes account of all the dimensions in which man moves, without however mixing them or simplifying them, but rather arranging them in a hierarchical order, cosmicizing them."[38] This view of cosmicization led Eliade to criticize Western scientific materialism and historicism for not being concerned enough with enduring spiritual values. Eliade's participation in the cultural symposium Criterion was an attempt to infuse Romanian culture with spiritual values, instead of having it rest on and torn apart by transient and sterilizing political interests.

But it was just this kind of interest in spiritual values that led Eliade to give moral support to the Legionary nationalist movement. He understood it to be a nonpolitical, spiritual movement aimed at the creation of a "new man."[39] This "new man" was not of blood (as in being racist), or of sex (Freud), or of economics (Marxists), but of the autonomy of the spirit.[40] This autonomy of the spirit, however, created its own form of xenophobia and violence. Though never condoning racism or violence, Eliade clearly demonstrated at one stage a xenophobic and prideful nationalism. The autonomy of the spirit and the cosmicization of the individual can, on the one hand, critique pragmatic and short-term self-interests. They can also qualify human life in light of its totality when human life is reduced to a single plane. On the other hand, the autonomy of the spirit and cosmicization of the individual can overlook or ignore the actual human interests that motivate social and individual action. And, often, with the aim of achieving spiritual values, these actual interests will subsume rightful means for exalted ends. In this regard, one way to evaluate interpretations made of human phenomenon whenever *homo religiosus* is assumed, is to determine how well these interpretations explicate, adjudge, and address the competing historical interests at hand.

It was not until he had been in exile for a few years and could reflect on the failed idealisms of his generation in Romania, that Eliade regretted not having been politically realistic enough. Failing to be so, he and his generation lost their chance at possibly constructing a different Romania. In an article in Gheorge Racoveanu's periodical *Indreptar* entitled "Politics ate up His Head!" Eliade said:

> This was the historical error and great fault of our generation, that instead of having begun in 1925 to participate in political parties—*all* political parties—and instead of having enhanced their ideological substance and regenerated their old leadership through the new and creative contribution of our youth, we remained outside political life and ignored political realities and techniques. . . . Such a detachment from political reality amounts almost to a moral deficiency—and it has been paid for, heaped up and running over, in the sad years that have ensued. The horror of "politics" on the part of the young generation led fatally to the ideological and moral debility of all the existing political organizations.[41]

Though Eliade came to a more sober view of politics, he never did aspire to hold political office, nor did he expect the history of religions to transform culture through political channels.[42] Indeed, except for his epic novel *The Forbidden Forest,* Eliade in exile became markedly detached from politics, often to the consternation of his colleagues.[43] Maybe in exile Eliade understood better Indian *maya* and his individual destiny for all culture, not just the Romanian, and thus retreated to scholarship and literature. Or maybe as an exile, and helpless except for his scholarship, he recognized the limits to his ability to affect change. Whatever the case, Eliade's early "political" involvements, even if veiled in nonpolitical terms, and his 1951 redressing—a conversion?—demonstrate a political element to his new humanism. Albeit concerned with the spiritual, the new humanism has a decidedly and necessary "political" nature. Humans are both social and political beings, said Aristotle. However "political" the new humanism is to be, the cosmicization of humans in the new humanism maintains the primacy of the spiritual over the political.

At whatever level, be it the material, the political, the metaphysical, or the religious, cosmicization occurs through symbols. And the greatest symbol, of which all humans are a part, is the natural world. The one thing that unquestionably unites humankind is the fact that we all share the same physical world; there is only *one* physical world from which humans can speak and understand themselves. However urbanized, secularized, and science-dominated humans are today (regardless of how much they differ from, or are the same with, earlier periods in time), Eliade believes the created order still shapes humanity's cultural and religious meaning, even if at the unconscious level. The created order is inseparably linked to human nature. In his last granted interview Eliade was asked if humans need nature to be religious. "Yes," he said, "in the sense that we are part of the same creation. Every animal has a mode of being based on fertility, and so on. Man is higher than the animals, but that does not destroy his inherited animal traditions. So, yes, we need nature . . . We live in the world, and the world is not only man's constructions."[44]

Eliade is quick to point out that to be open to the world of symbols does not mean one merely duplicates the rhythms of natural phenomenona. Symbols reveal and conceal, and they hold interrelating oppositions in meaning. To one's immediate perception the sun symbolizes light and life. As such, solar symbolism is associated with fertility, potency, the divine, etc. But the sun also manifests the "nocturnal," "evil," "funerary aspects," "death," etc., for as the sun rises it also sets, burns, consumes. This coexistence of opposites within a single entity or phenomenon is refered to as a *coincidentia oppositorium*. Symbols have a paradoxical quality. They "speak" to the whole person, to the conscious and the unconscious, the rational and the psychic, the diurnal and the nocturnal, to the good and to the shadow side of an individual. Combined, these polarities constitute the totality of the symbol.

In order for a person today to grasp the full significance of nature's symbols, therefore, both the poetic imagination and the rational mind must be brought into play. In an entry dated 9 April 1976, Eliade notes the need of modern society to integrate these two dimensions of human thought for grasping symbolic life:

> I think that contemporary man, and more importantly, men of tomorrow, will soon find themselves obliged and forced to integrate the two forms of knowledge—logical and rational on the one hand, symbolic and poetic on the other. I am also convinced that under the pressure of history we will be forced to familiarize ourselves with the different expressions of extra-European creative genius, such as are found in Asia, Africa, and Oceania. As I've repeated over and over for thirty years, only the history of religions furnishes the discipline that can bring to light the meaning not only of traditional, but also of "primitive" and Oriental, civilizations. In a word, this is a discipline— such at least as I envision and practice it—that will contribute decisively to "globalizing" culture.[45]

The primacy Eliade gives to intuition and to the poetic imagination, both essential componenets of the "creative hermeneutics" of his new humanism, has attracted many critics, Ivan Strenski being one of the more recent.[46] Eliade is criticized for invalidating or at least sidelining the deductive process in the interpretation of symbols. Eliade does not eliminate the deductive, since he stresses historical and ethnographic erudition and the formulation of hypotheses. He says, rather, that reality is not governed by Newtonian quantitative absolutes. Reality, instead, is marked by paradox, contradictions, illusion, and unpredictability. If reality is of the rational and the irrational, of the ordered and the unordered, of the seen and the unseen, then it is symbols, through their ability to integrate opposites, that can most comprehensively unite the totality of reality.

It is in *Patterns in Comparative Religion,* issued in its French version in 1949, that Eliade arranges morphologically the cosmic symbols humans have participated in and interpreted for meaning throughout time. *Patterns* is not a historical study; it does not trace the development of a symbol's meaning in a particular culture. Nor is it a sociological or an anthropological treatise. The symbols are not placed in a social structure nor looked at as human constructions. Neither is it a theological tome; it does not speculate on human belief but merely accepts human beliefs as various ways to construct meaning. *Patterns,* rather, is a morphology of religious forms that humans from across time and space have used to convey the presence of the sacred through nature into historical existence. Each form and the forms taken together serve, in the words of Lawrence Sullivan, as a "momentary center of gravity in the imagination."[47] Not the final word of a symbol's meaning, these forms, as momentary centers, orient the imagination for further inquiry and nuanced signification. Interpreters of religious symbols can then go on to contextualize how the symbols operate in a given context and throughout a tradition.

The chapters are arranged around the selected symbols of the sky, sun, moon, water, stones, the earth, vegetation and agriculture, and sacred space and time. Together, these symbols elucidate fundamental binary oppositions in nature and human culture: space/time, sky/earth, sun/moon, water (liquids)/stones (solids), vegetation/agriculture.[48] I will arrange the following discussion according to the cosmic symbols Eliade discusses in *Patterns*. These symbols are those which comprise a cosmic–human spirituality.

The Sky

As a symbol, the sky reflects that which is distant, highup, everywhere; it reveals transcendence. It communicates holiness, changelessness, and infinitude. Says Eliade:

> The transcendence of God is directly revealed in the inaccessibility, infinity, eternity and creative power (rain) of the sky. The whole nature of the sky is an inexhaustible hierophany. Consequently, anything that happens among the stars or in the upper areas of the atmosphere—the rhythmic revolution of the stars,

chasing clouds, storms, thunderbolts, meteors, rainbows—is a moment in that hierophany.[49]

However much the sky radiates power and infinitude, it remains too distant, too passive, to satisfy the human spirit. From its initial place as a god, the sky as symbol was found to be too removed, unchanging, and detached from the human sphere to serve as a ''personal'' god. Though it maintained its sacredness and presence, it came to be regarded as a functionless god, a *deus otiosus*. As a result, in the history of human spirituality, the sky as sacred symbol was subordinated to more specialized gods—the sun, moon, demiurges, storm gods—which were more active, dynamic, and involved in historical and physiological life, i.e., birth, death, fecundity. With the coming of historical consciousness and the activity of powerful conquerors, the sky gods came to be associated with kings, monarchs, emperors. They were the gods' representatives on earth. As history progressed, the sky gods themselves were devalued to the level of earthly powers. No longer were the sky gods the power and omniscient creators behind human activity. Instead, human activity became itself the agent affecting history; the economic, political, and social powers were thought to determine history's progress. In addition, being too removed from physiological life, the sky god was devalued to earth and vegetation deities. It is against these devaluations of the transcendent to the human plane, says Eliade, that there initiated the rise of the Yahweh cult in ancient Israel.[50]

The transcendent sky, lessened to the status of sky gods and to human sociopolitical powers, marks the first instance of the ''death of God'' in the history of religions.[51] To historians of religion the death-of-God theology in the 1960s was nothing new. In contrast to these theologians who wanted to sublimate absolutely the language of God and any transcendent to the secular, earlier cultures would simply raise another god in place of the ''dead'' god, hence maintaining the transcendent realm. Such a revalorization, says Charles Long, is a hope Eliade holds for the secularized modern.[52] Though the transcendent has undergone its own form of devaluation as history progressed into the age of scientific materialism, the longing for the transcendent persists as a structure of human consciousness, evident in all of the symbolisms associated with ''height,'' ''ascension,'' the ''center,'' sacred mountains, temples, ladders, and stairs.[53]

The Sun

As a sky deity, the symbol of the sun has been associated with sovereignty and power. In contrast to other sky deities, such as the moon and storm gods, the sun came to be associated with those civilizations where ''history is on the march" thanks to kings, heroes, and powerful empires. Eliade is not clear as to why the sun as a sacred symbol, a hierophany, became associated with historical force and with those who advance the course of history. Perhaps, as he says, it was the kings, monarchs, the elite, and the initiated—those chosen to become descendents or children of the sun hero—who monopolized for themselves the meaning of the sun as fecundator, creator, giver of life, and raiser of the dead.[54] Aside from these people, the sun as supreme being would not occupy a unique role among the peasant agriculturalists.[55] Other divinities—the moon, the waters, gods of vegetation readily associated with the human life process and which also symbolized and promoted fertility and creation—were substituted for the sun god. Eliade notes how the sun, in being associated with the elite, lost its full symbolic force when the elite prioritized rationality over intuition. For without the mode of intuition, the sun could not be perceived in its total nature as an ambivalent symbol of darkness and lightness, of destruction and creation, as raiser of the dead and as an omen of the apocalypse. It is not that rationalization is absent among the primitives, it is that when reason is prioritized over intuition the totality and paradoxes of the symbol are compromised.

The Moon

The moon did not, like the sun, undergo a degradation as a symbol. Apparently, says Eliade, the "nocturnal domain of the mind," evidenced most clearly by the moon, is less easily extinguished by rationalism. Perhaps it is because the moon more than any other sacred symbol reveals the basic condition of human beings, their becoming.[56] The moon waxes and wanes. Its oscillations between fullness and partiality denote the endless rhythms of life and death, of being born only to die again—constant temporality, endless becoming. It was in opposition to this cycle of becoming that the people of India seek Brahman, ultimate being, permanency.[57] Says Eliade of humans' need to break the cycle of impermanency:

> Though the modality of the moon is supremely one of change, of rhythm, it is equally one of periodic returning; and this pattern of existence is disturbing and consoling at the same time—for though the manifestations of life are so frail that they can suddenly disappear altogether, they are restored in the "eternal returning" regulated by the moon. Such is the law of the whole sublunary universe. But that law, which is at once harsh and merciful, can be abolished, and in some cases one may "transcend" this periodic becoming and achieve a mode of existence that is absolute.[58]

Because of its rhythmicality, the moon became a comprehensive, unifying symbol for the human condition. Processes relating to the human experience, such as birth, death, fecundity, immortality, light coming out of darkness, cycles, dualisms, reconciliation of contraries, were immediately grasped by the primitive mentality. For the primitive there is no lag time in the imagination between the symbol and its morphology of meanings. As Lawrence Sullivan describes in the cosmogony of the South American Campa of the eastern Peruvian forest, when the moon is said to have made its descent "in the beginning" it simultaneously created the first food, manioc, by blowing on termite nests and raised the fecundator sun, which impregnated the earth, mother of the sun, as she bathed in the river during her menstrual period. Today the Campa say that the moon is the author of life (in the form of the sun) and of the sustenance of life (in the form of manioc). In one movement the moon is associated with food, menstruation, sexuality, and birth.[59] The primitive grasps the whole intuitively, immediately, whereas for the modern, having the mentality of causation, the mind grasps the whole based on the proper functioning of its parts. The modern mind says "*Because* the moon governs the waters, *therefore* plants are subject to it"; the primtive says "Plants and the waters are subject to the moon *in the same way* as the moon governs the waters."[60] Both modes of thought reflect a contrast in ontology. The primitive worships the cosmos as a reflection of human life. The cosmos is seen wholistically, and humans are an integral part of that unity. For the modern the cosmos and nature operate independently of human life. Modern ontology, subsequently, is principally in an I–It relation to the natural world.

The Waters

Water, like the sky and like stones, gets its symbolic content from its very nature: its formlessness. Without form it precedes all forms. To be formless and to precede all forms, to be immersed in water, is to return to formlessness, to the time before birth, to the beginning of creation. By extension, any contact with water symbolizes life, regeneration, and the taking on of form. Water is "living water." By default, to be separated from water is to lose potentiality, since water fertilizes life. To come out of water, therefore, is to become subject to the laws of time and of life, and, subsequently, to change and decay.[61] Naturally, in order to halt continual decay, periodic regeneration by water is needed; so Hindus find spiritual renewal through periodic immersions in the sacred Ganges. Water symbolism, in short, suggests renewal and transformation through the collapse and reformulation of all forms.

The Stone

As symbols of the sacred, stones acquire symbolic meaning from their intrinsic quality: a stone *is;* it *strikes*. Stones are hard, firm, permanent. They bear the mark of a spiritual force of power. They seem to come from somewhere else and so point to a power beyond themselves. Meteorites, as a prime example, are thought to come from heaven. Piercing the heavens and falling to earth, they strike a connection between heaven and earth. The place where they lodge becomes the center of the earth, an *axis mundi*. Due in part to the heavenly origin of meteorites, metallurgy assumed a sacred, symbolic significance.[62] Not only meteorites, but all stones have the capacity to symbolize the center of the earth. Hence the biblical Jacob at Beth-el constructed a stone monument to mark the place and time when the transcendent entered the immanent. Prior to Jacob's apparition the stones meant nothing. Now, as a monument, they are sacred because of their association with a sacred space and time. Either by their unique form, place of origin, or by their association with a sacred place, time, or event, stones can assume a sacred or "hierophanic" power. Eliade is fond of commenting on how the Romanian sculptor Brancusi respected and revered stones in a manner approaching the early humans. Brancusi's sculpture "The Endless Column" is a clear symbol of an *axis mundi*, a connecting link of heaven to earth.[63]

The Earth

Aside from the sky, perhaps, the most inescapable symbol of the sacred is the earth itself, Mother Earth, *Tellus Mater*. The earth's existence is immediately accepted by all humans and cultures. The earth unifies all sacred symbols. As a wealth of symbolic meaning and natural forces, the earth is perceived as a procreator par excellence; it never wearies of procreating. The rhythms of vegetation symbolize the mysteries of birth, death, and rebirth. Agrarian cultures, henceforth, developed a cosmic religion centered around the periodic renewal of the world. And with Mother Earth considered as a womb, beliefs and practices centered around her birthing potential. Naturally the motif of fertility would attach women to the earth and its creative potential.

Examples are many of a spirituality centered around Earth Mother and of how, when that spirituality is intact, beliefs exist in the continuing vitality and productivity of humans. It was only when the scientific, rationalistic mindset prevailed, says Eliade, that the earth and humans suffered a breach. The earth became an object of study and a complexity of powers and resources for manipulation and exploitation. Drained of vitality, the earth and its resources were no longer considered perpetually regenerative. Instead they were seen as having a definite and fatalistic ending. The earth could give no more; thus it and humans would dry out.

Vegetation

The symbols and rites associated with vegetation and agriculture participate in the Mother-Earth symbol of the sacred. Although a complicated symbolic structure, vegetation symbolism focuses on the endless motif of regeneration. The sacred tree, of all vegetation symbols, best encapsulates the symbolisms associated with vegetation.[64] The tree symbolizes a microcosm of the whole. What takes place at the sacred place occupied by the tree extends into and represents the entire cosmos. Citing an interpretation of the cross, Eliade shows how the tree universalizes: "the blood of Christ, crucified at the centre of the Earth, on the very spot where Adam was created and buried, falls upon 'the skull of Adam,' and thus, redeeming him from his sin, baptizes the father of mankind."[65] In his novel *The Forbidden Forest,* Eliade describes the way in which a tree can universalize one's existence, the place upon which one stands. Stefan, the protagonist, watches as Ainsie cleans caterpillars from a tree:

> I watched him carefully and I felt that he was *present* in every motion. He wasn't thinking of anything else when he was working on a tree. His mind didn't wander. I perceived that the tree revealed itself to him in its totality. For him it wasn't a simple object, one among thousands of others of its kind, as it would appear to us, the majority of men. To him, at that particular moment, the tree that he was cleaning revealed the entire Universe. He saw it in its totality: roots, branches, leaves, parasites. . . ."[66]

Agriculture

Agriculture as symbol arose when humans no longer took a passive response to vegetation but actively participated in the vegetative process. Human rituals proceeded to alter and engage with the ways of nature. New Year celebrations of rites of sacrifice, ritual orgies, jubilees, and wild festivities fell at the closure of old, withered, and chaotic periods marked by the lunar cycles in order to open a new, regenerated, and abundant period for the coming agricultural season. Human sacrifices were also thought to affect the productivity of one's harvest. Whether they be sacrifices or ritual orgies, such creative acts were thought to restore the time of beginnings, of when creation first took place. The primtive, says Eliade, always lived in the "constant terror of finding that the forces around him which he found so useful were worn out."[67]

In order to prevent this sterility, nature had to be periodically regenerated.

One must be careful in interpreting the "barbarous" or "obscene" acts of sacrifice or ritual orgy as excessive and superflous if indeed nature was thought to never "weary of procreating." What is forgotten is that for the primitive no rational and effectual distance was thought to exist between themselves and nature; what humans did and what nature did operated in parallel. Humans were part of the whole. Agricultural religiosity taught them of the fundamental oneness of organic life: women to field, the sexual act to sowing, life as rhythmic, death as return, a hidden seed as a later resurrection. This cyclical-ness and organic oneness, adds Eliade, instilled in the traditional peoples a hopeful and optimistic view of existence: death is a provisional change, winter is never final, nature regenerates itself into new forms, and so on. Yet, Eliade continues, a pessimistic vision finds its origin here as well, "for man is like the flower of the field. . . ."[68]

The above lengthy overview of a cosmic religious orientation reflects a centrifugal positioning within the vastness of the cosmos. The anxiety of being in the world is overcome as one sees one's life as harmonious with larger cosmic rhythms. A centripetal positioning is more locative. One defines one's sense of place and time within tighter and more localized parameters. The two orientations are not mutually exclusive but a matter of emphasis among individuals and cultures.

The act of interpreting one's place centrifugally or centripetally is part of the morphology of symbolic space and time. Eliade concludes his morphology of symbols in *Patterns* with an exposition upon sacred space and time and the significance of myth in creating the distinctions between sacred and profane space and time for the spiritual-religious person.

Sacred Place

Every hierophany "transforms the place where it occurs: hitherto profane, it is thenceforward a sacred area."[69] The terrestrial landscape acquires meaning for the religious person when dotted with sacred places; space becomes non-relative and heterogeneous. It is no longer all of the same value. Manifestations of the sacred not only sanctify a profane space, they insure that sacredness lives on at that place as long as the manifestation remains viable. Whenever a person enters a sacred place communion with the sacred is possible. There at that place a person returns to the time of beginnings, to what is fundamentally real and meaningful. A sacrificial site, an altar, a temple, a place of residence founded upon a sacred spot are transformative and empowering centers. And for the primitive, the individual and the social group do not want to stray far from such centers. For it is at the center that one's self is rooted as a religious being. The important point to stress is the need of the religious person to break up space into meaningful centers. There must be distinctions of ontological value if the person is not to sink into chaos and meaninglessness. Such centers of value are many. And each one reveals to the person something about him or herself and about his or her relation to the cosmos.

Sacred Time

Sacred time functions in the same ontological way as sacred space: it breaks up time into periods of meaning and power. Symbolic, sacred time, or hierophanic time is that time 1) during which a ritual takes place—profane time precedes and antecedes that time—and 2) when a person enters into a sacred story, a myth, by means of a ritual or some action in imitation of a mythical model. For instance, in New Guinea, when a mariner sets out to sea, he is repeating the acts and story of the mythical hero Aori. The mariner dresses like Aori—with the same facial coloring and costume—dances and spreads his wings like Aori, and embarks on the fish hunt with the same attitude that Aori once had. The mariner does not invoke the mythical hero. The mariner imitates him as closely as possible to insure that he becomes contemporary with Aori. In this way the mariner repeats a sacred archetype, model, and makes the mythical time present, real. What would otherwise be a profane, ordinary, task is now given value and supernatural power. Along with the two other means, symbolic time 3) patterns itself after the rhythms of the cosmos, like the phases of the moon. Thus the annual New Year celebrates the recreation and reordering of the world.

The symbols of sacred space and time are the crux to Eliade's spirituality. By means of these humans order their world as a cosmos. They establish a place from which to define one's ''self'' in relation to the surrounds and a time for providing constancy amidst historical change and flux. Together they can perpetually restore a person and a group to new life and redefine their sense of purpose.

The cosmic spirituality that Eliade's morphology of symbols presents is not a form of pantheism, which denies any contrast, any dialectic, to the reality of the sacred within nature. Nor is the cosmic spirituality merely natural revelation, where all of nature is sufficient in itself to disclose the sacred, since Eliade's view of hierophanies demands that there be a *choice* made among objects and places in nature, and his morphology of symbols includes history and the person of Jesus Christ as manifestations of the sacred. It would be equally mistaken to equate Eliade's cosmic spirituality with the Catholic scholar Pierre Teilhard de Chardin's cosmic mysticism and his divine diaphany.[70] Whereas Eliade distinguishes the sacred from the profane, Teilhard poses no distinction between matter and spirit for those who have eyes to see.[71] Eliade's cosmic sacrality is a mystical faith of trust, more like the Jewish philosopher Martin Buber's definition of Jewish "faith." In the Jewish view of "faith" a person "'finds himself' in the relationship of faith." In the Christian view, the person is "converted" to faith. In the former it is the "status" which is the decisive point; in the latter it is the "act." Buber says that the trust inherent in faith ". . . has a beginning in time, but the one who trusts does not know when: he identifies it of necessity with the beginning of the contact."[72]

To the primitive this "faith" as trust is to see the reality of the cosmos as a vibrant, renewing, meaningful, and "salvific" force. And it is the hierophanies, the spatial and temporal particularities of the sacred, which establish for the primitive that existential point of contact wherein one becomes identified with the sacred. Nature is not the ultimate reality. Nature is but a symbol of a transcending reality. To *define* this reality becomes the task of particular theologies.[73]

The relative clarity by which the primitive is thought to engage with nature's symbols is an expression of Eliade's theory of symbols: symbols universalize one by opening one up to the structure of the world. Symbols provide meaning by actively engaging one with what is ultimately real.[74] Whether it is the waters, the sky, or the rhythms within the agricultural cycles, symbols "speak," and they do so at three levels, the cosmological (the symbol tells us something about the cosmos); the anthropomorphic (they tie the human as a microcosm to the macrocosm); and the anthropological (the symbol directs the human to increasingly higher modes of being).[75] The human person, therefore, in living the symbol, is removed from the anxiety and isolation of her or his historical contingencies. One is not susceptible to being dwarfed and trivialized within the expanse and complexity of life. Instead, one's existential place and mode of existence is enormously and joyously enlarged. For Eliade says that as one is made part of the cosmos one is rewarded with the feeling of joy. Contrary to the existentialism of Kierkegaard, Heidegger, and Sartre, Eliade's is joyful. In a statement from his 1934 *Oceanografie,* Eliade voices a spirituality of joy and love:

> The first and essential human duty is . . . love, that of an untiring justification of the joy of existence. Make of your life and of your consciousness a permanent joy—in spite of all the misery, the fear, the sin, the impotence and the dispersions—here [is] a duty truly viril, a duty of humanity and of your humanity. I believe that the good justifies itself and is recognized from the joy. I believe that joy is the true structure of the new humanity which we are waiting for. I believe that the greatest sin against humanity is the despairing sadness erected as the supreme value of spirituality.[76]

Here Eliade sets forth a spirituality of the new humanity whose end and means is joy. It is as one trusts in and engages in the cosmos that one acquires this rich and elevated state of being, similar to Goethe's own mystical nondoctrinaire "religion."[77]

This cosmic spirituality, Elaide says, is found among Romanian peasant pastoralists, hunting and fishing societies in Scandanavia and northern Asia, and within the Christian mystical tradition. From another source, Catherine Albanese, an historian of American religion, points out the presence of such cosmic spirituality in her latest book, *Nature Religion in America: From the Algonkian Indians to the New Age*.[78]

In his *Forbidden Forest,* Eliade introduces this cosmic spirituality into the profane world of the everyday in the character Ainsie. Ainsie does not live by the clock and the calendar as others do. Instead his sense of time operates in accord with cosmic events. Says Stefan of Ainsie, "the phases of the moon, the seasons, the rotation of the earth. He's content to exhaust the significance of each of these phenomena, living thereby an uninterrupted revelation."[79]

The nature of this spirituality is not, as Roland Chagnon refers to it, a twentieth-century deism. According to him it lacks any divine, historical character.[80] Certainly the mystical solidarity with nature, the cosmic, nondoctrinal, and noninstitutional character of Eliade's spirituality would seem to support Chagnon's view. But to take Chagnon's position is to overlook the historical and existential nature of Eliade's view of how the sacred manifests itself. The sacred cannot manifest itself in any other way except in history; yet it is not confined to history. Futhermore, as I have shown, the centrality of history to Eliade's thought prefigures his spirituality with a Christian inclination, particularly an Orthodox one. There is, therefore, an historical expression to the sacred in Eliade's cosmic spirituality.

To put into a broader context Eliade's spirituality of the cosmicization of the individual, the Hindu and the Buddhist see cosmicization only as the penultimate goal for humans. To enter into the natural rhythms of nature would be to remain in the samsaric cycle of "becoming." In their own different ways and toward different ultimate goals, both the Hindu and the Buddhist desire to be freed from any such rhythms and returns. Indian religions seek a liberation that preexists the cosmos. Humans, for the Hindus and Buddhists, must first see nature for what it is and then, for final release, be freed from all historic and cosmic contingencies.

Before I move on, I must mention how the Chinese, specifically Confucius', view of the cosmos might apply to Eliade's spirituality of cosmicization. Confucius prioritizes a strictly immanent cosmos over a transcendent one. In an immanent cosmos a person is cosmicized by integrating her- or himself with society and its rites, its ceremonies, and the basic human acts of civilized life passed down through tradition, such as meeting, greeting, showing respect, making promises and commitments, etc. It is *in* the actual performance of these, not apart from these, that the spiritual is articulated as meaning and power. As the philosopher of Chinese thought Herbert Fingarette says, "Spirit is no longer an external being influenced by the ceremony; it is that that is expressed and comes most alive *in* the ceremony."[81] Society itself becomes the cosmos. The individual is integrated with society and society with the individual. So to be cosmicized is not to transcend society and to enter the rhythms of nature, as much as it is to see society itself as the purveyor of meaning, as the realm in which human acts, and hence humans, acquire their meaning.[82] And insofar that there is a human-societal-cosmos homology in Confucius, we can speak of Confucian immanenence as interrelated with the larger cosmos.

The New Humanism and the Relation to the Whole

As it has been shown, to live out the new humanism is to live in the world of symbols. The world reveals itself as a symbol to be interpreted and experienced. By engaging in the life of symbols a person is opened up to the cosmos, to broader panoramas, to the whole. However capable the modern person is in interpreting nature's symbols, and however much they disclose the sacred, of what is ultimately real, symbols communicate totality, completeness, universality, and unity in paradox, in short, the whole. It is this totality, this ideal of the whole, which is the final arbiter of all limited symbolic conditions. All relative positions must be appraised in relation to the whole.

Yet, humans can only exist within the particular, in the contextual, in the relative. Mystical and intuitive visions of the whole are reserved for isolated moments and usually for the shamans and mystics of the world. Nevertheless, the dynamic and the dialectical tension between the whole and the particular cannot be erased. When Eliade accents the symbol as that which discloses the whole, he says that every personal, cultural, and—one might add—political, expression is to be evaluated in relation to the whole in order to approximate its most true and complete meaning. In this way one-sided interpretations are averted. To interpret symbols *only* in their "concrete," thus particular, mode is to destroy them, says Eliade:

> There is no heresy so monstrous or orgy so infernal, no religious cruelty, folly, absurdity, or religious magic so insane, that it may not be "justified" in its very principle by some false—*because partial and incomplete*—interpretation of a grandiose symbolism.[83]

Speaking in terms of racism, Charles Long mentions the way in which signs and how they are signified (their significations) can create "an arena and field of power relationships.'' By means of the manipulation of symbols (of signs and their signification), one cultural and racial group can oppress the symbolic world of another.[84] From an ethical vantage point, therefore, it is possible to exorcise a limited and potentially destructive interpretation and use of a symbol, as racial hegemony, by placing it in relation to the whole—which includes all races. No symbol is complete on its own; it requires others to complete its total meaning.

As totality is approximated, believes Eliade, subjectivism is overcome: ''. . . the cosmological valence of symbolism permits [a person] to step out of a subjective situation to recognize the objectivity of his [or her] personal experiences.''[85] So, he continues:

> The initiate isolated in the initiatory hut or the one who contemplates a *t'ao-t'ieh* mask and understands its significance, or the one who hears the myth of Maui or a story of the Jonah type intuitively perceives the unity of structure between his particular ''nocturnal condition,'' and all the others.''[86]

Particular symbols and one's own human state are grasped and validated through archetypal structures. For the modern person these archetypal structures are latent, submerged in the unconscious. It is for this reason that the new humanism through hermeneutics seeks to restore these archetypes to the conscious mode. As this process of recovery is followed, humans will see how their own particular symbolic position fits within the whole.

With the above comments stated, an obvious set of problems arises. What are the universal archetypes in which the symbols share? How is one to recognize them? And who is to do it?

From the late 1930s, Eliade postulated a unity among all peoples. Though the scope of human history is of enormous diversity, the history of humanity is not ultimately fragmented. History bespeaks an underlying unity and order, and this order and unity can be discerned in the aspirations and cultural, social, political, and technological constructions of humans.[87] These aspirations and constructions can be trusted in what they reflect, however dim, of the universal archetypes that underlie them. To get at these archetypes, Eliade follows the hermeneutical process of steeping himself in the archeological, anthropological, ethnological, and literary documents of a subject. Then, with the gained erudition, Eliade intuits the meaning of the phenomenon. In order to achieve as close an objective interpretation of the symbol's meaning as possible, a constant cycle of exchange occurs from text to intuition to text. In this way the archetypes are ''ferreted out,'' says Adrian Marino. Whenever the process of recovery and interpretation reaches an end point, its prime number, so to speak, where the ''original, irreducible situation . . . cannot be translated in any other way: by another image, symbol, myth, concept, etc.,[88] the universal archetype is thereupon perceived. And it is this archetype which integrates, "reduces," all the relevant symbols operating on the immediate plane of human experience.[89]

The hermeneutical circle, we find, is a process combining empiricism and intuition. Empirically, the interpreter works from facts and makes sure that subsequent interpretations of the facts cohere the vast array of facts in a meaningful synthesis. The interpretation is intuitive to the extent that the interpreter aims to draw out the irreducible element of the facts, that is, their spiritual meaning. That the hermeneutical process does not claim scientific objectivity demonstrates that the new humanism is an aesthetic spirituality. Nevertheless, because the hermeneutical process constantly self-validates itself by resorting to as broad and as deep an erudition as possible, the interpretation is kept from becoming arbitrary and solipsistic. The interpretations that come from the new humanism's hermeneutical process are a sort of grammar created for giving meaning to culture. This grammar is a heuristic device of the imagination serving to articulate that which would otherwise go unexpressed. It is not that the interpreter creates something *totally* new and imposes it upon the facts and the believers. Instead this language, this grammar, bridges the irreducible and the factual for others. Only as long as this language efficiently provides meaning to the facts, and people find a coherent structure to this meaning, is the language validated as true to the facts.[90]

However much, though, Eliade universalizes our particular position within the cosmos as symbolic beings opened to the whole, we presently do not live in the whole. Symbols at the same time reveal the universal and our own boundedness and contingency.[91] We might be able to conceive of the whole, but it remains a thirsted-for abstraction. Speaking to the issue of religious pluralism, the theologian David Tracy refers to the "whole" as that generic absolute denoting the Kantian limit in religion: the limit is that which can be thought but not known.[92] The whole is there, is coveted, but remains only faintly approachable. In the long meantime humans must remain amidst many ontological and moral particulars. When the whole (truth) is pluralistic (not a plurality of truths), we are forced to discriminate between competing orientations to the whole, unless, as some do, we accept truth as univocal and thereby eliminate the problem altogether.

Though it is difficult to settle competing ontological and moral claims, it seems that if we accept the fact of mutually coexisting relationships, as in the Christian *coincidentia oppositorium* and the Indians' acceptance of contradictions, we can avoid reducing a competing claim to one's own. Symbols, and myths, are less subject to how "true" or "false" they are in relation to other interpretations as they are 1) meaningful to a person and his or her culture, 2) "close" to their archetype, and 3) open to other interrelating symbolic forms.

For example, the historian of religions, Wendy Doniger O'Flaherty, speaks of the ontological and moral problems associated with the Hindu practice of suttee—the burning of the widow on the husband's funeral pyre.[93] To Westerners, this practice elicits abhorrence and invites moral condemnation. Before we judge it, however, we must understand it for what it means to a husband to have his wife follow him, what it means to the widow, to other Hindus, and within Hindu history and cosmology as a whole. The meanings gained and integrated with other structurally similar symbols in other cultures will help us then to understand the archetype upon which the practice of suttee is based. As we understand suttee more broadly and deeply, we see new ways of looking at it, ways which are more reflective of the Hindu position and of the universal symbol of sacrifice.

The point is, in the interpretation of a symbol, the interpreter should constantly be interpreting and validating the meaning of the symbol. Through an ongoing dialectical interchange between the symbol's own particular expression and its expression within the larger Whole the symbol will be understood and new avenues of meaning and founts of creativity will be revealed.

The new humanism is approached in such a manner. Humans are to understand and interact in their world by placing their own symbolic positions within the purview of the larger symbolic Whole. In the terms of Joseph M. Kitagawa, one is to live out of both an "inner" and "outer" meaning. The former is the meaning one acquires in one's own particular and limited religious, cultural, societal, and political position, and the latter is in how one understands and articulates this position in light of the plurality of other orientations to meaning.[94]

Notes

1. R. K. Narayan, *The Guide* (London: Penguin Books, 1958).

2. Marino, *L'Hermeneutique de Mircea Eliade,* pp. 177ff.

3. See the editors' introductory statements to the section "The Interpretation of Symbolism" in *Reader in Comparative Religion: An Anthropological Approach,* ed. William A. Lessa and Evon Z. Vogt 4th ed. (New York: Harper & Row, 1979), p. 90.

4. Mircea Eliade, "Methodological Remarks in the Study of Religious Symbolism," in *The History of Religions: Essays in Methodology,* ed. Mircea Eliade and Joseph M. Kitagawa (Chicago: University of Chicago, 1959), p. 95.

5. Mircea Eliade, *A History of Religious Ideas: From the Stone Age to the Eleusinian Mysteries,* trans. Willard R. Trask, vol. 1 (Chicago: University of Chicago, 1978), p. 3.

6. This anthropological concept underlay Eliade's notions of "personality" and of the "new man," concepts circulating at the time amongst the young generation of the 1930s in Romania. See Ricketts, *The Romanian Roots,* pp. 979–80.

7. While it is unanimously agreed that the word "primitive" connotes imperialistic and hierarchical terminology, and was itself a term Eliade only regretfully used, its ubiquitous usage among anthropologists and historians of religion makes it a sadly unavoidable term. I will use it to be consistent with Eliade but remain aware of its limitations and insinuations.

8. Eliade, *History of Religions: Essays in Methodology,* pp. 98–99.

9. James W. Heisig, "Symbols," in *Encyclopedia of Religion,* ed. Mircea Eliade, and others (New York: Macmillan Publishing, 1986), 14:204.

10. Anthony Storr, ed., *The Essential Jung* (Princeton, NJ: Princeton University Press, 1983), p. 17ff.

11. This interpenetration of the sacred with the profane seems to suggest the secularization of the sacred, a process the death-of-god theologians carried to the full. Thomas Altizer, one of Eliade's early interpreters and a founder of the death-of-God movement along with Kenneth Hamilton, saw, mistakenly, in Eliade's sacred/profane dialectic a sanction for the secularization of religion. See Altizer, *Mircea Eliade and the Dialectic of the Sacred* (Philadelphia: Westminster Press, 1963). For a response to Altizer see Mac Linscott Ricketts, "Mircea Eliade and the Death of God," *Religion and Life* (Spring 1967), 40–52. A more substantial and fruitful comparison of the sacred with the profane, is to compare the sacred/profane dialectic and interrelationship to the immanental cosmos of Confucius. See Herbert Fingarette, *Confucius: The Secular as Sacred* (New York: Harper & Row, 1972); and David L. Hall and Roger T. Ames, *Thinking Through Confucius* (Albany, NY: State University Press, 1987).

12. Ricketts, *Romanian Roots,* p. 878.

13. Eliade, "Methodological Remarks," p. 95.

14. Adrian Marino, "Mircea Eliade's Hermeneutics," pp. 40–41.

15. Mircea Eliade, *The Two and The One,* trans. J. M. Cohen (New York: Harper & Row, 1965), p. 68.

16. Ibid., p. 69.

17. Ibid.

18. Elaide, *The Quest,* preface, defines religion as referring "to the experience of the sacred, and consequently, [as] related to the ideas of *being, meaning,* and *truth."* More fully, "religion is the exemplary solution of every existential crisis. Religion 'begins' when and where there is a total revelation of reality; a revelation which is at once that of the sacred—of that which supremely *is,* of what is neither illusory nor evanescent—and of man's relationship to the sacred, a relationship which is multiple, changing, sometimes ambivalent, but which always places man at the very heart of the real. This double relationship at the same time renders existence human, 'open' to the values of the Spirit." See Eliade, *Myths, Dreams, and Mysteries,* trans. Philip Mairet (New York: Harper & Row, 1960), p. 18

19. Guilford Dudley III, *Religion on Trial: Mircea Eliade and His Critics* (Philadelphia: Temple University Press, 1977), p. 85.

20. See Eliade's article, "Prolegomenon to Religious Dualism: Dyads and Polarities," in *The Quest,* pp. 127ff. 173–75, especially the concluding remarks. Similar to the yin/yang polarity, the sacred/profane opposites cannot in all cases be distin-

guished as good vs. bad. In their capacity to provide meaning, though, Eliade would have his preference in that the sacred bespeaks cosmos, order, and meaning and the profane historicism, chaos, and meaninglessness. It is precisely because the sacred/ profane distinction is ambivalent in regard to moral distinctions, that the sacred/profane polarity is quite flexible for various ethical analyses.

21. Mircea Eliade, *Mircea Eliade: Autobiography; Vol. 1 Journey East, Journey West, 1907–1937*, trans. Mac Linscott Ricketts (San Francisco: Harper & Row, 1981), p. 322.

22. Ioan Culianu shows how Eliade is in line with the ''classicists'' and the ''new-wave'' anthropologists. But being a historian of religions and not an anthropologist, Eliade is really neither but occupies a third, mediating position. The ''classicists'' are of a Tylorian or Durkheimian trend, where symbols are associated with nature and society or with political and social structures, respectively. The ''classicists'' criticize Eliade for being too philosophical and for separating religion as autonomous from society, in the tradition of C. P. Tiele and Gerardus van der Leeuw. The ''new-wavers,'' ironically, are critical of Eliade for being too classical; he does not consider suprarational experiences. Culianu shows, however, how Eliade does valorize such experiences. See Culianu, ''Mircea Eliade at the Crossroad of Anthropology,'' *Neue Zeitschrift für Systematische Theologie* 27,2 (1985), 123–29. For other anthropological positions on symbols see Frank Whaling, ed., *Contemporary Approaches to the Study of Religion*, vol. 2 (New York: Mouton Publishers, 1985), pp. 191–25; and Brian Morris, *Anthropological Studies of Religion* (New York: Cambridge University Press, 1987), pp. 218–46.

23. Steiner, *Goethe the Scientist*, p. 63

24. Eliade calls for such contextualization when he says, regarding the morphology of the cosmic tree, ''The historian of religions will have to elucidate the reasons why such a culture has retained, developed, or forgotten a symbolic aspect of the cosmic tree. In so doing, he will be led to penetrate more deeply into the soul of this culture, and will learn to differentiate it from others.'' See his ''Methodological Remarks on the Study of Religious Symbolism'' in Eliade and Kitagawa *The History of Religions*, pp. 94–95.

25. Stephen J. Reno, ''Eliade's Progressional View of *Hierophanies*,'' *Religious Studies* 8 (1972), 160.

26. Eliade, *Patterns*, pp. 29–30, 30 n. 1.

27. Eliade, *Myths, Dreams, and Mysteries*, pp. 125–26.

28. Reno, ''Eliade's Progressional View,'' pp. 157–58.

29. Any book of Eliade's points out this obsession with the problem of history. See also Paul Ricoeur, ''The History of Religions and the Phenomenology of Time Consciousness,'' *The History of Religions: Retrospect and Prospect*, ed. Joseph M. Kitagawa (New York: Macmillan 1985), pp. 20–21. I disagree, then, as would Reno and as Eliade seems to be saying, too, with Douglas Allen who says, ''Eliade seems to evaluate those hierophanies that are most conditioned, limited, and relativized as 'lower' or less spiritual phenomena.'' Douglas Allen, ''Eliade and History,'' *Journal of Religion* 68 (October 1988), 560.

30. Although the forms in a morphology coexist, a morphology has its own "evolutionary history." See Steiner, *Goethe the Scientist,* p. 63 passim; and Walter Kaufmann, *Discovering the Mind: Goethe, Kant, and Hegel* (New York: McGraw-Hill, 1980), p. 54.

31. Ricketts notes that in Eliade's Romanian university lectures he appears to give a privileged position to Christianity. See *Romanian Roots,* p. 813.

32. Smith, pp. 253–59. *Map Is Not Territory.*

33. See Eliade's *Cosmos and History: The Myth of the Eternal Return* (Princeton, NJ: Princeton University Press, Bollingen Series 46, 1954).

34. It was not until his first article published in English, "Cosmical Homology and Yoga," in the *Journal of the Indian Society of Oriental Art* in 1937, that Eliade fully elaborated on the cosmicization of the individual. But the cosmicization of the individual is not solely of Indian inspiration. It has roots in Eliade's earlier discussions on "synthesis" in the late 1920s. See Ricketts, *Romanian Roots,* p. 573, 1323 n. 22. See also Culianu, *Mircea Eliade,* p. 47.

35. Ibid., p. 573.

36. See Eliade's *Yoga, Immortality and Freedom,* trans. Williard R. Trask (New York: Pantheon Books, Bollingen Foundation, 1958), p. 271.

37. The philosopher Leszek Kolakowski, arguing for a soberly conservative spirit, says that the presence of the sacred in society sets up natural and needed distinctions necessary for order and for differences in value. Without order and distinctions in value and a recognition of human limits, society settles into a stagnating and destructively uncreative homogeneity. Hierarchy need not be oppressive but can preserve the tension between structure and development, tradition and criticism. See Kolakowski, *Modernity on Endless Trial* (Chicago: University of Chicago Press, 1990), pp. 70–72. While I will demonstrate that Eliade's cultural hierarchy can be intellectually presumptuous and politically conservative, a hierarchy of planes of value can encourage creativity and moral accountability instead of suppressing them.

38. Ricketts, *Romanian Roots,* p. 572.

39. Ibid., p. 930.

40. Ibid., p. 896.

41. Translated from the Romanian, Ricketts, *Romanian Roots,* pp. 881, 930.

42. Political channels would serve him, however. Having arrived in the United States on a visitors' exchange visa, Eliade, after his time was up, would have to leave the country before seeking passage to come back in. So as to prevent his leaving in the first place (undoubtedly he would have had a difficult time getting back in again) Eliade was granted permission to stay in the United States because, according to the Department of Defense, he was "indispensable to the security and welfare of the United States." Eliade even entitles the last chapter of the second volume of his autobiography, "Indispensable to the Security of the United States." See Eliade, *Mircea Eliade: Autobiography, Volume II: 1937–1960, Exile's Odyssey,* trans. from the Romanian by Mac Linscott Ricketts (Chicago: University of Chicago Press, 1988), p. 213 n. 15.

43. Jerome Long, "A Letter to Kees W. Bolle," *Epoche: UCLA Journal for the History of Religions* 15 (1987), 92–95.

44. Mircea Eliade, "Mircea Eliade," an interview with Delia O'Hara, *Chicago* (June 1986), 179.

45. Mircea Eliade, *Journal III: 1970–78,* trans. Teresa Lavender Fagan (Chicago: University of Chicago Press, 1989), p. 226.

46. Ivan Strenski, "Mircea Eliade, Some Theoretical Problems" in *The Theory of Myth: Six Studies,* ed. Adrian Cunningham (London: Sheed and Ward, 1973); idem, "Love and Anarchy in Romania: A Critical Review of Mircea Eliade's Autobiography, Volume One, 1907–1937," *Religion* 12 (1982), 391–403; idem, *Four Theories of Myth in the Twentieth Century* (Iowa City, IA: University of Iowa Press, 1987).

47. Lawrence Sullivan, *Icanchus's Drum: An Orientation in Meaning in South American Religions* (New York: Macmillan Publishing, 1988), p. 701 n. 82.

48. Roland Chagnon, "Religion Cosmique, foi Humaine et Christianisme chez Mircea Eliade," *Questions Actuelles sur la Foi,* ed. T. Potuin and J. Richard (Montreal: Corporation des Editions Fides, 1984), p. 159.

49. Eliade, *Patterns,* p. 40.

50. Ibid., p. 110.

51. Charles Long, "The Significance for.Modern Man of Mircea Eliade's Work," in *Cosmic Piety, Modern Man and the Meaning of the Universe* (New York: P.J. Kennedy and Sons, 1965), pp. 142ff.

52. Ibid.

53. See the section, "Symbolism of Ascension," in Eliade, *Images and Symbols,* pp. 47ff.

54. Eliade, *Patterns,* p. 124.

55. This discrepancy between those who seemingly control history and those who do not, between the major and minor figures, between the force of great movements and the pettiness of the minutiae, represents two ways of looking at history, a debate very prevalent among social and political historians.

56. Eliade, *Patterns,* pp. 184–85.

57. The liberation from "becoming" is not only an Indian problem. To escape the contingencies of history is expressed in other religions as well. God or Allah could equally have been used here. See, for instance, Abdoldjavad Falaturi, "Experience of Time and History in Islam," in *We Believe in One God: The Experience of God in Christianity and Islam,* ed. Annemarie Schimmel and Absoldjavad Falaturi (New York: Crossroad, 1979), p. 70. He says, "it may be said that in the thought patterns of the Koran a static notion of space dominates and indeed totally overshadows a concept of time whose nature is sequential. The Koran lacks a notion of time which is the necessary basis for every scientifically comprehensible experience of history. Not only does the Koran lack a conception of history in the western sense, but such a concept simply could not exist in the Koran. The Koran affords no place for it."

58. Eliade, *Patterns,* p. 184.

59. Sullivan, *Icanchu's Drum,* pp. 39–40.

60. Eliade, *Patterns,* p. 157.

61. The Tewa of New Mexico refer to the world prior to their ancestors' emergence onto hardened land as *ochu* (meaning moist, green, unripe). After emergence life is

refered to as *seh t'a* (dry, hardened). It was in their ancestors' emergence that they became susceptible to time, and hence to illness, decomposition, and death. Alfonso Ortiz, *The Tewa World: Space, Time, and Becoming in a Pueblo Society* (Chicago: University of Chicago Press, 1969), pp. 13–16.

62. Mircea Eliade, *The Forge and the Crucible,* trans. Stephen Corrin (New York: Harper & Row, 1962), p. 19ff.

63. Mircea Eliade, *Symbolism, the Sacred, and the Arts,* ed. Diane Apostolos-Cappadona (New York: Crossroad, 1985), p. 83; see also Eliade's essay "Brancusi and Mythology" in Eliade, *Ordeal by Labyrinth,* pp. 193–201.

64. Inguild Saelid Gilhus says Eliade's understanding of the Cosmic Tree is limited when it comes to interpreting the symbol of the tree is Gnostic religion. Among Gnostics, symbols reflect human physiology rather than cosmology. "Gnostic symbols invite an investigation of their foundations in conscious and unconscious elaborations upon human biology and physiology, rather than an investigation of how they reveal the Sacred." She says the difference between Eliade's orientation, which emphasizes cosmology, and that of Victor Turner, for instance, who emphasizes the physiological dimension of symbols, is the difference between the Freudian and the Jungian perspective. Freud moves from the spiritual to the carnal, Jung from the carnal to the spiritual. Because it is more difficult to arrive at a consensus on the meaning of the symbol in the Jungian sense (since Jungian interpretations move outward from the phenomenon to plural meanings), Eliade's theory of symbols of the Cosmic Tree is less easily translatable to concrete expressions. In other words, Eliade resists reducing a symbol to any single interpretation or impulse. See Gilhus, "The Tree of Life and the Tree of Death: A Study of Gnostic Symbols," *Religion* 17 (1987), 348–49.

65. Eliade, *Patterns,* p. 293.

66. Mircea Eliade, *The Forbidden Forest,* trans. Mac Linscott Ricketts and Mary Park Stevenson (Notre Dame, IN: University of Notre Dame Press, 1978), p. 68.

67. Eliade, *Patterns,* p. 346.

68. Ibid., p. 361.

69. Ibid., p. 367.

70. Robert T. Francoeur, "The Cosmic Piety of Teilhard de Chardin: A Study of the Divine Ephiphany," in *Cosmic Piety: Modern Man and the Meaning of the Universe* (New York: P. J. Kennedy and Sons, 1965), p. 110. See also Pierre Teilhard de Chardin, *The Divine Milieu* (New York: Harper & Row, 1960), pp. 128ff.

71. Francoeur, "The Cosmic Piety," pp. 103, 110.

72. Martin Buber, *Two Types of Faith,* trans., Norman P. Goldhawk (New York: Harper & Row, 1961), pp. 7–9. This mystical faith of trust is intimately this-worldly; Buber's mysticism turns *to* the world, to the concrete, not away from it. See his classic *I and Thou,* trans. Ronald Gregor Smith (New York: Charles Scribner's Sons, 1958), pp. 11 et passim.

73. The Catholic theologian Avery Dulles provides a fine exposition of how symbols are themselves a form of revelation and function like revelation. Revelation is always mediated through symbols. "Revelatory symbols," says he, "are those which express and mediate God's self-communication." Dulles notes how symbolic commu-

nication parallels revelation: 1) symbols give participatory, not speculative, knowledge. Symbols move us to situate ourselves in a universe of meaning. 2) symbols, insofar as they involve the knower as person, have a transforming effect. 3) symbols have a powerful influence on commitment and behavior. 4) symbols introduce us to levels of awareness not normally accessible to discursive thought. They handle a multitude of meanings and the ingredient of mystery. Dulles finds that symbolic theory can correct the misleadings of the other five models of revelation he identifies: revelation as doctrine, as history, as inner experience, as dialectical presence, and as new awareness. Revelation as symbolic discourse has achieved wide popularity through Paul Tillich, H. R. Niebuhr, Karl Rahner, Paul Ricoeur, Langdon Gilkey, Ray Hart, John Macquarrie, Louis Dupré, and Gregory Baum. See Avery Dulles, *Models of Revelation* (Garden City, New York: Doubleday & Co., 1983), pp. 131–41.

74. See Eliade's essay on religious symbolism for his six axioms of religious symbols. *Essays in Methodology*, pp. 98–103.

75. Eliade, *Symbolism, The Sacred, and the Arts*, pp. 11–12.

76. Culianu, *Mircea Eliade*, p. 47. Translation from the Italian is mine. Also see Ricketts, *Romanian Roots*, pp. 595ff.

77. Johann Wolfgang von Goethe, *The Autobiography of Goethe: Truth and Poetry: From My Life*, ed. Park Godwin (New York: Wiley and Putnam, 1846), p. 31.

78. See for instance her discussions on the preservationist John Muir. Catherine L. Albanese, *Nature Religion in America: From the Algonkian Indians to the New Age* (Chicago: University of Chicago Press, 1990), pp. 99, 100.

79. Eliade, *Forbidden Forest*, p. 173.

80. Chagnon, "Religion Cosmique," pp. 169–70.

81. Fingarette, *Confucius*, pp. 16–17.

82. On the immanence of the cosmos of Confucius, on the Confucian interpretation of the individual in relation to society and tradition, and on human ontology as defined by the person's acts, see Hall and Ames, *Thinking Through Confucius*, pp. 12ff.

83. Eliade, *Images and Symbols*, p. 16.

84. Long, *Significations*, p. 2.

85. Eliade, *Symbolism, the Sacred, and the Arts*, p. 13.

86. Ibid.

87. See Joseph M. Kitagawa, *The Quest for Human Unity: A Religious History* (Minneapolis, MN: Fortress Press, 1990). Kitagawa shows how it is not only the idealists but also hard-core realists who make aspirations toward human unity. One can mention Western capitalism and democracy as present attempts to unite humans around certain pragmatic values.

88. Marino, *Imagination and Meaning*, p. 35.

89. Eliade is "reductionistic" in the sense of a "consideration and assumption of a basic reality whose decipherment necessarily requires recognition of the existence of coherent systems of sacred modalities," clarifies Marino, Ibid., p. 44. Wayne Proudfoot in *Religious Experience* (Los Angeles: University of California Press, 1985), pp. 196–97, 248–49 n. 5, is only partially right when he labels Eliade a "descriptive reductionist," as one who does not respect context and, thus, fails to "identify an

emotion, practice, or experience under the description by which the subject identifies it.'' Eliade does recognize a coherence to the sacred, as Marino states, which necessitates him to unite seemingly disparate religious experiences, sometimes with interpretations not recognized by the believer. So in this sense Proudfoot is right. But inasmuch as Eliade accepts the believer's own articulation of the experience, in contrast to a suspicion of it (as Freud and Lévi-Strauss practice), Proudfoot is incorrect in saying Eliade "fails" to honor the subject's identification of the experience.

90. Lawrence Sullivan speaks of myth functioning in this way, as a grammar that gives imaginative speech to the irreducible and ineffable element of experience. One can argue that this very process of reflection and (critical) articulation of a given reality is tantamount to philosophical discourse. See Sullivan and the debate between the purposes and functions of myth and philosophy in Sheryl Burkhalter, "Summary Report II," in *Deconstructing–Reconstructing the Philosophy of Religions*. Summary Reports from the Conferences on Religions in Culture and History, 1986–89, The Divinity School, The University of Chicago. ed. Francisca Cho Bantly (Chicago: The Divinity School, The University of Chicago, 1990), p. 29 et passim.

91. Marino, *L'Hermeneutique,* p. 184.

92. David Tracy, "Is a Hermeneutics of Religion Possible?" in *Religious Pluralism,* ed. Leroy S. Rouner (Notre Dame, IN: University of Notre Dame Press, 1984), p. 116.

93. Wendy Doniger O'Flaherty, *Other Peoples' Myths* (New York: Macmillan Publishing, 1988), pp. 20–21.

94. Kitagawa, *The Quest for Human Unity,* p. 3.

4

The Nature of the Human Condition: The Human as Mythic and as *Homo Religiosus*

In Eliade's *The Old Man and the Bureaucrats,*[1] the gentle, elderly Farama Zaharia, former principal of Primary School No. 17 on Mantulesa Street, undertakes a visit to Vasile I. Borza, a major in the Ministry of Internal Affairs (the Police), whom Farama believes is a former student of his. Farama hopes to renew contact and relive nearly forgotten memories.

Instead of having a warm reunion, however, Comrade Borza rejects Farama and claims to have never known him. Suspicious of the old man, Borza and his bureaucrats arrest Farama and subject him to intense questioning. In the process of their relentless interrogation of Farama, the military police discover that Farama's view of life is much different from that of their own. When pressed about his relations with Borza, Farama reconstructs the past through endless fantastic narratives. To make any point or to explain any story Farma must back up and narrate yet another story. Stories upon stories of an overarching story go into answering even the simplest of questions. After a while of endless narratives, the interrogators find themselves thoroughly puzzled by, and implicated in, the world Farama has constructed. Farama created a mythic net out of which the bureaucrats were unable to escape.

This short novel, a mythology of myth itself,[2] depicts well the stubborn interchange between the rationalistic, suspicious, authoritarian world of politics and power and the creatively meaningful, imaginative world of the mythological. It demonstrates how the mind attuned to narrative is able to ascribe meaning and survive under difficult circumstances. Moreover, as Claude-Henri Rocquet notes and Eliade acknowledges, the novel is an allegory of memory, of anamnesis, of the need to recover "beginnings" for the restoration of meaning for modern culture.[3] By extension, then, if modern culture is to realize a new humanism, it must rediscover and acknowledge the validity of the mythologic.

Humans as Mythic

The need to interpret and to acquire meaning is perennial to human existence. Even among those who see no need for the religious or the spiritual world, we find this need for meaning, nevertheless, as the sociologist Andrew Greeley has shown in *Unsecular Man*.[4] Notwithstanding the capability of the scientific method and of historiography to explain the "why" and the "how" of things, humans cannot cease from questioning life's mysteries and narrating stories about them. An individual, much less a culture, is incapable of living long in a demythologized state, a state of being indifferent to transhistorical, paradigmatic models serving to pattern and give meaning to one's life. To live oblivious of myth is to succumb to a mind-set governed by irreversible history, that is, to a historical consciousness not patterned after exemplary models taken to be true. This historical mind frame, instead, is marked by continuous change, revision, and desire for novelty. "Modernity," says the literary critic Matei Calinescu, "appears as the *history of the battle to give value to the present*. Ideally, modernity is the ability to delight sensually—aesthetically—in the fleeting instant of the present."[5]

Such a mind-set, Eliade believes, is prey to the whims and abuses of relentless historical progress. Only the models it itself creates are considered valid. But these models are transitory. For as soon as they are constructed they immediately become suspect in favor of newer ones. In the end, without any orientating and stabalizing models, history is found to be meaningless; it is without transhistorical rootage. The Spanish philosopher José Ortega y Gasset says that without any transhistorical models, ideals, prototypes to inspire, the modern person, though having all the potentiality to create, is unable to create, for the person does not know *what* to create, to emulate and rise above.[6] It is through overcoming such instability, sterility, and meaninglessness that Eliade's new humanism gets its justification.

So if, as Eliade claims, the human imagination possesses a mythological structure, and humans, a fortiori, require a mythology for orienting themselves in the world, then the new humanism must possess a mythopoetic mind-set. Appropriating the qualities of myth, therefore, we can say that the new humanism is characterized as a transhistorical manner of existence patterned after exemplary and communitarian models. And it is upon these paradigmatic models that individuals can universalize and enrich themselves within larger universes of meaning.

Humans Make and Live in Myth

In its simplest form a myth is a story. It is an account of what happened and of the way things are. And like stories do, myths entertain, instruct, encourage us to imagine, and give us meaning. In a sense, to tell any story is to mythologize. For in the telling and hearing of stories humans construct interpretive frames of reference for imagining their world and for acting within it in a meaningful way.

To demonstrate humans' need for narrative, Eliade is fond of referring to an example of Soviet internees in a Siberian concentration camp who survived their ordeal by listening to an old woman tell fairy tells. So desirous were they to hear the stories that they sacrificed part of their daily rations to keep the woman strong enough to continue her storytelling. In contrast to those in the other dormitories, who were dying at the rate of ten or twelve a week, these internees had a high survival rate. Perhaps more than any other factor, the hearing of stories meant the difference between survival and death. Says Eliade:

> The specific mode of existence of man implies the need of his learning what happens, and above all what *can* happen, in the world around him and in his own interior world. That it is a matter of a structure of the human condition is shown, *inter alia,* by the *existential necessity* of listening to stories and fairy tales, even in the most tragic of circumstances.[7]

In contrast to fairy tales, legends, or fables, myths are sacred stories. They are true[8] representations of reality. Myths speak of truth, meaning, gods or culture heroes, and of origins, and they give value to the transformative periods of human life—birth, marriage, adulthood, and death.

Recognizing that no single definition of myth is possible, Eliade offers a definition he feels is most adequate because it is the most comprehensive:

> Myth narrates a sacred history; it relates an event that took place in primordial Time, the fabled time of the "beginnings." In other words, myth tells how, through the deeds of Supernatural Beings, a reality came into existence, be it the whole of reality, the Cosmos, or only a fragment of reality—an island, a species of plant, a particular kind of human behavior, an institution. Myth, then, is always an account of a "creation;" it relates how something was produced, began to *be*. Myth tells only of that which *really* happened, which manifested itself completely. The actors in myths are Supernatural Beings. They are known

primarily by what they did in the Transcendent times of the "beginnings." Hence myths disclose their creative activity and reveal the sacredness (or simply the "supernaturalness") of their works. In short, myths describe the various and sometimes dramatic breakthroughs of the sacred (or the "supernatural") into the World. It is this sudden breakthrough of the sacred that really *establishes* the World and makes it what it is today. Furthermore, it is as a result of the intervention of Supernatural Beings that man himself is what he is today, a mortal, sexed, and cultural being.[9]

From the above quote we learn several things about the human condition in the language of the mythologic. First, humans interpret their world, their purpose, and their place in the world by means of narration, myth. Second, the world and humans have a divine origin. Third, humans and their world, the cosmos, gain meaning in the context of the "beginning," of creation. The cosmogonic myth for Eliade is the archetypal myth for all other myths. Four, only that which has been created by the gods is real and therefore significant for human life. Five, without the presence, the "breakthrough" of the sacred, human existence would be meaningless. Six, it is because of this "breakthrough" that there is a human condition to start with; the "Supernatural Beings" determined the limited, sexed, and creative quality of what it means to be a human being. Taking the mythologic as a structure of human consciousness, the above elements define the human as more than an historical, social, psychological, and biological being. And insofar as myth refers to and participates in other worlds of meaning beyond a given society to worlds of other times and places, myth is more than a function and creation of society. Because of the paradigmatic, existential, and ontological weight Eliade ascribes to myth, Eliade's interpretation of myth is far broader than most other interpretations.

In his book, *Mythography,* William Doty looks at several representative approaches to myth.[10] Each of these approaches in its own manner has something to say of the human as a constructor of myth. Against these approaches it will be possible to highlight Eliade's own distinctiveness.

Among sociologists and anthropologists, such as Émile Durkheim, Branislow Malinowski, Anthony F. C. Wallace, Clyde Kluckhon, and Melford Spiro, myth is a product of society and functions as a social-psychological glue. Humans construct myth as a way to bind society together and to satisfy certain social and psychological needs of power and prestige. Spiro says, for instance, "all human behavior, except for reflexive behavior, is purposive: i.e., it is instigated by the intention of satisfying some need."[11] The only thing that differentiates religion from politics in the satisfying of needs is that religion appeals to "superhuman beings," says Spiro.[12]

The problem with ascribing religion or myth to a function of, and for,

society is that what is explained is not religion but society. Religion and
are only a component of society and, so, cannot be explained merely in ten
of society.[13]

A "biogenetic" and "biofunctional" notion of myth sees myth as a product
of genetics and psychosomatic promptings. Loosely associated in this group
are Victor Turner, Mary Douglas, and Joseph Campbell. Campbell clearly
expresses the association of myth to biology:

> I realized that between mythology and biology there is a very close association. I
> think of mythology as a function of biology; it's a production of the human
> imagination, which is moved by the energies of the organs of the body operating
> against each other. These are the same in human beings all over the world [sic]
> and this is the basis for the archetypology of myth.[14]

Eliade does not dissasociate myth from the natural order or the sensual from
the cognitive. Myth is informed by the cosmos, tying humans to nature's
rhythms, cycles, topography, and its animal inhabitants, and the mythic imagination can operate in no other way except through the senses and the symbolism of the body. While the physiological and sensual are there for Eliade
(especially seen in his literature), his stress, however, is upon the psyche and
the spirit as what prompt the mythic imagination.

For Freudian and Jungian psychologists myth is a projection of the human
unconscious. For Jung the *collective* unconscious, the collectivity of human
creations since the beginning of time, gives rise to myth. Myth is not an outlet
for an aberrant or neurotic psyche, but is a natural and healthy expression of
the unconscious.

Eliade's view of the unconscious and of the function of myth closely parallels Jung's own interpretations. Eliade, however, arrived at his interpretations
prior to his exposoure to Jung. In contrast to Jung, Eliade roots the origin of
myth, its prompting, in eternity; the mythic consciousness antecedes human
history itself and, hence, the collective unconscious. Eliade refered to this
eternal consciousness as the "transconscious," a mental structure belonging
solely to the realm of religious experience. The "transconscious" has its root
in being, in the eternal itself. It is a "higher *logos*" beyond nature and all
historical and natural conditionings—time, sin, self, etc. It is encountered by
the mystic and belongs to the "fully awakened" person. For everyone else it
informs a religious thirst in the conscious and unconscious.[15]

The position of Freud hardly needs much elucidation. Myth, as is religion,
is a disease, an aberration of the human psyche in need of a rational cure.
Freud places the origin of myth at a primal patricide. And just as history
created myth, so will history through scientific rationalism render it obsolete.

Among literary theorists, the study of myth has received much attention.

earance of Sir James Frazer's *The Golden Bough,* published
ring lengths from 1890 to 1922, the construction, function,
h has been found to parallel the construction and function of
nform its symbolic and mythic content.[16] Literature, like
..., ... imaginative worlds of meaning and opens the reader to other
possible worlds of experience. Eliade frequently wrote on the continuity between literary fiction and myth.[17]

One of the most influential twentieth-century movements in the study of
myth has been Structuralism, founded on the work of the French anthro-
pologist-philosopher Claude Lévi-Strauss. Now largely a splintered movement and, in the vein of Lévi-Strauss, a disappearing one, Structuralism
continues, nevertheless, to have repercussions in philosophy, linguistics, and
anthropology.[18]

Lévi-Strauss sees myth as that which enables humans to order and resolve
the persistent contradictions of human life. These contradictions are represented as binary oppositions fundamental to creaturely existence, oppositions
such as nature/culture, existence/nonexistence, life/death, one/many.[19] Contrary to Eliade, Lévi-Strauss does not respect what the myths might mean to
the believer, since myths are the surface expressions of the unconscious and
so, in true Freudian fashion, cannot be trusted. Instead, myths are to be broken
down into "mythemes," logical constructions which are thought to make the
myth *work* and to *produce* "meaning" as a way to order what would otherwise
be a chaotic set of contradictions in meaning. Myth solves problems much in
the way that computers do. So in his latest work Lévi-Strauss says, "Every
myth confronts a problem, and it deals with it by showing that it is analogous
to other problems, or else it deals with several problems simultaneously and
shows that they are analogous to one another."[20]

To turn human thought, language, and meaning into a mechanistic science
fits in well with scientific, rationalistic, Western thought. But it is starkly at
odds with an aesthetic world of intuition, plural meanings, irreducible sentiments, and hope in the creative potential of humankind, a worldview consonant with Eliade's own.[21]

Each of the above approaches has something to contribute toward a serviceable humanism. In their own way these approaches restore the integrity of the
mythic dimension of human existence. And insofar as they broaden and
deepen our understanding of the human experience they enlarge the view of
what it means to be human. But whether the approach is history, sociology,
depth psychology, biology, or rationalism, it does not, in the end, complete
the totality of the human. For before all else, Eliade believes, the human is
homo religiosus. Humans thirst for meaning, being, and truth, in other words,
for that which is really *real*. Inasmuch as the above approaches fail to

account for the human as a religious being, they fail to recover the totality of the human experience.

The desire to address the whole person and to recapture for modern consciousness the mythologic is, I have mentioned, a powerful motivation behind Eliade's enormous productivity. The mythic consciousness has undergone various modifications and transformations from the traditional, archaic, societies to the modern, secular, scientific ones. The alteration in the mythic consciousness is not just chronological, however, since the archaic does not principally refer to a point in time but to a structure of the mind. The alteration, rather, is largely structural, spatial; the archaic and the mythic persist but have been relegated to another space, to the margins of intellectual discourse in society and to the unconscious in the human psyche.[22]

The historian of religion Wendy Doniger O'Flaherty identifies four types of "mythologized" people. The thoroughly "un-mythologized" are those who have never had, and never will have, any religious inclination; they are "tone dead." She says these will never be converted to myth. At the other extreme are the "un-demythologized (or still mythologized)." These are the devout churchgoers who never lost their original naivete. They are satisfied to remain among those of their own kind and tradition. No conversion to myth is needed here. In between these two extremes are the "demythologized" and the "remythologized." The "demythologized" have lost their first naivete and do not desire a second one. They are the "radical humanists," post-Enlightenment rationalists; they claim "God is dead." Lastly, the "remythologized" are those who react against the jettisoning of myth; yet they cannot simply remain in their first naivete. They hunger for a second naivete, a universe of meaning but a more plural one than that of the "un-demythologized."[23] All of these, in their own way, are Eliade's audience. The "un-mythologized" and the "demythologized" are to see the mythic structure upon which they still unconsciously operate and to recognize that through myths and symbols history is less susceptible to chaos, to the "terror of history." Of all his writings, Eliade's fiction would be the most likely to "reach" the "un-mythologized," since in fiction one is more willing to suspend disbelief and consider alternative possibilities. Eliade recognized that there were such "un-mythologized" people (such as many Marxists), though entire cultures, he thought, could not survive in such a state. But being forever confident of the human capacity for renewal and creativity, it is doubtful he would give up for lost the "un-mythologized."

The "un-demythologized" and the "remythologized" are to come into a larger network of meaning and overcome existential and hermeneutical parochialisms. It is among the "remythologized," perhaps, who, of the four types, are in the best position to bring about the new humanism. They are the ones most open to the spiritual world and given to creative, existential encounters with the other cultural universes of meaning. Eliade does not aim to have the modern person return to the ways of traditional societies, even if he or she could. What he does advocate is that modern culture adopt a plural, universal, wholistic, and cosmic presence in the world, one informed by exemplary models and archetypes. In this way humanity will approach a meaningful existence and overcome social fragmentation and individual alienation.

The New Humanism as Transhistorical[24]

Throughout his life, Eliade was persistently interested in the effect history, as a process of reversible or irreversible time, had upon people and culture. As a precocious and determined adolescent, he challenged the limits and conditionings of time, as in stretching the number of hours per day and in attempting to overcome time's wear on the body. He "waged war" against sleep to gain more hours for study and through the study of alchemy, peasant symbolisms, and yogic practices sought to discover how people in various cultures manipulated psychosomatic time. Eliade's preocuppation, even paranoia, with time had its social imprint as well.

During the interwar period in Romania (1918–39), Eliade wrote segments in the newspaper *Cuvântul* and mentioned in his literature on the lack of time the "young generation" had before losing their freedoms to the onrush of war and the occupying forces. These youth—those who had grown up between the wars—were the hope for the future Romania. But they had to act now! They had to create culture while there was still time. The end was imminent, both for Romanian culture and even for the West. After leaving Romania in 1945 in exile, Eliade's "sense of an ending" waned, though for a while he did feel World War III was inevitable. Though less impelled by some outside threat, the "sense of an ending" never left Eliade but would be a motivating factor behind much of his scholarly and literary writings. The apocalyptic is a hermeneutical theme for interpreting the Eliadean oeuvre.[25]

This living within two senses of eschatological time—the existential and the cultural—led the literary critic Virgil Nemoianu to note a "Great Divide" in Eliade's literature.[26] Pre-1940 the fantastic (the imaginative, fictional world) broke abruptly into the natural world as some outside, foreign force. This intrusion of the fantastic is especially evident in Eliade's 1936 neo-Gothic *Domnişoara Christina* (*Mademoiselle Christiana*) in which the spirit of a violent past, represented by the vampiress Christina, breaks and overcomes the order and energies of the present generation. In Eliade's post-1940 writings, evidenced clearly in the epic novel *Noaptea de Sânziene* (*The Forbidden Forest*) and in the short story "With the Gypsy Girls," the fantastic is more intimately woven into the natural world. There is less contrast between the two worlds and more contact. Everyday existence is subtly but forcefully transformed to new levels of meaning. History's pressures are overcome not at once but *in via*.

However radical the break between the way the fantastic worked in these two periods,[27] there is no doubt about the role of literature in helping one live in time and in constructing a world of meaning. The literary critic Frank Kermode says fiction speaks to the temporal and myth to the eternal; both serve to overcome that apocalyptic and anxious "sense of an ending" that threatens to bring one's physical and imaginative worlds to premature closure.[28] One could say, then, as Ivan Strenski does, that Eliade's literary shifts were a ploy to obscure his political past when he supported the Legionary movement and to escape the despair of failed idealisms.[29] There is no doubt that the mythic imagination can be used for twisting the historical memory. Myth and the imagination are especially malleable and easily manipulated. And the intensity of their use can increase during and after times of personal and cultural stress and for the propagation of an ideology. But it is equally true that shifts in a literary technique can be a way for the human imagination to adjust to and assimilate bewildering events into a workable worldview, a process natural and proper to the function of the human imagination. Says Kermode:

> [Literary fictions] find out about the changing world on our behalf; they arrange our complementarities. They do this, for some of us, perhaps better than history, perhaps better than theology, largely because they are consciously false. . . . It is not that we are connoisseurs of chaos, but that we are surrounded by it, and equipped for coexistence with it only by our fictive powers.[30]

Myth operates in a way similar to fiction, but on its own scale. Using the Romantic notion of "humor," the historian of religions Kees Bolle describes myth's own process of ordering the world. As "humor," myth becomes a "smile that liberates."[31] He sums up the function of "humor" in this way:

> True humor always concerns matters of ultimate importance. What is comical in this profound way suddenly opens a vista on matters of a most incomprehensible or unacceptable manner. . . . No human life which is lived consciously can forever evade all unimaginable realities. Humor is not the only solution of the dilemma between unimaginable facts and the limits of our imagination, but it is an important one. It distorts the facts, but it does not distort them at random. It does not lead to a bewilderment of human consciousness, but to a new acceptance of the unimaginable, and yet inescapable, reality.[32]

By seeking recourse from chaos in fiction and myth, humans demonstrate their inability to survive solely upon the historical plane and its vicissitudes. In the way that both literature and myth create meaning and "remove" one from chaos, they have a salvific, restorative function. Both belong to the "spiritual" person, to the one open to worlds of meaning and intellectual values unsusceptible to historical transcience. The nonreligious or nonspiritual person, or according to the type defined by Wendy Doniger O'Flaherty, the "unmythologized" and the "demythologized," is the one who most suffers from the abuses of history. Such a person is unwilling to ascribe ontological weight to historical paradigms or archetypes.[33] When faced with history's meaningless events, such as various conquests and brutalities, the historicist mind-set must look to history for their explanation. But those who find meaning in history are usually those in the position to shape and oversee historical events. In the historicist worldview, meaning is a function of power—social, political, and ideological power. The common people, the ordinary person, must resort to illusion, as Freud discussed in *Civilization and Its Discontents*,[34] and to the manipulation of the imposed order and of language,[35] says Michel de Certeau in *The Practice of Everyday Life,* to construct meaning and to find space for exercising freedom.

Since historicism requires the power of position to survive its own conclusions, Eliade argues that historicism is philosophically and ontologically weaker than myth.[36] In contrast to the irreversible, historical time of historicism, mythical time is reversible. Mythical time retells and relives paradigmatic stories and models. It repeats the time of "beginnings," the time of creation. All that which had decayed is subsequently restored anew. And to recover the time of "beginnings" is to participate in being, in that which is ultimately real. And being, whether it is God, gods, heaven in Chinese thought, even the endless arising of karma, is that which, according to the mythic mind, founded the exemplary, transhistorical archetypes in the first place. So to reenact the primordial archetypes is to participate in being and thus overcome or abolish temporal becoming and endless and unstable change. It is in reenacting the mythic archetypes that individual's "find" themselves: for humanness is not something discovered but something rediscovered, since the essential human condition, for Eliade, precedes the actual human condition. The essential human condition is more "consciously" one with being, the real. It is where the human is one with the fullness of existence and where there is no conscious awareness of the self; one fully is and acts with full spontaneity of action. Eliade discovered this state of being as a lycée student when he would read for stretches of time and notice that, during the time of reading, all memories of the "I" vanished. Only when he stepped back into passing time did he recover the "I," the collection of memories. This experience was an early insight to his later refined distinction between sacred and profane time.[37] This loss of the "I" and the spontaneity of action is recounted in all kinds of mysticisms, in primal ontology where the "I" is lost as the person merges with the god or culture hero in ritual, in Buddhist mindfullness, in a Taoist's harmonization with the Tao, in Confucian self-transcendence in ordinary life and social relationships,[38] and in various flow experiences in modern life.[39]

The actual human condition is a result of a mythic, primordial "rupture" where the "I," the self, came to be understood in contradistinction to any and all "others." No longer is there a cosmos–human homology, but a world of dualisms, of self/other, life/death, existence/nonexistence, nature/human, good/evil. It is in this condition that the majority of human life is lived, hence the need for escaping profane time, the time of decay and of dualisms, and of entering into sacred time.

For Eliade, the principal way in which profane time acquires meaning as sacred time is when it repeats a cosmogony, when through memory and ritual action one relives the time of beginnings, the primordial creative moment, and abolishes the weight and anxiety of the historical present. And all relivings, all repetitions, Eliade says, ultimately repeat the cosmogonic event. But as with various flow experiences in modern life and as with Chinese cosmology, which deemphasizes cosmogony,[40] we find that to give value to ordinary time and space one need not periodically repeat a cosmogony. The philosopher Paul Ricoeur, subsequently, qualifies Eliade's assertion that profane time must be regenerated by repeating the cosmogonic event. Profane time can be regenerated and be given meaning in other ways as well. Time can be abolished (as the East would put it) or redeemed (as the Hebraic mind would say) either 1) "continuously," occasionally," or "periodically"; 2) at propitious profane moments; 3) "rhythmically"; 4) as a "cumulative chain of efficacity" (karma); or 5) in a progression of history *from* "paradise" *toward* the kingdom of God.[41] In other words, even the chronological passage of time has its own cyclical patterns and pregnant experiences that charge and provide meaning to the moment. One can direct oneself toward the past through memory and toward the future with expectation. One need not consciously relive the original creation through myth in order to make the present moment meaningful.

Ricoeur gives greater nuance to mythical time by making it more readily available to ordinary life and to religious conceptions other than the primal and the Eastern. Ricoeur does not, though, question the conflict between myth and history nor disqualify the notion that authentic humanness can be found through myth. For, in reality, human life and myth cannot exist in any other way but *in history*. Although mythical time gives meaning to history, it does not hover above history as over some alien realm. Myth coexists in a dialectical relationship with chronological, irreversible history. Sacred time exists in profane time and can *only* be known *in* profane time. The progressive advancement of history itself can even be regarded as hierophanic, as a manifestation of the sacred.[42]

It is perhaps in Eliade's literature of the fantastic (*littérature fantastique*) that we best evince how the imaginative world subtly interweaves itself in ordinary events, making them meaningful and transformatively efficacious.

As a literary genre, the fantastic depicts the ambiguous coming together of two conflicting worlds, the natural world (the explainable) and the supernatural world (or the unexplainable). Authors such as Edgar Allan Poe, Franz Kafka, E. T. A. Hoffman, Henry James, Honoré de Blazac, and others, are included in this genre.[43] Various forms of science fiction can also fall into fantastic literature.[44] From youth Eliade often wrote in the fantastic mode while equally experimenting with various modes of realism. Ivan Strenski's assertion that Eliade took up the fantastic to cover over a tarnished personal history and that the "key to understanding his work lie[s] in his affection for fantasy" is simply erroneous.[45] The genre of the fantastic had long been a part of Eliade's writings. As a boy Eliade had already worked with the fantastic, as in his essays "How I Found the Philosopher's Stone" and "Travels of the Five Cockchafers in the Land of the Red Ants."[46] Eliade's interest in fantasy cannot be dated from the publication of Eliade's 1936 *Domnişoara Christina,* as Strenski asserts.[47] Eliade himself in his autobiography says at the writing of *Christina,* "After so many years of writing 'realistic' literature, I felt attracted to the 'fantastic' *again* [emphasis added]."[48]

The fantastic allowed Eliade to create new worlds of the imagination which were free to challenge ordinary perceptions of time, existence, and reality. In the fantastic the imaginative world vies with the empirical, the illusory with the tactile, the stable with the ephemeral, the cognizant world of the conscious with the hidden world of dreams and the unconscious, the understandable and meaningful with the puzzling and meaningless. Eliade weaves fantastic events with ordinary, mundane life to exploit the "unrecognizability of miracle." In Eliade's use of the fantastic, "miracle" and the activity of the supernatural do not clash with and freighten the ordinary world. Matei Calinescu describes Eliade's unique use of the fantastic:

> With Eliade . . . the transcendent or the supernatural is no longer a threat to the coherence of the world; on the contrary, it holds the only real promise of such coherence; and it is the everyday that, on closer consideration, turns out to be incomprehensible, cruel, and ultimately meaningless. Only when we recognize the secret but powerful pull of the *other* world of "miracle," the sacred, and the mythical, can we go beyond the inherent meaninglessness of quotidian life and

perhaps be given a chance of access to true meaning. This mere chance, however remote, is infinitely more precious than anything "reality" in the accepted sense might offer.[49]

Similar to the way myth functions, the fantastic operates as an instrument of knowledge. Its purpose is not to validate facts or history. Rather, it sets up an alternative way of seeing reality by providing new angles of vision and interpretations of what had been existing all along. But in contrast to myth, the fantastic maintains the functioning of the world as fundamentally ambiguous. The "true" nature of reality is never clear. At least in myth, however rich and conflicting are its messages, the nature of reality is clothed in such a way as to invite trust and suggest order. Whether it is the fantastic world created by the imaginative artist or the world of myth, in each case the world speaks, but mysteriously, incompletely, and by clues and symbols. And unlike the hermeneutics from suspicion of Freud, Nietzsche, and Marx which distrusts the reliability of surface realities and of the conscious life, these clues can be trusted as revealers of meaning. Myths and symbols must be interpreted for what they are saying, not for what they are covering over. To trust and interpret them provides the person with meaning in a world of chaos.

In Eliade's fiction, this act of interpretation is a responsibility the characters in and readers of his fiction must assume. Failure to do so leaves one in a meaningless and threatening world, as we find with the character Gavrilescu, a hapless and failed artist in the short story "With the Gypsy Girls."[50] Gavrilescu has a difficult time coming to terms with his own life. When he visits the seductive and mysterious world of a bordello on one hot day, his confusion with life becomes all the greater. His experiences at the bordello transform what would otherwise be a normal day into one of dizzing and strange entanglements where time itself is altered. Seemingly in the bordello for only a few hours, Gavrilescu finds out when he leaves that instead of a few hours twelve years of his life have passed. His world is no longer the same. His wife has since moved to the country and others he once knew have died. Eliade, through the manipulation of time, shows how the ordinary is at once what it is and yet far more. The fantastic (the sacred, the world of meaning) is depicted as effortlessly and subtly interweaving itself into banal existence. But because Gavrilescu fails to see and understand, he remains confused and bewildered. "With the Gypsy Girls" is as much a statement on the need for, and failure of, a hermeneutics as it is on the ambiguous functioning of time.

Eliade's use of the fantastic demonstrates the mysterious and ambiguous interweaving of the imaginative and the real. This use of the fantastic does not mean Eliade's literature and scholarship are interchangeable, that his literature was a testing ground for his scholarly discoveries, or that his scholarship was literature with footnotes. The fact that the two mediums shared discoveries and that, together, they formed a totality, does not mean they are the same. I am simply pointing out here that the fantastic, like religious facts, requires interpretation if one is not to remain in a state of chaos. Yet, as I mentioned, the internal ambiguity of the fantastic cannot be easily resolved. Regardless of one's hermeneutical skill and ability to acquire meaning, the world remains ambiguous and the process of interpretation elusive. In his scholarship, however, Eliade appears overly confident in the power of hermeneutics to interpret the mysteries of myths and symbols from around the world. Semantic, historical, and methodological obstructions that slow hermeneutics seem confidently circumvented. But meaning, and especially ontological meaning, is not so easily achieved. I think of the Holocaust and of the continuing search for explanations behind this incomprehensible event. Eliade's fantastic literature is a reminder, for Eliade too, that there is little room for overconfidence in the face of mystery and hermeneutical limitations. Even the gifted Orientalist scholars in Eliade's short story "Nights at Serampore" cannot eliminate their fear nor understand the mystery of the murder in the forests of Serampore.[51] It is in the nature of human existence that humans constantly live within the perplexities of persistent chaos.

In the way that Eliade's fantastic literature interweaves the mysterious and the transhistorical in ordinary life as the "unrecognizability of miracle," is it possible to interpret Eliade's own approach to scholarly and literary creativity as giving ordinary creations the power to reveal the extraordinary or some new angle of vision. Eliade's prolificacy can be seen as a conscious and unconscious hope that one of the products of his creation might bring some new mind-opening and conscience-awakening breakthrough, either for culture or his own personal desire for meaning, or both. For him the important thing was to create continuously, to bring a book, an essay, a journalistic piece, a short story, a journal entry, into history. Indeed, Eliade saw books acting as hierophanies: they bloom, yield their flower, and then pass away. Creativity, the *act* of creating, has ontological status. For to bring into existence, to give order to chaos, is to repeat what the "gods" did at the beginning—create a cosmos out of chaos. For Eliade, the writing of books and the synthesizing of religious facts constituted such creative activity.

But Eliade was not satisfied with the isolated book, the singular. He prized oeuvres. Eliade admired the Hasedus and the Goethes of the world.[52] He strove to create his own expansive oeuvre, and he challenged his Romanian generation to create oeuvres and to make of their life an oeuvre. Oeuvres represent totality, the complete body of material that defines a person, especially a writer. And in the sense that they represent totality, can oeuvres symbolize totality itself, Being. So through individual creative actions, each initiatory and potentially illuminating in their own way, the individual achieves existential meaning as the compass of her or his life attains a multi-form whole.

Eliade's fantastic genre, therefore, through its use of the ''unrecognizability of miracle,'' shows, by extension, how one's acts in history can assume creative and ontological status. All human acts—social, economic, political, artistic, and others however mundane—possess transformative potential for individuals and culture. Giving ontological value to historical acts parallels the incarnational quality of Eliade's symbols. In both cases we find a resource in Eliade's thought for giving value and power to social action, since any action now is seen to be pregnant with possibilities for effecting change. While it is true, then, that Eliade's morphological arrangement of religious facts does little to contextualize the facts and thus highlight their social, political, and cultural expressions, we cannot so quickly conclude that Eliade's interpretation of religion is contextually and historically indifferent and ineffective, as the theologian Harvey Cox suggests.[53] The dialectic of the sacred and the ''unrecognizability of miracle'' emphasize the *in history* quality of religious facts and that, since they are in history, their transformative potential can only be articulated through historical means—individual, social, political, cultural, etc. The important thing for a person to do is to act, to create; and, resultingly, one's actions, one's creations just might articulate some expression of the sacred and initiate some individual, social, political, or cultural transformation. The capacity of cultural fashions to align culture along new perspectives in meaning is one example of the above to which Eliade gives much attention.[54]

That concrete acts in history can be of value in giving meaning to one's life is but another way to stress how, for Eliade, myth can exist in no other way except that it be grounded in history. Eliade reels from philosophical assertions and religious statements not grounded in historical facts. The historian and sociologist of religion Joachim Wach even said, as Eliade recounts it, that Eliade ''had succeeded in demonstrating in a concrete way, with documents, that freedom and transcendence are constitutive dimensions of human existence.''[55]

While Eliade insisted upon a rootage in history, in facts, and stressed the need for living within history, in culture, he also knew that what ultimately mattered was an engagement with the real, the ''sacred.'' As in Indian thought, so for Eliade, the acquisition of wisdom is not an end in itself, to be used as a basis for argumentative proofs. To seek wisdom, or to do philosophy, is to seek one's ''liberation'' from the conditionings of history and from one's *vasanas*.[56] The whole basis of the new humanism is its ''soteriological'' aim, a point of contention for critics of Eliade's history of religions program.[57]

But this aim cannot be underemphasized. And in stating this, Eliade's understanding and use of history must be seen accordingly. Eliade knew the various ways history was understood and practiced among cultures and in the human psyche as well. Interpreters and critics of Eliade, such as Ivan Strenski,[58] Guilford Dudley,[59] and Jonathan Z. Smith,[60] among others, are justified in part in critiquing Eliade for his antihistoricism and his deductive approach to historical interpretation. They miss the totality of Eliade, however, when they critique him solely from these angles. Eliade is not the best model for the merely *historical* study of religion. His history is a *philosophy* of history and of culture. It combines both phenomenology and history to encompass the totality of the human as a religious and historical being.[61] Unless Eliade is interpreted in the way he saw history experienced, he will not be fully and rightly appreciated.

Even if we caution against quickly classifying Eliade as "antihistory," that does not mean his philosophical history is unaccountable to history and is heuristically self-serving nor does it mean that his "creative hermeneutics" is merely an exercise in the fantastic, as Ivan Strenski claims it to be, who practices a "creative hermeneutics" of his own. [62] In his reaction against Enlightment rationalism, Eliade may have gone too far in underappreciating empiricism, though he never denied the need for induction and empirical observations.[63] His dialectic of history and the "unrecognizability of miracle" are two history-linked themes already noted. In chapter 3 I mentioned how Eliade's theory of symbols maintains an internal dialectic between the parts and the Whole as a means for winnowing out erroneous or limited interpretations.[64] Adrian Marino notes how Eliade's circular hermeneutics of text (facts)–interpretation–text/interpretation–text–interpretation constantly reforms its interpretations.[65] Douglas Allen's study on Eliade's phenomenology mentions the degree to which an interpretation illuminates the data, gives coherence to a symbol's diverse meanings, and helps express the "actual situation of man" as means by which an interpretation is validated.[66]

On the psychological plane, Eliade asks whether a believer's interpretation of a symbol or a myth cultivates joy and hope and makes creative contributions to culture. Ethically, another validating (or falsifying) procedure is to note the extent to which an interpretation encourages "love," a term central to Eliade's own ethic.[67] Does one's interpretation of a myth or symbol encourage a humanistic regard for others? What kind of justice is it affirming? Is the myth used to destroy, to hate, to justify universally what can only be relative? What is meant by love is ambiguous and is principally a Christian ethical ideal. But if we were to use other ethical traits pertinent to other religions we could mention, to use Gerardus van der Leeuw's typology, "compassion" in Buddhism, "humility" in Islam, "obedience" in Judaism, and "asceticism" or detachment in Hinduism,[68] or other distinguishing elements from within the religions. The point is, there are other scales upon which to validate or falsify the interpretation of religious phenomena.

The New Humanism Patterned After Exemplary Models

The philosopher George Santayana said, "They who do not remember history are bound to repeat it." Eliade would concur, but he would transpose the adage's rationale. We do repeat history, but we repeat it regardless of whether we remember it or not.

In reality it is not history in its totality that we repeat but analogous structures and events. We repeat similar errors or parallel analogous periods. As we repeat them we are reminded of our flaws, and our period is set within a greater temporal scheme. Myth operates in the same way. It remembers and repeats certain structures and events from history. Through narration and the performance of ritual, the mythic mind remembers the necessary structures and events and corresponding personalities of its "history" in order for the imagination to provide the present with meaning. Memory in mythopoesis is two-sided: it is what *is* remembered, and it is what *is not* remembered, either by ignorance or selectivity. What is remembered from all possible details of history are the details and structures essential to the creation of meaning; all other details are regarded as irrelevant to the myth and to the performance of its rituals and are, therefore, forgotten, for what is not essential to giving meaning to one's place in the world is considered insignificant. This process of mythic remembering is refered to as anamnesis, the act of bringing to mind selective elements for consideration.

A presupposition behind the idea of archetypes and anamnesis is that the essential human condition precedes the actual human condition. True humanity is of the Edenic variety. All other is a "fallen" humanity. Eliade, in fact, proposes two "falls." The first occurred in "the beginning," at some mythical past. This "fall" marked a severing of intimacy between God or the gods and humans; it was a breakage in consciousness and gave rise to myth, whose existence as story and as language denotes rupture, the introduction of human autonomy from nature and from the divine beings. The second "fall" was the fall into historical consciousness. After the first "fall" the primitives still corresponded consciously as *homo religiosus* with the gods and the cosmos. But with the coming of historical awareness, the immediate relation with the cosmos was suppressed to the unconscious level. The historical person was distanced from the divine archetypes. Eliade summarizes these points:

[I]n the case of those moderns who proclaim that they are nonreligious, religion and mythology are "eclipsed" in the darkness of the unconscious. . . . Or, from the Christian point of view, it could also be said that nonreligion is equivalent to a new "fall" of man—in other words, that nonreligious man has lost his capacity to live religion consciously, and hence to understand and assume it; but that, in his deepest being, he still retains a memory of it, as, after the first "fall," his ancestor, the primordial man, retained intelligence enough to enable him to rediscover the traces of God that are visible in the world. After the first "fall," the religious sense descended to the level of the "divided consciousness"; now, after the second, it has fallen even further, into the depths of the unconcious; it has been "forgotten."[69]

In spite of these "falls," however, the archetypes of our divine nature survive, but in camouflaged forms. It is through the act of anamnesis, the physical and mental reenactment of mythical models, that we relive the archetypes. Whether reenacted in ritual or in conscious longings for higher states of being, anamnesis recovers the time of "beginnings," and, thus, one approximates her or his essential human condition—that spiritual condition beyond time.

As mentioned, the importance of the "beginning" lies in its association with being, with the absolute, with that which is really real. Whenever one returns to the "beginning," as when one repeats and participates in an archetype, one returns to the initial creative act. If so, then any act of creation—a sacrifice, sexual union, the founding of a home, the construction of a building, the enthronment of a king, the beginning of a new year, or the recitation of the cosmogonic myth in ritual—imitates the exemplary act par excellence, creation, and in the process achieves meaning and power. The important point here is the centrality of the creation myth as a paradigm for behavior. For Eliade, creation, and, a fortiori, any subsequent creative activity, is the principal ontological act. Jonathan Z. Smith, in his important essay "The Unkown God: Myth in History," may have shown that the creation myth and the creator god Io are not central to the Polynesian's mythology as Eliade purports them to be. But Smith has not explained why the Polynesians still hold onto and perpetuate a creation myth.[70] The desire to create, to see oneself and one's world renewed, is constitutive of the human condition. To create manifests a desire to *be,* to center and found oneself in the world. For when one creates one gives order to chaos, one affirms one's existence and gives it meaning.

A good example of the longing for being, to be, and for restoring one's world with meaning, is in the ritual of dance. In dance a person reenacts the primordial activity of the gods in the "beginning." Through the use of costumes, drums, prescribed choreography, and other symbolic mediums, the participants follow in the same movements and appropriate the same intentions of their mythical models. To do so is to imitate and return to the initial creative impulse, to the time of wholeness, unity, purity, to the time when humans and the cosmos were in close communion. One needs only to recall the Native American Ghost Dance where through dance it was hoped that the time when buffalo were plentiful and the white culture nonexistent could be restored once again.[71]

For the modern, demythologized person, however, this nostalgia for the time of "beginnings" has settled into the unconscious. It still exists in the modern person's psyche, but is greatly suppressed. Through a person's nostalgias, hopes, dreams, and actions, camouflaged traces persist of this desire to recapture the time of purity and wholeness at the "beginning," or as Eliade says, at *illo tempore*.

The following lengthy passage is a good example of how this nostalgia is found in contemporary experience. The writer Ian Frazier, visiting the town of Nicodemus, Kansas on its Founder's Day, witnesses a celebratory dance. Nicodemus was founded in the 1870s by African-American homesteaders and is one of the few such towns still surviving. The setting, the action of the dance, the various decorations, the significance of the event, all combine to produce in Frazier an experience of entering into another time and space. In a return to "beginnings," his mind is transported back to a time when all was right and to a time that could have been if history had not taken a different path. Frazier recounts his experience in the following way:

> When [the girls] were all lined up, they held their pose for a moment. Then the song "When Doves Cry," by Prince, began to play on the loudspeaker, and they began to dance. I looked past the people sitting on chairs against the wall, the women with their pocketbooks on their knees, past the portrait of Blanche White, who was like a mother to the kids in the town, through the tall open window, past the roadside grove of elms that Blanche White's 4-H club planted in the nineteen-fifties, past the wheat-field horizon, and into the blank, bright sky. Suddenly I felt a joy so strong it almost knocked me down. It came up my spine and settled on my head like a warm cap and filled my eyes with tears, while I stood there packed in with everybody, watching Mrs. Robinson's lovely daughters dance.
>
> And I thought, *It could have worked!* This democracy, this land of freedom and equality and the pursuit of happiness—it could have worked! There was something to it, after all! It didn't have to turn into a greedy free-for-all! We didn't have to make a mess of it and the continent and ourselves! It could have worked! The Robinson sisters danced; Prince sang about doves crying; beauty and courage and curiosity and gentleness seemed not to be rare aberrations in the world. Nicodemus, a town with reasons to hold a grudge, a town with plenty of reasons not to exist at all, celebrated its Founder's Day with a show of hats and a dance revue. . . . For a few moments, I could imagine the past rewritten, wars

unfought, the buffalo and the Indians undestroyed, the prairie unplundered. Maybe history did not absolutely have to turn out the way it did. Maybe the history of the West, for example, could have involved more admiration of hats, more unarmed get-togethers, more dance, more tasting of spareribs.

Joy! I leaned against the sturdiness of the McGhee sister by my side. From the wood floor came a dust that smelled like small town. Thoughts that usually shout down joy in me were nowhere in sight. I read in some magazine once that the most important word in American movies is "home"; that Americans, being immigrants, have strong associations with that word. The Robinson sisters turned and did a move that was mostly from the knees down. I was in the middle of America, in the middle of the Great Plains, in the midst of history, in the valley of the Solomon River, in the town of Nicodemus: in my mind, anyway, home. "Home on the Range," a song whose first verse ("Oh give me a home . . .") is familiar to millions, has a less familiar second verse, which goes:

> Oh, give me the gale of the Solomon vale,
> Where life streams with buoyancy flow,
> Or the banks of the Beaver,
> Where seldom is ever
> Any poisonous herbage doth grow.

All around me I observed an almost total lack of poisonous herbage. The life streams were flowing with bouyancy. I was no longer a consumer, a ratepayer, a tenant, a cardholder, a motorist. I was home. The world looked as I wanted it to. My every breath was justified. I felt not the mild warmth of irony, not the comfort of camp, not the cheer of success and a full bank account: just plain, complete joy.[72]

Through the ritual of anamnesis Frazier abolishes history by transcending it and by renewing the present with power and meaning. This repetition of archetypes belonging to the time of "beginnings" is what Eliade meant by the "myth of the eternal return." To recall the primordial archetypes is to give meaning to the present as a creative moment. In fact, it is only upon the existence of earlier experiences and events that we can interpret the present at all.[73] Anamnesis is "salvific" for its very ability to invest the present with interpretive models. Thus anamnesis is often associated with healing, and depth psychology itself is based on an individual's ability to recall latent neuroses.

The importance of memory, then, for a knowledge of selfhood and for uniting one to a cultural community, makes memory a creative and liberating process for a new humanism, since it is the memory of primorial and historic paradigms which help define us as human beings. For the primitive person, fidelity to the archetypes in anamnesis and ritual is essential to defining and preserving life and humanness. To forget and depart from the archetypes is a "sin" and means death. For Hindus, memory alone is what survives; the physical world is impermanent, illusory.[74] Even in the Jewish and Christian traditions, where history is regarded as linear and irreversible and whose renewal is projected to the *end* of history, memory continues to have importance. Jews are to remember the sacred traditions of the God of Abraham, Isaac, and Jacob. Christians recall the archetype of Jesus Christ through the ritual of the Last Supper. To be "saved," and thus to find life, is to be true to the remembered sacred history.

The historical traditions, however, differ from the archaic view of reality in that they allow for the possibility of reinterpreting the sacred tradition. In Matthew Jesus says, "You have heard it said . . . *but I* say unto you" (Matthew 5:21–22). In biblical Judaism the classical prophets like Amos reinterpreted the Mosaic tradition by emphasizing justice as what constitutes righteousness and not the perpetuation of the ritual sacrifices. The writers of wisdom like Job and the preacher of Ecclesiastes questioned the traditional Deuteronomic wisdom that from righteous living and the love of the Law success would come. Job even had the freedom to "curse God and die." Of Islam, one could say that in devaluing the revelations of the Hebrew and Christian scriptures for the final, complete, and perfect revelation of the *Qur'an,* Islam reinterprets the sacred traditions thus far. The historical traditions, in other words, could discredit former archetypes and not repeat them because of their belief in humans' "absolute emancipation from any kind of natural 'law'."[75]

Such freedom grants humans the ability to define their own ontological constitution, and, even more responsibly, as Eliade points out, to "intervene even in the ontological constitution of the universe."[76] This creative break from the archetypes and from an archaic spirituality preset the advent of the modern, historical consciousness—that which is conscious of its individual freedom and of evolutionary linear time. The demythologization in secularism is the radical extension of this human autonomy from the archetypes.

Though Eliade concedes to the transcending of archetypes as a creative venture, the preponderance of his work favors an archaic ontology and its cosmic order of containment. We are reminded of this when Eliade affirms that the essential human condition precedes the actual, the second "fallen," human condition. Yet, if we assume that with the coming of historical consciousness history itself is valued as ontologically creative (humans as free and as historical), then the ontological and moral distinction between the sacred and the profane becomes less clearly distinguishable. The profane sphere, in other words, defined as pertaining to ordinary time and to continual becoming, might just indeed be creative in its own right. In matters concerning the seeking of justice, the demythologized secular person can, on many occasions, exemplify higher moral ideals than the Church and the mythologized person. Moreover, the "killing" of God, as in the death-of-god theologies, is creative in its helping to break through cemented and outdated interpretations of the sacred's activity in human society. Eliade's ontological structure is not given to valuing change and becoming; his emphasis is on the stability of being. This stance not only undervalues secularism but also proves somewhat limited in valuing Chinese religions, since it is in the very nature of the Tao that change or becoming is the principal ontological constitution of the universe.[77]

To return to anamnesis, I stated above that it has two sides, that which is remembered and that which is forgotten. Any recollection presupposes the selection of certain facts over against others. It is as important to know what to forget as it is to know what to remember. It is this mythic characteristic of needing to remember and selectively forget which is foreign to the historically obsessed mind-set. Modern historiography is intent upon recalling everything, *all* historical facts. On a positive note, total anamnesis helps universalize the West through the West's insistence on amassing all possible cultural information, Western and non-Western. Negatively, it indicates in the modern person an existential anxiety before the abyss of death, where, unless we are remembered, death is a transition to nothingness.[78] John Updike's defroked preacher Thomas Marshfield voiced this fear when he said, "I still have a memory, a soul (let us pray the two not prove at the end of time to be synonymous)."[79]

This distinction between historiography (total anamnesis) and myth (selective anamnesis) raises a serious tension in modern, pluralistic societies. The increasing pluralism within and among cultures and the inter-cultural permeability that blurs the boundary lines between cultural-religious groups have virtually eliminated most of the isolated, mythically self-contained communities. Today one group's myth becomes or affects another's. An insignificant event to one culture is another culture's pivotal event. And one religion's archetype is another's type among many other types. No longer are we asked just to remember our own stories and archetypes. Now we are forced to know others' as well. In her latest book, *Other Peoples' Myths,* Wendy Doniger O'Flaherty inquires into the befuddling complexities of living upon, interacting with, and speaking of and for other peoples' myths. If, as she says, we do not live the stark, primordial archetypes, which are "dead coral," but rather their multiple and present variants and manifestations,[80] then after which archetypes or models must we pattern ourselves? Which events must we, as individuals and as a culture, recall and which be forgotten? Which events do we honor and which do we question? If the new humanism is a patterning after exemplary models—undeniably many are only unconsciously lived and must, therefore be hermeneutically derived—which, in their present, variant form, do we imitate, remember, forget, etc.?

Eliade had his own "immediate" archetypes and put forward some of them for the Romanian "young generation." Throughout his life Eliade modled himself after various figures,[81] such as Papini and Nietzsche; encyclopedic and Renaissance men like Goethe, Hasedu, Eminescu, Voltaire; historians of religion like Tylor, Frazer, Müller, and Pettazzoni;[82] writers like Dante and Balzac; and literary heroes, such as Don Quixote and the Norwegian pastor Bran; the theological-philosophical thoughts of Nicholas de Cusa, Meister Eckhart, and Sören Kierkegaard, and after the lives of alchemists and yogi ascetics. The nationalism of his youth was inspired by Hasedu, Nae Ionescu, Gandhi, and the Oxford Group Movement of Frank Buchman. Such a nationalism was to involve a continous "spiritual revolution" for a "new man" as inspired by the Christ model, a model signifying an inner transformation of the soul, the cultivation of spiritual values of charity, hope, and love, and a willingness for personal sacrifice, even unto death.[83] In 1927–28 Eliade recommended to his lycée friends that they must read A. G. Chamberlain, Descartes, Bergson, Gustave le Bon, the New Testament, the novelists London, Kipling, Papini, Unamuno, D'Annunzio, Rilke, Thomas Mann, and the classics Pascal, Racine, L. Rouchefoucauld, Gracian, Machiavelli, etc. Although Eliade would grow out of (such as Papini), reevaluate (such as the model of the Legionary Movement[84]), and keep (such as Goethe, Pettazzoni, Balzac) certain of the above models, the point is, in the shortrun, the new humanism is governed as much by the archetypal models a person or a culture chooses for itself as by the latent archetypes operating within the structure of the individual and cultural psyche.

Eliade, though, especially in his post-Romanian period (1945 onward), does not prescribe any particular models that might define the contours and thrust of a new humanism. In addition, his attention to hermeneutics and to the camouflage and suppression of the sacred in modern consciousness tends to prioritize unconscious motivations over the conscious ones humans do and must choose for themselves. True, Eliade encouraged encounters with primal and Oriental cultures. But these cover an amorphous mass of ethnographic facts and religious positions. And as for those he studied, Eliade had little interest in making ethical judgments, be it of Aztec human sacrifice or of mystical visions. To make judgments was simply not a part of the way he approached the religious subjects under study. This detachment can be explained, in large part, by the fact that Eliade considered himself to be an author and thinker without a model. He says in a journal entry on February 10, 1981:

> Ordinarily I don't read many articles about myself (especially those published in
> Romanian in recent years), but in the ones I have read, I've never seen anyone
> bringing out this fact; that I am an author *without a model*. I resemble, or want to
> resemble, Hasedu, Cantemir, and Goethe. But look very closely at our writings
> and ideas, our belief and *lives:* which of my great predecessors, indeed, has
> constituted for me a model? Their example gave me courage, that's all.[85]

Though easily misconstrued as a dodge from any guilty associations—
scholarly, literary, political—this quote is important for understanding, and
where to trace (or not so clearly trace), Eliade's scholarly thought, literary
styles, and why he was so nonprescriptive. For, as Mac Linscott Ricketts
never fails to emphasize, Eliade is fundamentally a self-taught scholar and
writer.[86] Subsequently, the evolution of a new humanism should progress, if it
takes Eliade as its paradigm, somewhat randomly, letting cultural and religious creations come as and where they may with only "destiny" being their
guide.

We can also explain Eliade's non-normativeness by what one would expect
from an historian of religions who takes a descriptive approach to her or his
subject,[87] though I have shown how an ethical analysis can emerge from
Eliade's theoretical system. What Eliade does try to have us see, in the end, is
that whether or not one is a spiritual or religious person, one follows some
archetypal and mythic model which provides meaning to one's view of the
world. It is out of such a mythic framework—often making use of a plurality
of myths—that humans (as individuals or as a culture) construct the world into
what they think it should be. The image of this "should be" is largely governed by how the world was thought to exist at the "beginning," at "paradise," or will be thought to look like at the endtime.

It is his stress upon uncovering the mythic impulses behind individual and
societal action that Eliade becomes a psychoanalyst of culture. The value to
this psychological hermeneutics is that the historian of religions can contextualize cultural fashions and political ideals within the framework of human
history. The conscious and unconscious impulses underlying these fashions
and ideals are more fundamental than what historigraphy can explain and
provide. These impulses arise from both the human desire to construct a
cosmos and to transcend the human condition. So, for instance, the Holocaust
is the result of more than the seemingly innocuous historicist Nazi goals of
desiring political and economic freedom and strength. Nazism, more fundamentally, pursued a myth of a pure race of the Aryan people. Hitler and his
movement wanted to recapture the purity of paradise, to be at one with the
gods. While this interpretation might be as obvious as the historistic, it at least
places the Nazi phenomenon in the broader scope of universal, human mythic
aspirations. The Holocaust and the conquest of Europe are but human expres-

sions of humans' unrelenting desire and need to continually recreate the world by first destroying it, which no amount of political or economic maneuverings can contain. The goal, then, for societies and nations is to rechannel this unavoidable human drive into more constructively creative ways so that it need not explode into such grossly evil consequences. We cannot, in the end, avoid repeating history, as Santayana thought a historical memory could do. The best we can do is diffuse the repeated history's vehemence.

So despite our best intentions, it is idealistic to think that—even in acknowledging the psyche's mythic structure—we will be able to recognize, avoid, and possibly eliminate personal, societal, and international evils. For it is the nature of myth to recall the *whole* picture at the "beginning." As in many cosmogony myths, malevolent and disruptive powers along with benevolent and constructive ones are part of the creation process. Or as in the yin/yang creation from chaos, creativity emerges and proceeds through an ongoing interrelationship between polar opposites. Myth simply but profoundly articulates, without moralizing or resolving, the way things were and are. "In the beginning . . ." is also now; what happened then happens still. Good exists along with evil; the sun symbolizes a new dawning and inaugurates the apocalypse; the gods create and they destroy and so on. The new humanism, therefore, in taking seriously the nature of myth and the plurality of myths, does not proffer any specific normative directive, nor could it really do so. It can only bring to view the fullness and totality of the human–cosmic homology. Although no normative directive is forthcoming, the new humanism does suggest a direct or indirect correlation between a person's and a culture's cosmogony—view of the beginnings—and their biological, psychological, cultural, and ethical rationales for the way things are and should be. For it is the cosmogonic myth that tells how the world came into being and which focuses and unifies all other myths—healing myths, myths of battle, of death, of cultural creations, etc.

But to identify *the* cosmogonic myth in many cultures is difficult. It is especially problematic when there are not one but several cosmogonic myths. Though the Hebrews' two creation accounts in Genesis may seem to be their primary cosmogonic myths, Douglas Knight identifies not two but six different types of Hebrew cosmogonies.[88] Moreover, there is no single interpretation of the cosmogonic myth that is valued over all others. Elaine Pagels, in *Adam, Eve, and the Serpent,* reviewing and reevaluating the interpretations given to the Edenic myth in the first few centuries of our era, will undoubtedly be criticized for her own interpretations of the Genesis cosmogonic myth.[89] In spite of the problem of interpretation, to get at *the* cosmogonic myth poses a methodological problem as well. For methodologically speaking, there are several ways the hermeneute can choose to reach what is thought to be the principal creation myth, especially if one must cut through several cultural and historical layers. Eliade's "creative hermeneutics" is frequently criticized for its methodological subjectivism on this matter.

Whatever the problematics of identifying and arriving at the cosmogonic myth of a culture and then interpreting it, there is still value to Eliade's audacious attempts to integrate the multivocality of humans' religious expression around the archetypal cosmogonic myth. He brings into bold relief the healthy tensions of moving between synthesis and analysis, order and chaos, unity and plurality, the particular and the universal, subjectivity and objectivity, etc. Whether a formal, semiformal, or empiricial approach is taken toward arriving at some prescriptive ethical order,[90] a morphological structure appears to remain as the most suitable arrangement by which to handle the plural, latent, and present models after which individuals must pattern themselves. Robin Lovin and Frank Reynolds, in their introduction to *Cosmogony and Ethical Order: New Studies in Comparative Ethics,* seem to suggest as much:

> [B]y drawing attention to the fact that different patterns of choice and action are related to different myths of origin and understandings of reality *even within a single tradition,* an empirical, history-of-religions approach calls into question the formalist proposition [of Kant] that rationality in morals can be reduced to a single pattern which will be independent of humanity's substantive preferences and diverse beliefs about the facts. But such an approach also shows that the diversity which does, in fact, exist within cultures is not necessarily destructive or debilitating.[91]

I have not answered the earlier question: after which archetypes should we pattern ourselves? That cannot be easily answered, nor does Eliade facilitate its being answered. What he does have us do is recognize that the exemplary models we choose for a new humanism have roots in our deeper assumptions as to the way the world is. As we trace our immediate archetypes to the deeper ones, we begin to uncover what is truly real and essential for us in the making of our world. It is upon this process of present–past–present/past–present–past reflectivity that Brian Smith establishes a humanistic definition of religion. We define ourselves as "religious" when we rely upon past authoritative sources ("canons") to legitimate present action.[92] Even without Eliade's "superhuman" referents in his definition of myth, Eliade's mythic structure, vis-á-vis Smith's definition, is "spiritual" and humanistic.

The New Humanism Patterned After Communitarian Models

No myth can operate in isolation. All myths are part of a larger group of narratives, a "mythology." For Eliade this communitarian quality of myths is true not only within a particular culture but equally among all cultures. Myths share a universal, primordial structure. Humans across space and time share common mythical patterns.[93] It is Eliade's universal communitarianism which challenges any kind of individualism and isolationism. Only within the community of others—of other myths, symbols, cultures, religions—is meaning attainable and personal, cultural, and religious authenticity achieved. In this regard Eliade is a contextualist. His context is simply larger than what many anthropologists and historians of religion are willing to allow.

The communitarian quality of myth is further evidenced by different people sharing similar religious experiences. Because manifestations of the sacred, for Eliade, demonstrate a structural continuity across space and time with other similar and differing religious experiences, the experience of a monotheist is not necessarily precluded from sharing in the experience of a polytheist, and vice versa. All that is required for a polytheist to share in the experience of a monotheist, for instance, is the presence of a celestial god within a polytheistic culture. The Jewish scholar Jon Levenson skillfully demonstrates such a sharing in the experience of the sacred between the polytheistic Babylonian culture and the monotheistic culture of the ancient Israelites.[94] In elevating the warrior god Marduk over the pantheon of gods for defeating the goddess of chaos, Tiamat, the Babylonians express a type of monotheism. Similarly, refering to Psalm 29, Levenson notes how monotheistic Israel echoes a polytheism-made-monotheism when it enthrones YHWH over all other competitors for having vanquished the forces of chaos.[95] YHWH is singular because YHWH conquers. In this relatively close historical connection we see how, despite one's historical context, a person or a community "practices"—consciously or unconsciously—many and a variety of religious experiences. That one's religious experience and, potentially, tradition is a syncretism of other religious experiences can be quite troubling. Salman Rushdie's novel *Satanic Verses* depicts a syncretism of polytheism and monotheism in the Islamic experience. And the incendiary reactions against Rushdie's book have been all too obvious. Eliade stresses that even chronological history cannot obliterate the innate structural complexity to the collective human religious experience. And though particular religious experiences have their rise and fall among and within cultural traditions, the innate structure of human religious experience cannot be extinguished.

Humans are social beings united in their common thirst for the real, the sacred. Through its own individual historical and cultural vignettes, each religious tradition exemplifies this quest for the real. The particular–universal dialectic in Eliade between a common thirst for the sacred and the individual expressions it takes, implies an ecumenical syncretism. There is no pure blood here. It is in ritual, perhaps more than any other form, that the irruptive presence of the sacred is most creatively harmonized in all its particular and universal expressions. For it is in ritual where myths are concretized, mythic models repeated, time is made full through the imagination, and where communities both share in other peoples' myths and demonstrate their own unique set of convictions.[96] Returning to the example of dance, though dance today is less consciously patterned after mythic models, its choreographies suggest such patterning. The behavior of a totemic animal, the arrangement of the stars, or the stages and gestures associated with an initiation are frequently consciously or unconsciously acted out in dance rituals. All dance then, Eliade could say, repeats mythical behavior. In the end, it is in the participation in ritual that a person and a community can be opened to a greater complexity of meanings, to other mythologies and symbols, and to new understandings of being in the world, as the writer Ian Frazier so emotionally described.

The Human Being as *Homo Religiosus*

In a journal entry dated November 3, 1959 Eliade wrote, "I repeated what I've said over and over again so many times in so many books: that *homo religiosus* thirsts for the real. That he wants to *be,* fully and at any cost. I show how nature, for him, was full of signs and hierophanies."[97] The presupposition that a human being is by nature *homo religiosus* underlies Eliade's theories on the behavior of humans toward the world in which they live. Humans have an essential desire to *be,* to live in Being, to live in a world that has meaning and is taken as sacred. It is this ontological view which makes the new humanism into a decidedly "spiritual" enterprise. The new humanism involves the spirit, the eternal, and the nonchanging in human life. If the condition of *homo religiosus* is assumed, the new humanism, then, is to awaken the demythologized and isolated person of modern culture to the myths and symbols which propel and inform the person's existence. For, as Adrian Marino reminds us, Eliade cannot be understood except from the standpoint of his aim to redirect a wayward West toward a new spiritual impulse.[98]

Eliade uses the term *homo religiosus* to refer to all humans. It is not meant for only the charismatic individual, such as a mystic, as it does for Schleiermacher, Max Scheler, and Joachim Wach. For Eliade, *homo religiosus* designates a quality of the human condition. The phenomenologist of religion Gerardus van der Leeuw uses it in this way, but, in contrast to him, Eliade says the quality of *homo religiosus* remains in the secularized person, though obscured or camouflaged. The structural condition of *homo religiosus* manifests itself through the secularized person's nostalgias, dreams, ambitions, fictions, initiations, political movements, New Year festivals, etc. In a 1983 lecture entitled *"Homo Faber and Homo Religiosus,"* Eliade argued that even the purely scientific mentality of *homo faber* (human being the maker), which envisions the endless progress of humanity, demonstrates a religious structure in its aspiration to refound the world.[99] While there are "unmythologized" and "demythogolized" people, an individual, much less a culture, cannot long survive without some degree of transcendence or of the "magical," as in the "secular" worldview of Confucius.[100] History cannot erase the inherent need to participate in being. Eliade does not say this religious quality in humans is the only quality of a human being. For humans are characterized also as *homo sapiens* (the human as rational), *homo faber, homo viator* (the human as voyager), and *homo ludens* (the human at play). But it is in the human as *religiosus* that we find all these united; we come to an understanding of the "total person."

A criticism of the assertion that a human being is structurally and inherently *homo religiosus* is that such a quality is unverifiable in the earliest anthropological documents of the human species, contrary to the observation that humans have always been the maker of tools and technology (*homo faber*). To posit *homo religiosus* is to assume an archetypal postulate, a purported state of being that bases all human actions and aspirations as religious in motivation, that is, as motivated by the desire for meaning, being, and truth. Although there is no way to prove the primordiality of the human as religious, there is equally no way to disprove it.[101] Like Eliade's "transconscious," it survives by being nonfalsifiable. The only way that humans can be perceived as religious in nature is by observing how they articulate their religious impulse—thirst for meaning and transcendence—in the concrete acts of history. What we have is a circular logic: human activity is symbolically religious, but it is religious because of the *homo religiosus* postulate. Furthermore, if what humans do is interpreted from the premise of religion, then some of the other, perhaps more immediate motivations out of which humans operate—the political, economic, social, and psychological—in their day-to-day concerns are glossed over or given short shrift. To postulate *homo religiosus* for interpreting human behavior can, at times, fail to attend to the particularities of concrete, give-and-take existence. Humans can be seen to ride above the mundane.[102]

In defense of Eliade, however, his purpose is not to elucidate *homo faber* or the practical life of *homo religiosus*. The human as the maker of technology gets enough attention in modern society. And how religion plays a part in fashioning societies, in setting up trade and commerce, creating culture, or in informing the psyche, these practicalities have been well studied by Durkheim, Weber, Malinowski, and Jung, respectively. Eliade responded to a need in a Western civilization that was just coming out of the rationalism of the

Enlightenment and into the scientific technocracy of the twentieth century. Eliade discerned a crisis of meaning and an absence of the transcendent. The root to this crisis was religious and its solution, Eliade believed, was also religious.

One can argue whether a thirst for meaning is endemic to human consciousness or whether the problem of meaning is as much an issue—scholarly or otherwise—when environmental and survival concerns and deconstructionism relativize and undermine meaning. But meaning is not so easily dissociated from physical survival, and a great many people still refer to meaning and speak of it being found. Meaninglessness is very much a part of human existence, but it cannot be its perpetual condition lest all order collapse and all hope dry up. Moreover, human survival becomes an ontological and existential issue when biology and ecology are said to inform how we interpret ourselves in the world and define what we feel constitutes us as being human. By positing the human as *homo religiosus,* Eliade infuses the dimension of meaning as a necessary and serviceable construct into all other characteristics that make up the totality of the human person.

Notes

1. Mircea Eliade, *The Old Man and the Bureaucrats,* trans. Mark Park Stevenson (Notre Dame, IN: University of Notre Dame Press, 1979).

2. Matei Calinescu, "The Function of the Unreal: Reflections on Mircea Eliade's Short Fiction," in *Imagination and Meaning: The Scholarly and Literary Worlds of Mircea Eliade,* ed. Norman J. Girardot and Mac Linscott Ricketts (New York: Seabury Press, 1982), p. 153.

3. Eliade, *Ordeal by Labyrinth,* p. 184.

4. Andrew M. Greeley, *Unsecular Man: The Persistence of Religion* (New York: Shocken Books, 1985), pp. 94ff.

5. Matei Calinescu, *Faces of Modernity: Avant-Garde, Decadence, Kitsch* (Bloomington, IN: Indiana University Press, 1977), pp. 264–65.

6. José Ortega y Gasset, *The Revolt of the Masses,* trans. (New York: W. W. Norton, 1932), p. 31.

7. Eliade, *The Forbidden Forest,* p. vii.

8. Myths are not literally true but are true in their implicit meanings, says Wendy Doniger O'Flaherty. "Myths are perceived as true when the reality to which they point has 'always' been perceived as true or becomes newly perceived as true. And a myth becomes newly perceived as true either by inspiring people to change the way things are or by enabling people to project their view of reality over the world, even when that world remains the same." See Doniger O'Flaherty, *Other Peoples' Myths,* pp. 31–32. See also Eliade, *Myths, Dreams, and Mysteries,* p. 24. Also see Bruce Lincoln on the distinctions between fable, legend, history, and myth based on the criteria of their

"truth-claims," "credibility," and "authority," in *Discourse and the Construction of Society* (New York: Oxford University Press, 1989), p. 25.

9. Mircea Eliade, *Myth and Reality,* trans. Willard R. Trask (New York: Harper & Row, 1963), pp. 5–6.

10. William G. Doty, *Mythography* (University, AL: University of Alabama Press, 1986), pp. 45–47. See also Hans H. Penner, "Myth and Ritual: A Wasteland or a Forest of Symbols?", in *On Method in the History of Religions,* ed. James S. Helfer (Middletown, CT: Wesleyan University Press, 1968), pp. 48–53.

11. Spiro, "Religion: Problems of Definition and Explanation," in *Anthropological Approaches to the Study of Religion,* ed. Michael Banton (London: Tavistock Publications, 1966), pp. 104–06.

12. Ibid.

13. Penner, *On Method,* pp. 52–53.

14. Cited in Wendy Doniger O'Flaherty, "Review of *Historical Atlas of World Mythology* by Joseph Campbell," *The New York Times Book Review,* (December 18, 1983), 25. On myth and religion originating through human biology, also see Robert F. Brown, "Eliade on Archaic Religion: Some Old and New Criticisms," *Studies in Religion* 10,4 (Fall 1981), 428.

15. On the "transconscious" see Mac Linscott Ricketts, "The Nature and Extent of Eliade's 'Jungianism,'" *Union Seminary Quarterly Review* 25,2 (Winter 1970), 229–30; Eliade, *Images and Symbols,* p. 120 and Eliade, *Patterns In Comparative Religion,* p. 454. The existence of some "other" raises questions on how objective an entity this "other" was for Eliade. I tend to think it is more objective than imaginary, as Matei Calinescu, the literary interpreter of Eliade, takes it. See Calinescu in the introduction to Mircea Eliade, *Youth Without Youth and Other Novellas,* ed. Matei Calinescu, trans. Mac Linscott Ricketts (Columbus, OH: Ohio State University Press, 1988), p. xiv.

16. What has undercut the connection between myth and literature in modern literature is the genre of the *nouveau roman.* The "new novel" rejects the fictional for the scientifically real and concrete. It equally rejects any dependency of the author upon literary precedents, and, because it rejects historical dependency and development and all prototypes, the "new novel" eliminates the role of narrative. Every creation, every act is existentially unique and, hence, is unrepeatable and unshareable. Without the presence of fiction and narrative it wipes out any continuity with myth. See Arnold Hauser on the "crisis of the novel" in *The Sociology of Art,* trans. Kenneth J. Worthcott (Chicago: University of Chicago Press, 1982), pp. 716–26.

17. Mircea Eliade, *Tales of the Sacred and the Supernatural* (Philadelphia: Westminster Press, 1981), p. 12.

18. Edith Kurzweil, *The Age of Structuralism: Lévi-Strauss to Foucault* (New York: Columbia University Press, 1980), p. 4, 14ff.

19. Claude Lévi-Strauss, "The Structural Study of Myth," in Lessa and Vogt, *Reader In Comparative Religion,* pp. 185ff.

20. Claude Lévi-Strauss, *The Jealous Potter,* trans. Benedicte Chorier (Chicago: The University of Chicago Press, 1988), pp. 193,171.

21. Matei Calinescu even speaks of an antihuman, despairing tendency in Lévi-

Strauss. See "Imagination and Meaning: Aesthetic Attitudes and Ideas in Mircea Eliade's Thought," *The Journal of Religion* 57,1 (January 1977), 10–12.

22. The historian Jonathan Z. Smith, wanting to reclassify the implied periodization in Eliade's "archaic–modern" classification, prefers a spatial means of designation. Smith prefers to speak of a "*locative* vision of the world (which emphasizes place) and a *utopian* vision of the world (using the term in its strict sense: the value of being in no place)." See *Map Is Not Territory*, p. 101. Smith's designation does not alter the "archaic" and "modern" worlds Eliade describes, but it does, as I will show later, put greater weight on space as what defines an ontology and less upon time, or myth, as that which gives space its ontological value.

23. Doniger O'Flaherty, *Other Peoples' Myths*, p. 120.

24. "Transhistorical," we must always remember, does not mean parallel to history or detached from history, in the sense that meaning or interpretations of experience can exist apart from history. Recall the definition of a *hierophany*. There are certain experiences—such as initiation, ecstasy, the thirst for the center, nostalgias—which are, structurally, nonhistorically conditioned. But the values ascribed to them are historically conditioned. See Douglas Allen, *Structure and Creativity in Religion* (The Hague: Mouton Publishers, 1978), p. 179 n. 9.

25. See Frank Kermode on the effect of the apocalyptic or the "sense of an ending" in the interpretation of literature: *The Sense of an Ending* (New York: Oxford University Press, 1967).

26. Virgil Nemoianu, "Wrestling with Time: Some Tendencies in Nabokov's and Eliade's Later Works," *Southeastern Europe* 7,1 (1980), 84–85.

27. For in the same year in which he wrote *Christina*, 1937, Eliade wrote *Şarpele* (The Snake) in which the fantastic was found to be essentially indistinguishable from ordinary experience, or the sacred from the profane. See Ricketts, *Romanian Roots*, p. 1058; and Eliade, *Mircea Eliade: Autobiography*, 1:322.

28. Kermode, *Sense of an Ending*, pp. 39, 63, 123.

29. Strenski, *Four Theories of Myth*, pp. 78–79.

30. Kermode, *Sense of an Ending*, p. 64.

31. Kees Bolle, *The Freedom of Man in Myth* (Nashville, TN: Vanderbilt University Press, 1968), pp. 36–37.

32. Ibid.

33. The "demythologized" person, who can be a religious person, can posit archetypal models, such as death-of-god Christians who look to Jesus as a moral example. But in that no outside reference to human language, hence no transcendence, is allowed, the archetype fails to have ontological weight.

34. Sigmund Freud, *Civilization and Its Discontents,* trans. Joan Riviere (Garden City, NY: Doubleday & Co. 1961), pp. 13ff.

35. Michel de Certeau, *The Practice of Everyday Life,* trans. Steven Rendall (Berkeley, CA: University of California Press, 1984), pp. xii–xxiv, 30.

36. Eliade, *Cosmos and History,* pp. 148–51.

37. Ricketts, *Romanian Roots,* p. 69.

38. Tu Wei-Ming, *Confucian Thought: Selfhood as Creative Transformation* (Albany, NY: State University of New York Press, 1985), pp. 26, 126.

39. Flow experience is best found when a person is at play. To be engaged in play, in a pleasurable and semistructured activity, a person flows with the activity itself in a goalless process of spontaneous action and self-forgetfulness. ''A person in flow has no dualistic perspective: he is aware of his actions but not of the awareness itself,'' says Mihaly Csikszentmihalyi in his study *Beyond Boredom and Anxiety: The Experience of Play in Work and Games* (San Francisco: Jossey-Bass, 1975), p. 38.

40. Tu Wei-Ming, *Confucian Thought,* pp. 35, 126–28. Without a stress on cosmogony it does not mean that there is no primordial archetypes or exemplary models after which a person is to pattern and ontologically give meaning to his or her life. Even given the Confucian stress upon the here and now and upon present social relations, humans participate in the way of heaven, which created human nature in the first place, says Tu Wei-Ming. And, in that one is informed by heaven, one's social models— parents, rulers, elders—become ''archetypes'' of meaning. In addition, even Confucius himself spoke of archetypal, exemplary models of behavior, principally the kings of the Chou Dynasty. See Eliade, *A History of Religious Ideas, Vol. 2, From Gautama Buddha to the Triumph of Christianity,* trans. Willard R. Trask (Chicago: University of Chicago Press, 1982), pp. 25.

41. Ricoeur, ''The History of Religions,'' p. 20–28.

42. Mircea Eliade, *Shamanism: Archaic Techniques of Ecstasy,* trans. Willard R. Trask (Princeton: Princeton University Press, Bollingen Series, 1964), pp. xi–xxi.

43. For a representative text of this genre see Tzvetan Todorov, *The Fantastic: A Structural Approach to a Literary Genre,* trans. Richard Howard (Ithaca, NY: Cornell University Press, 1973).

44. Ibid., p. 172.

45. Strenski, *Four Theories,* pp. 97, 118–22.

46. Eliade, *Autobiography,* 1:55–57. See also Ricketts, *Romanian Roots,* p. 40; and Ion Balu, ''Les debuts litteraires,'' in Constantin Tacou, *L'Herne: Mircea Eliade* (Paris: Editions de L'Herne, 1978), p. 377.

47. In making this assertion Strenski quotes Matei Calinescu. See Strenski, *Four Theories,* p. 82.

48. Eliade, *Autobiography,* 1:315.

49. Matei Calinescu in Eliade, *Youth Without Youth,* pp. xiii–iv.

50. Eliade, ''With the Gypsy Girls,'' in *Tales of the Sacred and the Supernatural.*

51. Mircea Eliade, ''Nights at Serampore'' in Eliade, *Two Strange Tales* (Boston: Shambhala Press, 1986).

52. Bogdan Petriceicu-Hasedu (1838–1907) was a Romanian historian and encyclopedist; and Johann W. von Goethe (1749–1832) was one of Germany's greatest poets. See Ricketts, *Romanian Roots,* p. 945.

53. Harvey Cox, *Many Mansions* (Boston: Beacon Press, 1988), p. 203.

54. See Eliade's essay ''Cultural Fashions and the History of Religions,'' in his *Occultism, Witchcraft, and Cultural Fashions* (Chicago: University of Chicago Press,

1976). Harvey Cox, *Many Mansions,* pp. 196ff., in his ruminations on the future of religion, forsees religion dissapearing as some compartment separate from the rest of life. He cites the contributions of the French philosophers of the age of Reason, of Freud, and of Lenin as what will help lead to such a diffusion of religion into all areas of life. But that religion is diffused throughout all dimensions of life and that questions of meaning will continue to command central importance for tomorrow's "religion" are precisely issues which Eliade has us see. See especially Eliade, *Myths, Dreams, and Mysteries,* p. 107.

55. Eliade, *Autobiography,* 2:173 n. 7. Wach was referring to passages that would be written in Eliade, *Myths, Dreams, and Mysteries,* pp. 106–10.

56. Eliade, *Yoga: Immortality and Freedom,* pp. xv–xix.

57. Ursula King, "Historical and Phenomenological Approaches," in *Contemporary Approaches to the Study of Religion,* ed. Frank Whaling (New York: Mouton Publishers, 1983), 1:113–14.

58. Strenski, "Love and Anarchy in Romania," pp. 392–93.

59. Guilford Dudley III, "Mircea Eliade as the 'Anti-Historian' of Religions," *Journal of the American Academy of Religion* 44,2 (1976), 44–48. See also for greater treatment Dudley's *Religion on Trial.*

60. Jonathan Z. Smith, *Imagining Religion* (Chicago: University of Chicago, 1978), pp. 25, 29.

61. Dudley's provocative suggestion to tie Eliade to the structural, antihistory philosophy of Michel Foucault in order to sidestep Eliade's own view of history and to ground Eliade on a philosophical antihistoricism, is interesting but shortsighted. Dudley tries to take Eliade out of an empirical framework, yet he evaluates him by one. Dudley forgets that Eliade is exposing us to *other* valid histories besides the West's. Dudley and Strenski both almost totally ignore Eliade's Indian influences. Furthermore, Eliade's phenomenology cannot be removed from the "raw data of history." As for Eliade's phenomenological orientation, which Dudley wants to preserve, to tie it to Foucault would undermine it, since Foucault rejects the phenomenological approach. See Dudley, "Mircea Eliade as the 'Anti-Historian'," 44–48; and Michel Foucault, *The Order of Things* (New York: Vintage Books, 1973), p. xiv.

62. Strenski, being highly critical of Eliade's "creative hermeneutics," and claiming it is of the "fantastic," ends up practicing his own creative hermeneutics, as an excerpt from Strenski's *Four Theories* demonstrates: "There is, then, more than enough material here for an important and *enlightening story.* I shall try to tell as much of it *as the available data permit.* If the reader is *willing to accept some limited goals and some historical reconstruction,* we can at least begin to see Eliade's theory of myth within its time. If the conclusions we reach have to be *qualified by ignorance,* at least the questions raised may provide a stimulus for scholars in possession of better data" [emphasis mine], p. 79.

If Strenki is so critical of Eliade's hermeneutics, he can at least avoid doing it himself. Or maybe he realizes how valuable and valid it is for helping illumine ("enlighten") still unrecovered data.

63. Eliade's life-long mentor, Goethe, reacted overly strongly against the New-

tonian mathematical hegemony of his day which, in the end, limited his appeal among scientists who *do* take mathematics seriously. Eliade carried out empirical studies as a boy in Romania, and in a 1937 review on the sacred bee he argued for the need for the inductive method and empirical testing. See Ricketts, *Romanian Roots,* pp. 864–65. Moreover, Eliade always stressed the need to consult the specialists in the field.

64. See Joseph M. Kitagawa's and Gregory Alles' comments in the chapter "Afterword: The Dialectic of the Parts and the Whole: Reflections on the Past, Present, and Future of the History of Religions," in Kitagawa and Alles, *The History of Religions: Retrospect and Prospect* (New York: Macmillan Publishing, 1985).

65. See Adrian Marino, "Mircea Eliade's Hermeneutics," in Girardot, *Imagination and Meaning.*

66. Allen, *Structure and Creativity,* pp. 207–8, 239–43.

67. In conversation with Joseph M. Kitagawa (12/9/87), he said Eliade's conception of love is principally Johannine; that love is more important than right or truth. Love is beyond justice, even. One *is* love. Eliade's views on love are principally found in his novels. See especially his *The Forbidden Forest.* Love could even take on a sociopolitical scale. While a cultural advisor for Romania in Lisbon between 1941 and 1945, Eliade praised the Portuguese dictator Antonio de Oliveira Salazar for building a state on love: "The Whole social and governmental concept of Salazar is based on the family and, as such, on love." See Ricketts, *Romanian Roots,* p. 1111.

68. Joseph M. Kitagawa, *The History of Religions: Understanding Human Experience* (Atlanta: Scholars Press, 1987), p. 40.

69. Eliade, *The Sacred and the Profane,* p. 213.

70. Smith, *Imagining Religion,* pp. 88–89.

71. See the classic ethnographic study on the Ghost Dance by James Mooney, *The Ghost Dance Religion and the Sioux Outbreak of 1890* (1896; rpt. Chicago: University of Chicago Press, 1965).

72. Ian Frazier, "A Reporter at Large (The Great Plains—Part III)," *The New Yorker* (March 6, 1989), 44. As it is included in the book see his *Great Plains* (New York: Farrar, Straus & Giroux, 1989), p. 166, 173–75.

73. Ricoeur, "The History of Religions," p. 18; and see Walter J. Ong, *Interfaces of the Word* (Ithaca, NY: Cornell University Press, 1977), p. 60, in which he describes how the writing of literature relies on previous paradigmatic models, models like myth, which are fictionalized in the imagination. "If the writer succeeds in writing, it is generally because he can fictionalize in his imagination an audience he has learned to know not from daily life but from earlier writers who were fictionalizing in their imagination audiences they had learned to know in still earlier writers, and so on back to the dawn of written narrative."

74. Doniger O'Flaherty, *Other Peoples' Myths,* pp. 64ff.

75. Eliade refers to the notion of faith in Christianity as allowing for this emancipation. See *Cosmos and History,* pp. 160–62. Martin Buber says there is a comparable reference in the Hebrew scriptures to Christianity's notion of faith emancipating one from natural law. Martin Buber, *Two Types of Faith,* pp. 20–22.

76. Eliade, *Cosmos and History,* pp. 160–61.

77. I show under the section "Humans as Authentic" that Eliade's thought on authenticity as occuring at the juncture of being and becoming can appropriate the Chinese thought of the Tao.

78. See a full treatment on modern anxiety in Eliade's chapter "Religious Symbolism and Modern Man's Anxiety," in *Myths, Dreams, and Mysteries.*

79. John Updike, *A Month of Sundays* (New York: Alfred A. Knopf, 1975), p. 41.

80. Doniger O'Flaherty, *Other Peoples' Myths,* p. 95.

81. To whatever degree Eliade modeled himself after various individuals, the fact that Eliade got inspiration and courage from them and not from others is enough to refer to them as models. He still speaks of models, but qualifies the degree to which he is indebteded to them. See below in the texts.

82. Eliade admired Tylor, Frazer, and Müller for their willingness to propose bold hypotheses and for their cultural impact. Eliade did not share in their principal theories. Pettazzoni remained a life-long model for Eliade. Though Pettazzoni's historicism differed from Eliade's phenomenological and morphological approach, Pettazzoni's position, nevertheless, remained in complementary tension to Eliade's. Eliade especially admired Pettazzoni's universal approach to the history of religions as *Allgemeine Religionswissenschaft.*

83. Eliade's great admiration for, and sorrow over, the sacrifical death of his friend Ion Mota (d.1936), contributed to Eliade's belief in the value of the Legionary Movement for the renewal and edification of the Romanian nation. Ricketts, *Romanian Roots,* p. 922.

84. It appears Eliade never completely rejected the essential virtues he saw in the Legionary Movement. For in its essence as a spiritual, Romanian, and ascetic-sacrificial movement, the Legionary exemplified qualities Eliade would always admire. See Eliade, *Autobiography,* 2:62–69. But, once in exile with an outside and more sober perspective, Eliade disparged the zealous naivete the young generation had in blindly accepting the spiritual-political idealisms of the Legionary. In its idealistic protest against democratic and Marxian politics of party negotiations and class liberation, the Legionary became an off-balanced and unrealistic, therefore, extremist political movement. See Ricketts, *Romanian Roots,* pp. 929–30.

85. Mircea Eliade, *Journal IV: 1979–1985,* trans. Mac Linscott Ricketts (Chicago: University of Chicago Press, 1990), p. 41.

86. Ricketts, *Romanian Roots,* pp. 1211–15.

87. How normative comparativists and historians of religion can be has been the focus of much discussion. A recent series of conferences between anthropologists, historians of religions, and philosophers has been discussing the very problematics of the "when," "how," or the "should" in evaluating other peoples' practices and beliefs. See the summary reports from the conferences on Religions in Culture and History, 1986–89, at the Divinity School, the University of Chicago, in *Deconstructing, Reconstructing the Philosophy of Religions,* ed. Francisca Cho Bantly (Chicago: The Divinity School, 1990).

88. Other religious traditions similarly have multiple cosmogonies and cosmogonic interpretations. Robin W. Lovin and Frank E. Reynolds, *Cosmogony and Ethical*

Order: New Studies in Comparative Ethics (Chicago: University of Chicago Press, 1985), pp. 23–24.

89. Elaine Pagels, *Adam, Eve, and the Serpent* (New York: Random House, 1988).

90. The formalist approach relies on identifying a priori structures to human religious reason and then applying these to the evaluation of human behavior from across religious traditions. The semiformal approach begins by identifying the human need to cooperate and to manage scarce resources. Based on these two practical realities, differing religious traditions are analyzed as to how they practically guide human behavior in balancing cooperation and competition. Differing with the formal approach, the semiformal makes no use of a priori rational structures to the human mind. Lastly, the empirical approach uses the process of scientific investigation to continually revise what we think should be done with what the facts and situations may indicate and demand. See Lovin and Reynolds, *Cosmogony and Ethical Order,* pp. 12–20.

91. Ibid., p. 29.

92. Brian K. Smith, "Exorcising the Transcendent: Strategies for Defining Hinduism and Religion," *History of Religions* 27,1 (August 1987), 52–53.

93. This broad communitarian quality given to myth naturally offends diffusionist theories of myth. These theories say we cannot suppose cultural interchange between cultures known to have had no cultural or physical contact. Eliade hurdles the problem of disconnectedness in three ways: 1) by presupposing a *sui generis* value to religious experience wherever it is found, 2) saying that manifestations of the sacred (hierophanies) have a structural continuity across space and time, and 3) by accepting with qualifications the Graebner-Schmidt-Koppers theory of culture circles (*Kulturkreis*). See Eliade's preface in *Shamanism* and his *Quest,* pp. 24–25. This theory holds that within a given area, and based on evidence of shared "forms" and "quantity" of commonalities, a uniform material culture could have existed. See Eric J. Sharpe, *Comparative Religion: A History,* 2d (La Salle, IL: Open Court, 1986), p. 181. As early as 1925, Eliade saw the need for a structural hermeneutical approach to myth. Ricketts, *Romanian Roots,* pp. 79–80.

94. Jon D. Levenson, *Creation and the Persistence of Evil: The Jewish Drama of Divine Omnipotence* (San Francisco: Harper & Row, 1988), pp. 131–39.

95. Ibid., p. 133.

96. Wendy Doniger O'Flaherty terms the kind of myth that shares and continues in, yet modifies without severing the roots of, another peoples' myth as a "metamyth," a myth about a myth. Christianity's appropriation of the suffering servant myths of ancient Israel is an example. She also claims that people tend to be more orthoprax than orthodox. People are more willing to shape and alter their myths than they are their rituals. She concludes that people will become more heteroprax and heterodox through encounters with others' myths. See *Other Peoples' Myths,* pp. 112–13, 125, 144–45.

97. Eliade, *No Souvenirs,* p. 71.

98. Marino, *L'Hermeneutique de Mircea Eliade,* pp. 297–300.

99. Eliade, *"Homo Faber and Homo Religiosus"* in Kitagawa, *Retrospect,* pp. 1–13. See also Julien Ries et al. ed., *L'Expression du sacre dans les grandes religions,* vol. 3 (Louvain-La-Neuve: Centre D'Histoire des Religions, 1986), pp. 337–38.

100. Fingarette, *Confucius: The Secular as Sacred*, p. 3.

101. Culianu, *Mircea Eliade*, p. 88. In 1945 Eliade said to a friend that though others may not see the inner meanings of a symbol, that does not mean they are not there. Eliade, *Journal I: 1945–1955*, pp. 8–9.

102. Recall that the incarnational, dialectical quality to Eliade's theory of symbols and myth prevents his thought from being overly abstracted from everyday life.

5

The Goals of the New Humanism

If humanity is to approximate a new humanism, there will naturally be some goals toward which it aims. Eliade never elaborated on the particular implications and expressions of the new humanism. So there are no definitive goals that he had in mind to which we can point. Nevertheless, it is possible to extrapolate recurring concepts throughout Eliade's life work which constitute certain individual and cultural ambitions. We can refer to these ambitions, or goals, as archetypal variants on the primordial archetype of the new humanism. In fact, all the forms which comprise the morphology of the new humanism are archetypes which imitate the central archetype of the new humanism. And because these forms recur through innumerable variations, are we able to articulate what the new humanism might look like. For, true to the nature of archetypes, each time an archetype is repeated, in whatever guise, the repetition constitutes a return to the "beginning." And though the designation "goals" implies ending, every ending is but another beginning. To modify, slightly, the archaic phenomenon of ritual repetition, each return to the "beginning" will differ somewhat from the previous return so that, whether it is at the personal, national, or global level, each step toward the new humanism will always be creatively "new."

Within the morphology of the new humanism, therefore, each goal of the new humanism is but one particular expression, or form, of the new humanism. Like Eliade's morphology of the sacred, these goals interact and overlap, they complement and supplement each other, but together they build toward what we know as the morphological whole of the new humanism. As such, they share in those forms constituting "the nature of the human condition" in the new humanism, and they equally share in those forms that will constitute "the challenges of the new humanism." The goals rest on the anthropological assumptions of myth, symbol, and *homo religiosus* and contain ordeals or challenges necessary for the achievement of a new humanism.

The following four goals are extracted as archetypes of the new humanism: 1) humans as authentic, 2) humans as free, 3) humans as of culture, and 4) humans as at the center. As "authentic," the new humanism suggests a particular mode of being in the world. As "free," it concerns the ability of humans to be fruitfully creative. As "of culture," we find that the new humanism adopts a sophisticated cultural status. Finally, as "at the center," the new humanism organizes a place upon which to stand; a place, however, never free from disruptive forces.

Humans as Authentic

We can define Eliade's existentialism as that of "being in the world." Amidst the expanse, plurality, and mystery of the cosmos humans find themselves, in the philosopher Martin Heidegger's term, "thrown" into the world. From out of this condition humans symbolically and mythically construct their sense of belonging and narrative of meaning. Humans squarely face their "being in the world," formulate its significance for their lives, and then responsibly live out its conclusions. In so doing, humans live authentically. To live as authentic human beings is to live at the heart of the real and realize true humanness. For Eliade, authenticity, to be authentic, implies a religious, philosophical, and behavioral mode of existence.[1]

In order to define more precisely what is meant by authenticity for Eliade, we must take into account what it meant to the German poet Goethe, to the philosopher Martin Heidegger, and in the Romanian sense. Much of Eliade's inspiration as a scholar and as a humanist came from Goethe. Heidegger is one of the most influential existentialist philosophers of the twentieth century and one in relation to which Eliade posited his own type of existentialism. And it is from the Romanian context that we get some of the principal sources to Eliade's view of authenticity.

For Goethe, authenticity means to live one's life autonomously. One is to be free from external conventions and unfettered by internal complexes for the creative development of one's selfhood. This free and unfettered mind allows the mind to be in a continual state of development and one's thought and actions in close harmony with the spontaneous impulses of nature.[2] For Heidegger, to live authentically means to accept the reality of one's finiteness and then act resolutely as "being unto death," in other words, to live in light of one's imminent end.[3] As for the particular Romanian sense of the word, Sergiu Al-George defines authenticity as:

> A certain mode of engagement in the real which aims at apprehending the most dense, *concrete* zone of reality: its *primordial nucleus*. This type of engagement

is conceived of as an "experience" or "lived experience" (*trăire*) of certain acts (*fapte,* things done), thereby becoming an act of "understanding."[4]

From a composite of the Goethian, Heideggerian, and Romanian views of authenticity, it is possible to discuss authenticity for Eliade in terms of four components. Authenticity means: 1) a *free* 2) *engagement, encounter, active experience* with 3) *concrete* and *pristine facts of existence,* which 4) leads to *understanding,* to an apprehension of what is real, undefiled, and nonimitative.

The Centrality of Authenticity to Eliade's Work

Because "authenticity" is an existential term and is relevant to hermeneutics, it is easy to see how it would assimilate well with the many dimensions of Eliade's life and thought. It is not surprising, therefore, that Günther Spaltmann and Sergiu Al-George have, accordingly, identified it as the "primordial plant" to Eliade's work. They say it captures the motivation behind Eliade's desire to uncover, depict, and elucidate for present existence the real. No doubt the hermeneutical potential of the term makes it a likely primordial archetype to Eliade's vocation. But to stop at authenticity and make it "the basis of the entire Eliadian corpus"[5] does not break the Eliadean swing and follow through with the pitch to the new humanism. For the ultimate aim of Eliade's work is not just that we be more fully human, but that we attain a humanness of a universal consciousness. The new humanism is a "new" order of existence. So among interpretive paradigms, the "new humanism" carries us further than the category "authenticity." After all, Eliade never wrote an article exclusively on authenticity in the manner of his new humanism article. Neither did he refer to authenticity in the same ultimate terms for individuals *and* for culture as he did to the new humanism and the "new man," a romantic ideal of his generation. Authenticity, in the end, is only a penultimate goal within the morphology of the new humanism. The notion of a new humanism is the central archetype to the Eliadean corpus. Defined, then, in accordance to the primordial archetype of the new humanism, the variant archetype of authenticity, based on the above components, characterizes the new humanism as an existential encounter of concrete experiences where at the juncture of being and becoming the real is apprehended and attained. Before I address this thesis, though, it serves to trace the influences on Eliade's use of the term. From these sources of influence we will be in a better position to delineate the above four components to authenticity.

Influences on Eliade's Use of Authenticity

In temperament, Eliade seems to have been born with an extreme sensitivity for experiencing things firsthand.[6] From his earliest years, Eliade evidenced a probing intuition and a relentless urge to grasp the essence of human and natural phenomena. In his autobiography he recalls how as an infant he crawled into his parent's drawing room and there discovered a new world. He describes this room as like a "fairy-tale palace" of "green velvet" curtains and of an "eerie iridescent light" that gave him the impression of being within a "huge grape." He looked into the room's large "venetian mirrors" and saw himself as "grown-up, more handsome" as if "ennobled by that [iridescent] light from another world."[7] He recalls other such probing and searching encounters as when, at five, while on a walk with his grandfather, he had an eye-to-eye, I–Thou meeting with a young girl his age. On another occasion, he came eye-to-eye with a blue-green lizard while on an outing through the woods. He recalls the incident in his autobiography: "Once, in the forest, creeping on all fours through the grass, I unexpectedly found myself in front of a glittering blue-green lizard. Both of us were dumbounded, and we just stared at each other. I was not afraid and yet my heart was throbbing. I was over-whelmed by the joy of having encountered, for the first time, a creature of such strange beauty."[8] These intense, searching encounters indicate the premium Eliade gave to undisguised engagements with the "other." It is this sensitivity to undisguised encounters, coupled with later adolescent insecurities, that drove Eliade to explore and capture in words as starkly honest as possible, in his two autobiographical journal-novels *Romanul adolescentului miop* (The Novel of the Nearsighted Adolescent, partly published in Romania between 1926 and 1927) and its sequel *Gaudeamus* (1927–28), the moods, motivations, and behaviors in his own life and in the lives of his friends and acquaintances.[9] Eliade suffered to express the authentic self, the authentic person behind the masks, contexts, and terminologies that define the persona. This ravenous need for authenticity helps explain Eliade's "sacred persistence" in delving into the mentality of pristine cultures. Eliade sought the irreducibly human.

A second source of Eliade's view of authenticity came through his Romanian mentor, Nae Ionescu (1890–1940). Ionescu was a university lecturer, logician, metaphysician, and, for several years, editor of the newspaper *Cuvântul*. Ionescu's philosophical term *trăire*,[10] "lived experience," became the codeword for the intellectuals of the "young generation," whose movement, consequently, became known as *Trăirism*.[11] *Trăire* is an existential concept that means to live life directly, spontaneously, and to arrive at one's personal philosophy through concrete experience. One is not to come to one's philosophy by consulting philosophical tomes, especially those coming from the rationalism of the Enlightenment and Western European currents of thought.[12] Along with its existential expression, *trăire* also means living life on the proper planes of reality. According to Ionescu, the three planes of reality are 1) the scientific (which stresses induction and reason and is of the hard sciences, and of politics and economics), 2) the metaphysical (of "essences," logic, and ethics, and includes the aesthetic realms of art and literature; this plane is absolute only for the individual), and 3) the religious (of revealed truth, and is absolute for all. This plane includes faith, and, along with the metaphysical plane, sees love as an instrument of knowledge). These planes act independently, with methods of their own, and are mutually irreducible. Living authentically, in "lived experience," means, based on these planes of reality, that religious meaning, behavior, and encounters with the Absolute can only occur on the religious plane. And for Ionescu, to be religious meant for the Romanian to act and believe in obedience to the tradition of the Romanian Orthodox Church, the truly indigenous church of Romania. Protestantism, he felt, being primarily a religion of ethics, and Catholicism, one of power and of the material, were repudiated since they were, first of all, nonindigenous to Romania and, second, in error for confusing the ethical and the material planes with the religious.[13]

Consciously in some cases and unconciously in others Eliade appropriated in part the thought of Ionescu. Ionescu's thoughts on the planes and structures of reality and on "lived experience" were picked up by Eliade. Eliade differed strongly, however, with Ionescu's views of Orthodoxy, and he qualified Ionescu's view on the separation of the planes of reality. Eliade did not believe that by necessity one had to go through the Orthodox church to reach the absolute. Through "adventure," experiments, and concrete experiences, a person could attain the absolute at various points, but only completely by "grace" and at death.[14] Instead of following the singular ways of the Church or renouncing culture (which makes use of the scientific and metaphysical planes), one could encounter the real, the absolute, at isolated moments in one's cultural vocation. In this way authenticity occurs as an ongoing experiential engagement with life through culture en route towards one's alloted destiny. Eliade chose this philosophy of engagement through culture when he decided against staying at a Himalayan ashram and living the life of a "saint."[15]

A third source of influence on Eliade's view of authenticity came through the Romanian existentialist literary genre by the same name.[16] The autobiographical novel or journal-novel, in which personal experiences were directly transcribed into the narrative, characterized this genre's medium as the way to achieve authenticity. Eliade's adolescent writings, his first best-seller *Maitreyi* (1933), and *Şantier* (a "work in progress," 1935), exemplified this life-to-fiction genre. The author's aim in this genre was to be completely realistic and to depict as authentically as possible the way things were experienced and perceived by the author. In its attempt to be authentic and nonimitative, this genre was characterized by its rebellion against established European, especially French, genres and the Romantic melancholy many Romanian writers had for previous periods in Romania's history. In Eliade we find a similar kind of personal rebellion. His 1927 "Against Moldavia," a tirade against a territory and a mindset from his own background, his high regard for the Italian novelist Papini, an individualist and reactionary in his own right, and his brusque and brutal *Huliganii* (1935), all evince a desire to arrive at personal autonomy through rebellion.[17] As a literary genre, authenticity has a rich appreciation for the concreteness of ordinary life and for the relentless exploration of the imagination which, in exploring the parameters to ordinary life, entertains a fine line between fact and fiction. Moreover, in its attempt to develop itself as a Romanian genre, authenticity, along with *Trăirism* had a nationalistic edge.

A fourth influence on Eliade's view of authenticity came through his Indian studies of the *Bhagavad Gita, bhakti,* Mahayana Buddhism, and especially of yoga and tantrism.[18] In these Eliade saw a side of Indian religion that affirmed history instead of denying it. A person could reach the absolute through the renunciation of her or his actions and through disciplined, ascetic techniques. A person did not have to abandon the world, become a *sannyasin,* a "renouncer." "Set thy heart upon they work, but never on its reward (2:47)," says the *Bhagavad Gita*. "Both renunciation and holy work are a path to the Supreme; but better than surrender of work is the yoga of holy work (5:2)," it continues. Eliade's 1931 doctoral thesis on yoga included an initial, but still unelaborated, morphological canvassing of India's "in-history" spirituality as found in tantrism.[19] Authenticity as the overcoming of history while in history is strongly brought out in Eliade's 1932 *Soliloquii* and 1934 *Oceanografie*.

The New Humanism as Concrete Experience

I stop before this monumental Jesus, beardless and as luminous as an archangel, and I feel that a memory coming from very far away is trying to reach me as I am today. I wait, fascinated by this fragment of my forgotten life, a fragment which is trying so hard to come to recognition. And suddenly, I have it. It was in the spring of 1926. We had arrived late the night before, and, as it ought to be, our first visit in the morning had been to San Marco. I had left the others clustered around the guide, their heads tilted back, listening to his explanations of the scenes from the Old Testament, and I had gone into the basilica. I was convinced that I should *go see for myself* [emphasis added], without the guide's comments, that it was the only way for me to be able to discover. Discover what? I didn't know, I didn't even wonder. I only had a feeling that something would be "revealed" to me.

And it was at that very instant that I was greeted by that Christ in mosaic, a Christ that I couldn't even recognize as such for an instant, it resembled an archangel so much. *Christos Angelos.* One of the first mysteries that I couldn't be aware of, much less understand, at that time. I had an idea, nevertheless, that in the beardless youth an incomparable beauty of the Christ was hidden also the mystery of the androgyne. Suddenly I find myself again as I was in 1926.[20]

Eliade wrote this journal entry during a tour of Venice in 1957. In seeing for himself in an anamnestic reflection, Eliade discovered the mystery of the Christ symbol. The personal encounter brought him a new awareness that he might not otherwise have had had he stayed and passively accepted another's (the guide's) interpretation. The concrete encounter, in short, acted as a hermeneutical device.

This example is another indication of Eliade's distaste for imitation, pastiche, kitsch. He always wanted to get at the original source of inspiration. Though never a field anthropologist like a Malinowski, Eliade did go to India, the source for his Romanian interests in Orientalism. In India he lived for a week in the community of Santals (a non-Aryan tribal people), he retreated to an ashram, took up yoga, and became proficient in Sanskrit, all serving not just to understand the Oriental mind but to search for the absolute as well.

One can say that for Eliade what remains in abstraction, in its idealized forms alone, does not exist. That is, the idea alone has no significance for actual existence unless it *is* actualized, much in the same way the sacred is made to manifest itself in profane forms. Only when the sacred is actualized in concrete experience—as when rituals imitate archetypal, mythic models—can the sacred be said to be real.[21] The primitive did not consider him or herself "real" until he or she imitated the mythic archetypes. The concrete experience of ritual actualizes the power of the real into daily life and invests it with meaning and efficacy. Sacrality and meaning, consequently, are not confined to the performance of isolated rituals. All activities of life can have the power and import of ritual. In other words, the sacred is both passively and actively infused into ordinary life, such as through specialized celebratory rituals and through activities taking on the quality of ritual, or in contemplation in action, as in Buddhist mindfulness, for instance. To be authentic is both a state of being and a form of activity. One is both detached from, and engaged in, concrete experiences. The authentic life is a combination of moving with the rhythms of the cosmos—similar to primal and Taoist philosophies—and of engaging with life in human activity—as in implementing a Christian ethic.

Eliade developed his thoughts on the incarnation of the real in temporal activity when in Romania in the late 1930s. At the time he struggled with how to reconcile the life of experience (*trăire*) and culture with that of contemplation and retreat from the world. The problem was not so much on how the absolute can be encountered in the world, for Eliade's notion of the sacred identifying itself in the profane resolves that. The problem was in how to prevent the encounter with the absolute in concrete existence from sinking into positivism and empiricism. In other words, what is to keep the sacred from disappearing into the secular, the profane? The emphasis, for Eliade, had to fall upon the *dialectic* in the coexistence of the concrete with the transcendent. The profane was always more than what it appeared. The life of culture, of concrete experiences, never fails to remain as a symbol of greater universes of meaning.[22] Even in the immanental Confucian cosmology there is always the presence of a distinguishing spiritual dimension (as cosmos and heaven) to the material life.

If authentic existence articulates the real in concrete experiences, inauthentic existence is the *failure* to realize the real in concrete experience. Failing to articulate one's dreams, imaginations, and perceptions of the self into deeds, however ridiculous the deeds may be, is to fail to bring oneself into existence. It is to deny being and one's inner spirit the right to *be*. So Eliade praised the literary figure Don Quixote who, despite his lunacy, lived out the color of his imagination into concrete acts. Contrarily, in Eliade's short story, "With the Gypsy Girls," Gavrilescu is inauthentic since he failed to live by his dream to be an artist, remaining instead a failed piano teacher.[23] Authentic existence, in short, is being true to one's archetypes, to the models one holds for oneself.

Authentic existence comes at a price, though. One must be responsible as one brings one's dreams and imagination into concrete life. Not to live in accordance to one's nature nor to accept the consequences of one's behavior is to deny the fact and significance of one's presence in history. Thus, it is to be inauthentic, to be not concretely in history. We find a fictional example in Eliade's *Mademoiselle Christina* (Romanian publication, 1936). In this novel the protagonist Christina returns from the land of the dead to the real world as a *strigoi*, a ghost who embodies itself in human or animal form. In this case she returns in the human form of Christina's niece, Simina. By returning to the world of the living and corrupting the world around her Christina violates her immaterial nature in coming as a *strigoi*. It is not so much the return to the living that constitutes her as inauthentic as it is, as Eliade says, her "lingering, contrary to Nature, in a paradoxical condition (a 'spiritual' being behaving like a living body)."[24] This "lingering" of the spirit in the human realm *for too long,* being "contrary to nature," violated the separation of planes—the spiritual from the material. Although a hierophany, a manifestation of the sacred, constitutes a breach of the two planes as well, breaching the material and spiritual, the breach is only momentary. The dialectic is always preserved. In the case of Christina, like in positivism and empiricism, the dialectic collapses.

To refer to a nonfictional example, Eliade became disillusioned with the Legionary Movement when he saw it fall from its mystical, spiritual ideals into those of oppressive and brutal politics, as when members of the Legionary murdered the great Romanian historian Nicolae Iorga.[25] As an initially spiritual movement it came to linger in the realm of the political, the historistic.[26] By surrendering its true nature, the Legionary Movement became an inauthentic rebellion unwilling to accept the responsibilities and the consequences of its ambitions.[27] In his novel *Huliganii,* of brutally idealistic youths overturning history to begin anew, Eliade, who seemed to tacitly condone such revisionist behavior, depicts only certain youth, notably Petru, as willing to assume full responsibility for their actions.[28] In *Huliganii,* at least, it seems authentic living is unavoidably the domain of the individual; groups are more susceptible to compromise.

This failure to take responsible action in accord with one's true nature parallels Heidegger's concept of "authenticity." For Heidegger, "authenticity" (*Eigentlich*) is to obey the "call" of one's "conscience" as a mortal being (as "being unto death") and accept the ethical responsibility of that "call."[29] Inauthenticity (*Uneingentlich*), by implication, is being "delusive, self-destructive, or evasive of the truth of oneself," avoiding the responsibility of one's true nature.[30] Whereas Eliade, in his notion of authenticity, acknowledges an outside realm of reference in a dialectical, paradoxical relation to the individual, Heidegger does not.[31] For Heidegger no outside "caller" or "power" impinges upon a person's "resoluteness" (*entschlossen*) toward authentic action.[32] "Authenticity" comes simply, yet with difficulty, as one reacts against, and identifies oneself apart from, the "They" (*Das Man*), from all material, sensual, and human distractions. Once done, one faces squarely one's aloneness before death, nonbeing. Like Heidegger, Eliade locates one's most authentic condition at the time of death, though, for Eliade, death does not have the pessimistic finality that it does for Heidegger.

In line with Heidegger's denial of an outside referential realm to the person as "being unto death," his existential individualism lacks the contextual reference of the whole that is found in Eliade. It was Heidegger's philosophical failure, says Richard Schmitt, "to provide the vocabulary in which to express the distinction between individuals and their lives and the community to which they belong."[33] A repercussion of this failure was Heidegger's avowed support as rector of Freiburg University for the National Socialist Party.[34] Heidegger associated the authentic "individual" with the state itself as a collective "individual." Eliade's continual dialectic between the part and the whole qualifies in part the individualistic self-regard of Heidegger. The collectivity in Eliade is never simply the summation of all individuals, as it was for Nae Ionescu. The cosmic Whole transcends the sum of the parts. So the state cannot be an end in itself.

During the middle to late 1930s, Eliade was, however, highly nationalistic. His nationalism was xenophobic and messianic in its ambitions. He argued for a Romanian messianism inspired by the creative vitality of such exemplary figures as Eminescu (1850–1889) and Hasedu (1838–1907) of the nineteenth century Romanian Renaissance and the later Nicolae Iorga and Nae Ionescu. These possessed a strong love of country. Their nationalism and poltical involvement were of a spiritual kind. They sought to shape culture and the values of the masses toward spiritual values fed by the deepest roots of the distinctly Romanian genius. In their zeal for taping and preserving the pure Romanian roots, these nationalists became decidedly anti-Semitic. Eliade knew of this but downplayed it to emphasize instead the "creative genius and prophetic vision" in which these figures excelled.[35] As a nationalist himself in this prestigious line, Eliade did not steep to anti-Semitism, however. His xenophobia was pronounced, and he ridiculed Hungarian and Bulgarian minorities and resented at the time the profusion of non-Romanians in the governing bodies of provincial cities. But he did not seek to forcibly oppress minorities, and he rejected anti-Semitic postures.[36] Eliade can be seen providing theoretical ammunition for right-wing groups, but he himself saw no gain in "intransigence and intolerance," and his intellectual studies preclude homogeneity and nationalistic provincialism. Eliade respected the intellectual vitality that comes with diversity and maintained a receptivity to foreign currents of thought. His own scholarly studies into Indian philosophy and alchemy were criticized for seeming to be counter to Romanianism.

Contrary to the exaltation of the state over the individual as one finds in fascism, Eliade's nationalism never did diminish the right and freedom of the individual to create. Even Eliade's views on the "new man," an ideal adopted by the Legionary, demonstrated an individual autonomous from society, one who "signifies above all a complete break with the hypocrisy and cowardice of the society in which we live. A young man, tied down to nothing, without fear and without stain . . . ," as he stated in a 1934 article.[37] And although fascism is characterized by its own form of mysticism and spirituality, Eliade's own mystical and spiritual ideals for Romania did not reject intellectualism nor blackball many of the intellectuals of the day, as Romanian fascism did.[38] Nor did Eliade see religion as the means for political ends. For Eliade, the primacy of the spiritual *always* ruled over the political, a position not finally held to by the Legionary. In short, whether in his attitude toward minorities, in all its ambivalences, or in his position on the individual and on religion in service to the nation, Eliade maintained the referential paradigm of the whole as that which both validates the individual and the state and adjudges them. It would be in exile (1945 onward) that we find Eliade's nationalism giving way to a greater universalism (though he forever remained devoted to his native Romania), the kind that would exemplify his mature new humanism.

It is in light of the political turbulence in which Eliade grew up in Romania and of his own life-long personal struggles that we can draw an aspect of Eliade's life and work that has been ignored, the existential and physical fact of suffering, paralleling Heidegger's view of authenticity as "being unto death" in which the individual confronts her or his aloneness in the face of ultimate finality. In an 1932 article Eliade wrote:

> To live in [concrete] reality is our first duty. And never do we verify reality more decisively than in our suffering and in the happiness we bring to others. . . . If we propose to live a real life, we must renounce every act . . . which is oriented toward our *own* happiness. . . . If it is given to us to know true happiness someday, we will meet it, unexpectedly and unsought, from another. It will be bestowed, not won.[39]

And he adds, "We do not do this because it is *good;* we do it because we cannot do otherwise, because this is *reality;* we live *concretely* in this way . . ."[40]

The element of "suffering," whether it be at the existential level, as in the separation from being, or at the physical (and equally existential) level of actually living under the political forces of the "terror of history," is a significant impulse to the construction of symbolic and mythic discourse. The primordial rupture between being and nonbeing constitutes the existential angst in the mythologic. We find such a rupture in Hinduism's separation of *purusha* (the self) from *prakriti* (the physical and sensual world), in Buddhism's belief in *dukkha* ("suffering"; the unsatisfactoriness of existence), in the disharmony with the Tao in Chinese thought, and in Christianity's notion of sin. Primal cultures, as the anthropologist Clifford Geertz points out, must also deal with the problem of suffering as they "formulate conceptions of a general order of existence."[41] In short, to postulate the ubiquity of existential suffering in its broad sense as some form of rupture, amplifies Eliade's symbolic theory to include and address a universal condition.

Suffering in Eliade's own life included years in Romania spent under the uncertainty and oppressiveness of political authoritarianism. In 1938 he became himself one of its detainees,[42] and his works would be censored. From 1945 he would undergo the emotional and professional traumas of having to live in exile, never once to return. Other personal sufferings were the loss of his first wife, Nina Mares, to cancer and, for most of his later years in Chicago, his debilitating struggles with acute arthritis, cataracts, and ulcers. His last published journal is a testament to the physical ordeals he constantly combated in his obsession to write, whose incessancy, for him, meant the continuance of life itself.[43] Through each of these ordeals never was the formation of Eliade's thought detached from concrete experiences. Mythopoesis, the construction of myth, arises under the weight and randomness of history, what Eliade calls the "terror of history."[44] Eliade's journals and autobiography were exercises in his "creative hermeneutics" as a way to understand the internal meaning of his life. From studying other cultures Eliade knew mythopoesis was a structure of the human imagination, and so it would naturally come into play to interpret his own retrogressive look over his life. The point in attending to Eliade's own mythopoesis is not to subjectivize theory to autobiography or to label Eliade's scholarship as myth, for his scholarship made no pretense at setting up paradigmatic truth claims. Rather it is to show how theory cannot be divorced from the universal condition of suffering, an unavoidable and yet potentially fertile soil for acute insight. Ivan Strenski, therefore, is right to attend to the "external" influences on a scholar's life in the formation of a scholar's theory. It is naive and unrealistic of him, however, to think that theory will cease and scholarship be purified of grand theorists once "catastrophic times" are past. Says he:

> One hopes the history of the first half of the twentieth century, with all its displacement and shattering of lives, will not be repeated. Yet, perhaps because we may live in less catastrophic times, we may not see such theorists again [Cassirer, Malinowski, Lévi-Strauss, Eliade]. If the social stability of the industrialised West translates into stability within the professional academic realm, then we may expect the professions to be able to maintain boundaries and even (with the help of demographics) to reinforce them. Such stability would militate against the appearance of theorists such as ours, who at crucial points in their lives found themselves unable—doubtless against their wills—to act as professionals.[45]

I am not advocating a need for grand theorists, with theory development being a thorny issue in the history of religions.[46] I am only drawing a connection, however proportional, between creative and theoretical thought and the perennial condition of suffering; reflection cannot occur apart from the human condition and the ubiquitous threat of chaos. It is not coincidential, then, that Cassirer, Malinowski, Lévi-Strauss, and Eliade became so popular during tempestuous times. To follow Strenski's argument is to divorce creative thought from one of its principal founts of stimulation and creativity. What

Strenski hopes for would only sterilize the academic profession, not to mention general culture.

The suffering Eliade knew and the suffering which spawns myth allows Eliade's works to address not only intellectuals and those in the position to shape culture, it also gives voice to those who, silenced by historicism and Western colonialism, have had little or no voice in shaping the direction of world culture: the archaic and the Oriental peoples. Much of this is changing, naturally, in a world of geopolitics, economic interdependence, and cultural interrelatedness. But through Eliade's "creative hermeneutics," as in the works of the Jewish author and philosopher Elie Wiesel, the "dead," the silent and suffocated voices of history, are allowed to speak *as they would speak if they could.* An early indication of this practice in shown in Eliade's adolescent novel *Gaudeamus* in which he gives voice to a character, Dinu, based on an actual friend of Eliade's by the same name. His friend Dinu later accuses Eliade of putting words into his mouth. Eliade responds in defense, "you didn't say the words, but only you *could* have said them. By keeping the name Dinu I had precisely *you* in my mind, as you really are. I let you speak as you wanted to."[47] Despite his attempt to articulate the authentic voice of others, Eliade recognizes his own limits as an intepreter and voice. The complete character of those he depicts cannot be fully depicted, since humans can only know partially.[48]

In giving voice to the "others," the silent, distant, or oppressed voices, Eliade demonstrates that if we are to approach authenticity as human beings, then these voices from throughout history and culture must also be heard. For they constitute reality as well and must be acknowledged if the modern person is to know the *total* human condition. The historian of religions Charles Long undertakes a similiar hermeneutics when he argues for giving voice to blacks, Native Americans, women, and others who have suffered under the oppressiveness of history.[49] It is in the element of suffering—in this case, the suffering of being denied a voice—that we find in Eliade's "creative hermeneutics" an ability to transcend any "certain worldview."[50] At the level of "suffering," authenticity becomes a universalizing hermeneutics.

Another point can be made here. As a concrete experience *par excellence,* suffering is fundamental to initiation, to the ongoing transformation of human beings. In a sense, even to achieve authenticity suffering must be willed, for suffering precedes any transition to greater states of consciousness, even for the Buddhist who postulates the inherent, unavoidable condition of suffering.[51] As long as the suffering can fit within a sacred history, a myth, it is less likely to succumb to the "terror of history," to meaninglessness. When a myth or a mythology, however, is found inadequate in giving meaning to the suffering, can we speak of the humanistic and universal scope of Eliade's "creative hermeneutics"—of giving meaning "even when it is not there"—as a type of theodicy, or to put it in the Eliadean context, as a type of "hierodicy," the justifying of meaning in the face of meaninglessness. In fact, one could say Eliade's whole system is a "hierodicy of suffering," a restoration of the multiform "sacred" to a painfully meaningless existence. Yet in spite of a "creative hermeneutics," it is questionable whether one can always create enough meaning to satisfy many a troubled spirit or critical mind.[52]

The New Humanism at the Juncture of Being and Becoming

For some of us, "authenticity" meant revolt, at all costs, against our parents, against the "old ones," bourgeois society, and contemporary values.[53] —Eliade

But because Dasein is *lost* in the "they," it must first *find* itself. In order to find *itself* at all, it must be "shown" to itself in its possible authenticity. In terms of its *possibility,* Dasein *is* already a potentiality-for-Being-its-Self, but it needs to have this potentiality attested.[54] — Heidegger

Authenticity comes through the breakage of static forms. Social convention, traditional patterns, internal complexes, or recurring *vasanas* can obstruct human freedom and smother a creative imagination. The constant breakage of all forms and of all models characterizes the modern consciousness in which humans are thought to *make* themselves. In this regard Eliade is a "modernist." He spent his life resisting and overturning sterilizing, superficial, and false structures in order to discover what is ultimately real, which for him meant the primordial, spontaneous, creative impulse of the cosmos. Although Eliade values being—permanency—over becoming—ceaseless change—and stresses repetition over innovation, there is no lack of dynamism to his system. The creative, transformative hermeneutics of the new humanism is continously encountering and conversing with "other" worlds of meaning. Eliade himself remained passionately curious of, and receptive to, orientations different from his own. And the breakthrough of meaning for Eliade never ceased to reveal richer interpretations of religious symbols.[55]

Eliade's view of the breakage of static forms differs from that of modernity's, whose rebelliousness and flux disallow any fixed condition, in that it seeks "a place upon which to stand," a "center." The mentality of the modern is to reside upon no place and prioritize no time as better than any other. There is only relative space and endless becoming. Heidegger, as a modern philosopher, attempted to root the rootless modern mentality in authentic "being unto death." Humans find being in the finite moment as it is informed by the imminence of death. But this existential state only exists from one moment to the next; it is not given a wholistic context within a larger cosmic scheme of meaning. In spite of the finality of Heidegger's existential moment (there being no eternal time for Heidegger), Eliade saw a *coincidentia oppositorium* (a coexistence of opposites) in Heidegger where at death even nonbeing is taken into being.[56] The point for Eliade is that even in nonbeing (what is becoming and inauthentic) there is the presence of being, of authenticity. In the breakage of forms there is the possibility of achieving a ''center.'' That is, *as* a person resists limits by challenging and breaking all limits the person confronts the real, that which ultimately and finally *is* beyond (and within) all human constructs. Heidegger's ''being unto death'' is itself a resistance against the inevitable limit of death; as one authentically lives the moment death's finality is declawed.

The state of approximating being-in-becoming is similar to the Australian Arunta aborigines who carried a sacred pole, their ''cosmic axis,'' their ''center,'' with them wherever they went. As long as they were at the center they were attached to that which was most real.[57] Being-in-becoming is also similar to the negative theology of the mystic Dionysius which held that we know and are known as we cease to know. God is more than, and is beyond, any theological language. Moreover, one can find this being-in-becoming in those philosophies that put change and becoming at the very nature of all sentient and nonsentient existence. The process philosophies of Alfred North Whitehead and Charles Hartshorne, the Buddhist philosophy of impermanence, and the Chinese philosophy of the Tao, all make room for the empty, full spaces within the macro and micro processes of change wherein authentic existence can be found.[58] This combination of finding the permanent (being) in the transitory (in becoming, in nonbeing), returns us to the dialectic of discovering the absolute within culture and history. To phrase this dialectic in another way, Eliade speaks of combining the ''mystical'' life with the ''magical.''

The ''mystical–magical'' dichotomy is the surface expression of the ''nature'' versus ''human freedom'' dichotomy. The ''mystical'' side is tied to the cosmic rhythms, whose regenerative, circular movements from life to death to life ultimately balance out the effects of human intervention in nature. The ''magical'' side is that of human freedom ostensibly acting autonomously from nature. Taken together in their dialectical relationship, cosmic movements assist and equilibrate human action. So however iconoclastic humans are against social, political, cultural, or religious structures, chaos will not be the final condition, since for Eliade the cosmos fundamentally moves toward order. At some point the individual and the social aggregate will achieve authenticity by ''destiny,'' by some cosmic pattern. Eliade did not fear the Romanian ''young generation's'' rebelliousness, for he knew it would eventually come to its ''synthesis,'' its unifying order. In the same way, he felt that to choose the life of "adventure," of culture, over the "absolute," of world renunciation, a person would equally come at death to the absolute, as would a person who had renounced the life of culture. On the macro scale, Eliade believed in the ultimate survivability of the human race, despite all odds and indications to the contrary. We gain a literary premonition of this in his novella *Youth Without Youth,* in which one of the characters actually speaks of the human race continuing after a nuclear holocaust.[59]

This dialectic between human will and nature's "will," here refering to cosmic movements, underlies many of today's methodological dichotomies: the dichotomy between empirical science and poetic intuition, between specialized technique and artistic freedom, between history and phenomenology, between achieving objectivity and in seeking intentionality, between nurture versus nature, etc. Whether it involves personal or global crises or methodological debates, Eliade trusted in the ultimate centering force of the cosmos to bring humankind to its new humanity.

In light of cosmic time, and returning to Heidegger, it is in their perceptions of time that we find no clearer difference between Heidegger and Eliade. For Heidegger "time" is finite. From the time a person is born to his or her death the possibilities for action are limited. A person faces the future with dissolution and the past with "guilt" with each passing moment not lived authentically.[60] For Eliade, contrarily, time is expansive, eternal. Mythical time precedes and impels a person's existence. It provides resources of symbolic meaning which nonregenerative history has difficulty providing. In Eliade's novel *The Forbidden Forest,* Ciru Parternie, the double (*Doppelgänger*) of the protagonist Stefan Viziru and who represents the "historical" Stefan, suffers a senseless and tragic death due to a mistaken identity. It was Stefan whom an assassin meant to kill. Parternie's being killed instead of Stefan symbolizes how life on the plane of history alone is a finite and senselessly tragic existence. And Stefan, who manages miraculously to survive repeated threats to his life, symbolizes the eternal mythical in which authenticity is "being unto death" *and* being unto life. For in death authenticity achieves its completion. In life authenticity is best incarnated in "love" (as *philo,* agape, and eros), prompting some to tie the two together as love sanctified by death. Authenticity, therefore, occurs in historical existence at the juncture of death and life, of historical and mythical time, of becoming and being. In sum, authenticity is being-in-becoming in and through concrete experiences. It continuously penetrates static forms—of cultural complexes, religions, methodologies, etc.—to illuminate their internal, creative, cosmic impulses. And in the paradoxical state of authenticity, one becomes an authentic human being.

Humans as Free

In his influential and incisive *Map Is Not Territory,* Jonathan Z. Smith refers to a presupposition in Eliade's understanding of sacred space and time. For Eliade, ontology prescribes sacred space. It is upon an ontology that the primitive as *homo religiosus* repeats the archetypal models. In being dependent upon an a priori ontology, the human as *homo religiosus* differs from the autonomously free *homo faber* in the post-Kantian view of human nature. Says Smith:

> Since Kant it has been commonplace to define man as a world creating being and human culture or society as a process of world construction. Taking their clue from the third *Kritik,* philosophers and social scientists have sought to elucidate the mechanisms of human creativity and to explore the limits of human possibility and freedom. Complex theories have been proposed—all starting from a fundamentally anthropological base ("man makes himself"). Eliade [however] . . . implies a fundamental reversal. World creation and world founding are not anthropological categories expressive of human freedom. Rather, they are to be understood as ontological (perhaps even theological) categories. Man's fundamental mode is not freedom and creativity but rather repetition. Or, perhaps more accurately, man's creativity is repetition.[61]

Smith is most troubled with Eliade's notion that modern historical consciousness constitutes a "second fall."[62] When Smith defines the post-Kantian anthropology, "man makes himself," as more "free" than Eliade's pre-Kantian concept of the human as fundamentally *homo religiosus,* Smith goes straight for Eliade's jugular. According to Smith, *homo religiosus'* founding of space is less an act of human choice and free will than it is a repetitious, subserving, automatic obedience to what the real, the mythical gods, have already instituted. The anthropology of *homo religiosus* becomes nothing but a conditioned ontology. In every creative act humans simply imitate the gods by repeating what the gods did at "the beginning." Humans do not freely and willfully make themselves, freely organize the relativity of space and time, but merely absolutize space and time by ascribing to them an ontological status.

If this is what Eliade's suppositions imply, then his new humanism has lost its freely creative impulse. Personality and individuality would be abolished and moral and ethical responsibility skirted. Instead of encouraging creativity, the new humanism would restrict it or at least predetermine it.

Although the new humanism makes use of universal archetypes, it would be erroneous to say the new humanism restricts creativity. Nor is it a logical deduction from the postulate of *homo religiosus* to say creativity would be predefined, that is, that the freedom to create is limited. Smith, I contend, has a limited view of freedom and is inconsistent in his argument. It is in response to Smith that I will show how freedom in Eliade's new humanism allows for unlimited and meaningful creativity. Eliade does not limit freedom, he expands it.

Homo Faber *and* Homo Religiosus

Smith's misgiving concerning *homo religiosus* rests on the Kantian notion that humans stand over against nature as subjects to object. As rational beings, humans define and structure nature according to the constructs of "space" and "time." Nature becomes what humans make it to be. Kant believed that humans can only know the world of sense experience, the "phenomenon" (that which is manifested). The essence of things, the "thing in itself," the *numenon,* is unknowable by the rational mind. The only way the *numenon* can be apprehended is by practical reason, that is, by moral choice and behavior. In choosing in our freedom to act morally we articulate our essential human capacity to be moral, rational beings. And as we make and act upon right moral choices, we approach perfection; and we have all of eternity to reach the goal. It is only in moral action, in practical knowledge, that humans can presently and partially approach God, the *numenon;* in eternity humans shall know God fully.[63]

When it is stated, therefore, that "man makes himself," this says we can know the essence of things, of who we are as human beings, only by what we produce, create. Our creative acts are an expression of our free will. We are most free and most human when we create, for it is in this activity that we control nature and approach, through successive moral actions, the *numenon.* Anthropology, therefore, is founded upon deeds, freely chosen and nonconditioned. Kant is so persuaded of the mind's ability to make moral choices in full confidence of its unconditional freedom, that he says a person at any moment is capable of choosing the good over the bad as if she or he were making the choice for the first time. Says he:

> For whatever his previous deportment may have been, whatever natural causes may have been influencing him, and whether these causes were to be found within him or outside him, his action is yet free and determined by none of these causes; hence it can and must always be judged as an *original* use of his will. He should have refrained from that action, whatever his temporal circumstances and entanglements; for through no cause in the world can he cease to be a freely acting being.[64]

This radical and naive (Kant did not have the advantage of Freudian depth psychology) understanding of the nonconditionability of the will vis-à-vis free action, places the onus of human freedom on the ability of humans to *act* morally. The proof of the pudding is in the deeds, in the choice of one act over that of another. So if we grant to *homo faber* the integrity of the deed as that which constitutes human freedom, then Smith, to be consistent, must grant the same to *homo religiosus*. The way Smith frames his argument, it is *homo faber*'s autonomy over nature as demonstrated in the person's acts which designates the existence of freedom. But the creative acts of *homines religiosi* are less free because they repeat an ontology. That is, Smith validates the freedom of *homo faber* in theory *and* practice but judges *homo religiosus only* on the plane of theory. The way to validate freedom and free will, however, is on the plane of everyday action. As the philosopher Charles Hartshorne says, "Determinism is not a doctrine anyone lives by."[65] On the plane of empirical behavior *homo religiosus* is as free as *homo faber*.

Although primitive behavior founds space and time and creates through repetition, the individual's actions, that which she or he does, is still based upon a choice to found space or not, to repeat the archetypes or not, to choose the sacred or the profane. What the primitives create is an expression of freedom, since in their relation to nature they can choose to make some space and some time sacred and leave other space and other periods of time profane. The element of *choice* is in the very nature of hierophanies.[66] Even though primitives act symbolically within a worldview inhabited by the divine and informed by a higher order, thus making choices in view of that higher order and therefore allowing for no purely purposive or pragmatic choices, they nevertheless make choices.[67] The fact that among the primitives there is the confession of sin is an indication of choice; their remorse and confession is for an act wrongly chosen.[68] So if we stick with Kantian arguments, the freedom of the individual[69] is evidenced in his or her ability to choose one form of behavior over another, to separate the value of one deed from that of another. What I am emphasizing is that both the primitive and the modern act freely on the level of deeds, whether in repetitive or singular action. Through their deeds each approaches the *numenon*. In the case of the primitive the *numenon* is "known" immediately in the repetition of the divine archetypes. For Kant, contrarily, it purportedly occurs in eternity. In the end, I center Smith's argument upon "deeds" and not theory. It is at the level of deeds, as a matter of fact, that Eliade ultimately establishes freedom anyway. That is, it is through authentic concrete experiences (deeds) that a person comes to "know" the deeds of the sacred and therein discover the true nature of reality. Goethe in his theory of colors used the same argument to counter Isaac Newton's theoretical study of light. Goethe said that to know light you do not study it merely in theory, as refractions through a prism, but by stepping outside and seeing the deeds of light in all its color. So even if we were to stay with Kant's argument, Smith is misleading in ascribing freedom to *homo faber* and insinuating its absence in *homo religiosus*.

I would be amiss, however, to keep Eliade within the Kantian sphere. After all, Goethe is the antipode to Kant. Goethe knew aesthetics, plurality, novelty, development, and, according to the philosopher Walter Kaufmann, the moral sphere better than Kant. Goethe enriched humanness and the human mind rather than having sterilized and constricted it as Kant did.[70] To speak of freedom in Eliade, who operated from a Goethian paradigm rather than a Kantian, we find that freedom includes not just our Western perceptions of the term but archaic and Eastern ones as well. As I speak of freedom in the new humanism, then, I note the manifold usage of the term in Eliade. For as Eliade said in the last line of his *Yoga: Immortality and Freedom,* "Everything depends upon what is meant by freedom."[71] In order to make the term "freedom" workable for our purposes, however, we might say that freedom in the new humanism is the ability to create in likeness with the unpredictable potentiality of the real, the sacred. And insofar as the Real manifests itself in and through human deeds, human creativity becomes significant and meaningful.

The Free Potentiality of the Real

Eliade does not define the real, the sacred. It is simply taken as a given with no univocal expression. What is important for our purposes is its freedom of expression. As manifestations of the sacred, hierophanies can take any form whatsoever. From a stone, to an idea, to a word, (such as the Hindu OM), to a person, the sacred is unfettered in the way it expresses itself. As *deus otiosus* it can even choose *not* to engage itself, choosing instead to remain withdrawn and idle. The free unpredictability of a hierophany's "irruption" into concrete existence confirms its dynamic quality. As was shown above, at the level of concrete existence the deeds more than the ontological fact attest to freedom. The nature of being in Eliade might be absolute, universal, and found order and stability, but in its deeds it is dynamically diverse as it expresses itself among cultures and adapts itself to a variety of interpretations. The sacred is as pluralistic as our imagination allows it to be. In Eliade's fantastic literature, we find how unpredictable and unsettling the activity of the real can be. Eliade's definition of religion and of the sacred are necessarily ambiguous and versatile because the sacred and human religious experience are themselves ambiguous and versatile in expression. The virtue of a morphology is its ability to integrate the multivocality of the sacred into symbolic patterns while remaining fluid enough to contextualize the sacred's radical diversity throughout human existence. In sum, Eliade perceives the sacred as acting fully free.

But as for human freedom, humans can only be as free as the ground (*Grund*) of its ontology allows it to be. That is, humans are only as free to exercise their will as nature, society, the divine, the psyche—or whatever is said to define the person—allows it to be. Historians and social scientists acknowledge that history and society determine human activity only so much if humans are to have any freedom at all. Acknowledging the existence of chaos in nature, physicists concede an internal freedom in nature; nature exercises only so much control over itself. In regards to Eliade's ontology, therefore, we can ask, "*does* the sacred limit itself in order that there may be such a thing as human freedom in the first place?" And by logical necessity, "*is* the sacred free enough to limit itself?" To both questions we can say Eliade would answer "yes." Hierophanies, as manifestations of the sacred, are the self-limitation of the sacred within concrete existence. As I showed in chapter 3, Eliade attests to degrees in the self-limitation of the sacred: Jesus Christ is a greater limitation of the sacred in history than is a stone. Subsequently, the primitive has as much freedom as the "later" Christian does. In addition, the "unrecognizability of miracle" in Eliade's literature demonstrates how, for Eliade, the sacred can so limit itself as to become almost synonymous with the profane. So as Eliade understands it, the sacred can and does limit itself to give unlimited potential to human freedom for creativity.

The Plurality of Human Creativity

The inherent freedom of the real, sufficient to limit itself, allows for the possibility of unrestricted and spontaneous human action. While the potential exists for unrestricted and spontaneous action at the level of deeds, for the primitive freedom is measured in how efficacious are one's actions in ritual. Ritual makes the primitive free because she or he loses her or himself in the divine in imitation of the archetypes. Their actions have meaning and performative power. In like manner, the modern, for one alienated in a fragmented world and susceptible to the "terrors of history," freedom occurs through the repetition of archetypes in ritual anamnesis. By repeating mythic archetypes one enters into mythical time and is freed from temporal becoming. The spiritual person (one who lives in mythic and symbolic existence) has a variety of ways for escaping the meaninglessness and banality of ordianry existence. One can choose to engage in ritual, found a special place—as in the construction of a home, temple, or sacred center—create a work of art, write a piece of literature, or construct a philosophy. In each case the person places the creative act in a larger universe of meaning. This universe need not be confined to any singular frame of reference or worldview, such as the historicist or the Western. Nor must one conform to any singular worldview for defining what constitutes creativity. In the Confucian view of creativity, the human creates *from within* a context where the "self" is organically united with its context. This view differs, for instance, from the Hebraic notion of *creatio ex nihilo* in which the person creates *upon* a context by patterning his or her actions after a transcendental model.[72] Among the possibilities for creative activity, the spiritual person has many options for meaningful existence, for "miracle." The nonspiritual person, the demythologized or unmythologized, on the other hand, commited to one plane of reality, the historical, must rely on the historical plane for validating his or her creative acts.

The ability of the spiritual person to live on and integrate all planes of reality—the historical, metaphysical, and religious—is what Eliade meant by a person becoming "cosmicized," a thought introduced in his 1932 "work in progress," *Soliloquii*.[73] To be "cosmicized" is to be open to the world of symbols where, as the historian of religions Lawrence Sullivan says, "the cosmos [itself] becomes the proper context for human freedom."[74] Symbolic living exemplifies a greater positive freedom since a person is freed *for* so many other meaningful possibilities. The cosmos (the universal) is reflected in individual actions (the particular); and the actions, in turn, are cosmicized, are made universal. Though the archaic or the historically "mythologized" or "remythologized" person perceives past models as having interpretive and ontological significance for present action, such individuals, as I mentioned, do not exercise any less freedom of action as does the "demythologized" nonspiritual person who interprets freedom as spontaneity and being autonomous of all models. In the Eliadean perspective, however, these seemingly free and spontaneous actions are simply camouflaged desires to regain paradise, to return to pure freedom and to when humans lived at one with the gods and the animals.

It goes without saying that freedom for Eliade implies responsibility. Just as mythic and symbolic expressions cannot exist apart from concrete existence and temporal history, so freedom must be grounded in the concrete. The fifth-century Christian theologian Augustine said, "Love, and do as you please." Such a statement can only take place in a "community of love," says Eliade. Only there will actions be responsible.[75] In other words, where there is the acceptance of, and allowance for, creative acts—as in a community of "love"—one is most free to create and to express the quality of one's humanness. Thus, a totalitarian state or any kind of communal oppression, retards, even if it cannot completely abolish, the freedom to create. Reflecting back on what he wrote in 1927 and on and in 1934, Eliade said "nothing, *absolutely nothing,* can sterilize spiritual creativity so long as a man is—and realizes himself to be—*free*. Only the loss of freedom, or of the consciousness of freedom, can sterilize a creative spirit.''[76] Despite this position, however, Eliade came to realize, after first supporting a dictatorship for its apparent vitality,[77] that creative, intellectual freedom cannot merely exist in abstraction but consistently works best when accompanied by actual physical freedom, as he discovered when he left totalitarian Romania and settled in the United States. While not exactly a "community of love," the United States did provide Eliade the space and means for free expression. In 1983, on the day he concluded his last seminar at the University of Chicago, Eliade wrote, "I don't regret that I remained at Chicago. . . . Nowhere in Europe would I have had the freedom to teach what I wanted as I wanted.''[78]

In addition to providing freedom for creativity, a "community of love" has creativity inducing resistances, individual and social. Without various resistances challenging one to accountability, a person becomes complacent and sterile and, finally, unfree; absolute license is no freedom. The importance of resistance for encouraging a free, creative, and authentic life is similarly found in Heidegger's notion of "being unto death.''[79]

A word must be said about how freely creative is Eliade's hermeneutics. As a "creative hermeneutics," Eliade's hermeneutics retrieves and articulates for contemporary culture hidden worlds of meaning long since camouflaged by history. At face value this retrieval through anamnesis does not sound freely creative. It only seems to draw upon what has already been. There is nothing "new" about it. Instead of contributing to novelty and human potential, it appears to put a ceiling on them. But if we go by what was said earlier, that on the plane of present action there is no such thing as determinism—or as the philosopher of science Rudy Rucker says, "stable reality is a mere construct!''[80] —then each and every day offers new possibilities for action. We have no prescribed determinism. The circular hermeneutical process, therefore, is always a new process. New interpretations and breakthroughs occur precisely because we, as physio-psychic beings, change, as does the context of our environment. Though Eliade's hermeneutics informs modern culture of its preexisting unconscious structures, at each renewed retrieval of these structures the information is new, "novel," in relation to the changes that have occurred in a person's and a culture's life with each passing period. Hence, correspondingly new choices for present action are made at all times.[81] As Eliade's circular "creative hermeneutics" deepens and broadens its knowledge base it increases the potential for new options and creative breakthroughs at every "new" and developing moment. Says Eliade:

> The fact that a hermeneutics leads to a creation of new cultural values does not imply that it is not objective. From a certain point of view, one can compare the hermeneutics to a scientific or technological "discovery." Before the discovery, the reality that one came to discover was there, only one did not see it, or did not understand it, or did not know how to use it. In the same way, a creative

hermeneutics unveils significations that one did not grasp before, or puts them in relief with such vigor that after having assimilated this new interpretation the consciousness is no longer the same.[82]

In the end, Eliade's ontology radically encourages free and creative action. And insofar as it also cosmicizes one, it frees one's "self" from the fleeting conditionings of temporality.[83]

Meaningful Creativity Through Memory

Hindu and Buddhist wisdom says that if one were to peel back the layers of oneself one would discover, in Hinduism, one's ultimate self ("atman") or, in Buddhism, nothing (*anatta,* no permanent self). For the Hindu of the Vedantist philosophy, the self empties into Brahman, the eternal and enveloping self. For Buddhists, there being no self at all, there is only emptiness. In either case, what endures throughout a person's successive reincarnations is the memory of the true nature of things. For the Hindu it is the atman, which recalls its unity with Brahman and moves toward being reunited with Brahman. For the Buddhist it is only the "dharma," the Buddha's teaching, that survives and must be remembered if one is to be liberated from the world of suffering and ignorance. To recall the true nature of things enables a person eventually to be released from the cycle of "samsara" (rebirths) for liberation. Memory is also associated with "karma" (action), since in karma what is sown will be remembered.

Christians, Jews, and Muslims also speak of being known in memory in that from God's memory humans will be judged according to their actions during life. One's actions are immortalized in the memory of God.[84]

The above viewpoints highlight the importance of memory for giving meaning to present action. Memory draws to the present former experiences and images, and one becomes associated with such experiences and images. The ritual of anamnesis regains the time of "beginnings" and transforms profane time into meaningful, sacred time. Memory draws the presence of the sacred into concrete experience. Unlike *homo faber,* whose freedom and humanness receive their value "in the making" and requires historiography to "remember" its creations, the human as *homo religiosus* achieves her or his freedom and humaness based on an ontology that precedes any creative activity. The sacred archetypes founded by the gods precede the act, and it is memory that keeps these archetypes alive. For the human as *homo religiosus* it is not historiography that is required to validate and immortalize one's deeds, but a sacred ontology. By actively implementing the sacred into present life in ritual or by passively appropriating the sacred in one's deeds (itself a form of ritual, as in the Confucian practice of rites), one's deeds are given meaning and remembered.[85]

In this section, I have shown how the person charaterized as *homo religiosus* is as free for action as the person characterized as *homo faber* and as being potentially more free for creative actions since the deeds of *homo religiosus* are seen to have meaningful and transformative value. It would be wrong, however, to suggest that *homo religiosus* and *homo faber* are polar opposites and that one can exist without the other. Whether "human the maker" existed prior to "human the religious" is a long and controversially debated chicken-or-egg question. The world is both a familiar and terrifying place, "home" and a wasteland needing domestication. One can suppose that from the time of the protohumans to now humans have symbolically constructed a world of meaning and have "made" it fit for habitation and created political-social structures to keep it so. *Homo religiosus* complements *homo faber* in defining an anthropology. In the end, humans express their freedom by harmonizing these two modes of being: humans create from a need for meaning for continued meaningful existence.

Humans as Cultural

The new humanism is concerned with universal culture. As far back and as far away as the mind can travel, humans are affected in various degrees by the creative acts of other people. Taken in their totality, these creative acts define the human condition as preeminently cultural. If the total human condition interests Eliade, then the new humanism would appropriate and encourage a concern for a "planetary consciousness." Eliade expressed this belief in *The Quest:*

> Today history is becoming truly universal for the first time, and so culture is in the process of becoming "planetary." The history of man from paleolithic to present times is destined to occupy the center of humanist education, whatever the local or national interpretations. The history of religions can play an essential role in this effort toward a *planetisation* of culture; it can contribute to the elaboration of a universal type of culture.[86]

According to Eliade, the history of religions is in the position to create and transform culture out of its fragmentation and provincialism to a universal interrelatedness among cultures past and present.

But if the achievement of a universal culture is a goal for the new humanism, what will this culture look like? And through which individuals and communities will it come about? Assuredly, because the character of the new humanism develops and is constantly given to change, it would be difficult to predict the character of this universal culture. We cannot say what kind of cultural creations will emerge in the arts, literature, among the religions, in the human psyche, or will come to influence the social and political realms. Instead of trying to forecast what a universal culture might look like, I want to examine how Eliade viewed culture and the cultural program through which he saw a new humanism evolving. In this way we can approximate the image of the culture of a new humanism.

It is my view that the new humanism necessitates and effects an elitist culture, one shaped by the intellectually and politically "powerful." By "powerful" I mean those who have a transhistorical consciousness *and* an ability to shape history. The "ability to shape history" is important to Eliade's interpretation of culture. For autochthonous peasant cultures have a transhistorical consciousness, but they are limited in their ability to shape history. The ability to influence the course of history is part of the requirement for a new humanism.

The New Humanism as Cultural Creation

To reiterate, before all else, according to Eliade, a human being is *homo religiosus*. As religious beings (*homines religiosi*) humans thirst for transcendence and a desire to *be*, to be in touch with other universes of meaning and to understand their "place" in the cosmos. From out of this structural condition culture is created. Culture is a composite of all humans' spiritual thirst to transcend material and biological existence and to *be*. To the primitive, culture is "the sum of the values received from supernatural beings."[87] In short, culture has a spiritual import since it seeks to create spiritual values—those which transcend the transitoriness of time and help provide meaning to one's place in the world. The creation of art, the writing of literature and history, the formulation of a philosophy, of an ethic, of a religious belief constitute the creation of cultural, spiritual values. Such values are concerned with more than physical survival and the maintenance of human affairs, being the concerns of politics and economics. Spiritual values, rather, address and express the very essence of the human person—the human spirit. In the following paragraph Eliade connects culture with the ontological thirst for being:

> On the one hand, [theologians] are rather suspicious of historico-religious hermeneutics that might encourage syncretism or religious dilettantism or, worse yet, raise doubt about the uniqueness of the Judeo-Christian revelation. On the other hand, the history of religions envisages, in the end, cultural *creation* and the *modification* of man. The humanist culture poses an embarrasing problem for theologians and Christians in general: What do Athens and Jerusalem have in

common? . . . [I]t would be futile to ignore the fact that nearly all the contemporary philosophies and ideologies recognize that man's specific mode of being in the universe inevitably forces him to be a creator of culture. Whatever the point of departure for an analysis that seeks a defintion of man, whether one utilizes the psychological, sociological, or existentialist approach, or some criterion borrowed from classical philosophies, one comes, explicitly or implicitly, to characterize man as a creator of culture (i.e., language, institutions, techniques, arts, etc.). And all the methods of liberation of man—economic, political, psychological—are justified by their final goal: to deliver man from his chains or his complexes in order to open him to the world of the spirit and to render him *culturally creative*. Moreover, for the unbelievers or the irreligious all that a theologian, indeed, simply a Christian, considers heterogeneous in the sphere of culture—the mystery of faith, the sacramental life, etc.—is included in the sphere of "cultural creations."[88]

A theologian would inquire into the impulse "behind" these cultural creations and whether these creations are worthy of ultimate trust. Eliade does not broach theological inquiries into religious truth claims. He only points out how religious distinctiveness is itself a cultural creation. A person merely chooses certain cultural paradigms over others. As Eliade would have it, a historian of religions would consider a synthesis of all religio-cultural expressions as her or his "religion."[89] Those who are eager and able to transcend religio-cultural parameters will most likely approximate the universal consciousness of the new humanism. Such a "compassion for the universal" is itself an element of elitism, says Louis Massignon.[90]

To be a person of culture is, unavoidably, to be elitist. A person must be initiated into becoming a person of culture. One moves out of the natural, profane state of ignorance, animality, and childishness to a state receptive to spiritual values and knowledgeable of the nature of the universe. It is to develop beyond ignorance and the survival instinct to wisdom and creativity. In the demythologized and fragmented society of today, initiation has lost its spiritual import. Individuals in modern culture no longer purposefully sense the need to be initiated into becoming a total human being, total in the sense of including the physical, mental, and spiritual qualities of the human person. Subsequently, they fail to develop in their capacity to perceive the spiritual world of meaning and to create meaning for others. But since initiation constitutes humanness from animality, the modern person becomes a person of culture nevertheless, if only incompletely.

In that Eliade's view of culture includes the spiritual and has a salvific intent, his view differs from many prominent definitions of culture used by anthropologists and historians of religion.

One might begin with the definition of the late and influential anthropologist E. B. Tylor:

> Culture or Civilization . . . [is] that complex whole which includes knowl-
> edge, belief, art, morals, law, custom, and any other capabilities and habits
> acquired by man as a member of society.[91]

Such a definition proved, in time, to be too static, rationalistic, and dominated
by evolutionary theories. Cultures were defined by what they should contain
(i.e., belief, morals, law, etc.), and primitive cultures, not necessarily con-
taining all the elements, are, thus, incomplete as cultures, and certainly as
"civilizations," in comparison to modern cultures. The definition superseding
Tylor's and widely used among anthropologists, social scientists, and students
of religion during the 1930s to the 1960s was Bronislaw Malinowski's. Culture, for Malinowski, was defined as "partly material, partly human, and
partly spiritual" for meeting humans' organic and organizational needs.[92] In
defining culture according to its function and context, Malinowski's definition
lacks the spontaneous, organic, purely creative impulse found in Eliade's view
of culture. Moreover, because culture is contextually imbeded, Malinowski
could not give to cultural creations the same universal and salvific potential
Eliade does.

For many anthropologists, students of religion, and historians today, the
definition of culture put forward by the anthropologist Clifford Geertz com-
mands much respect. Culture, says Geertz,

> denotes an historically transmitted pattern of meanings embodied in symbols, a
> system of inherited conceptions expressed in symbolic forms by means of which
> men communicate, perpetuate, and develop their knowledge about and attitudes
> toward life.[93]

Insofar as Geertz gives central importance to "meaning," "symbols,"
"knowledge," and their perpetuity through history, he shares common
ground with Eliade. But here the sharing stops. Geertz does not make universal claims about cultural symbols and patterns, nor does he interpret a symbol
by placing it within a synthesis of a plurality of symbols. A symbol's meaning
is gathered from constructing a "thick description" of the culture from which
the symbol derives. Like Malinowski, Geertz stresses context over any universal themes the symbol might share with other symbols from other cultural
contexts.

Eliade's hope for culture and for what the history of religions can accomplish is more than what many anthropologists and historians of religions would
ever conceive for their respective disciplines.[94]

A Cultural Collectivity

Although Eliade's view of culture has a mythical, noncontextual, and semi-
institutional character, it assumes nevertheless a collective, somewhat static

quality of its own. Culture is defined in contrast to civilization, generally defined as material, atomistic, secular, and provincial to the Western avant-garde. In addition, civilization disregards paradigmatic history; it does not prescribe normative models of behavior.

The distinction culture–civilization has long been used by such theologians as Albert Schweitzer and Emil Brunner, such anthropologists as Robert Red-field, and such historians as Oswald Spengler. In these cases "culture" refers to the traditional, barbaric societies and "civilization" to that of the progressively rational, moral, aesthetic, differentiated, and decentralized peoples of the Renaissance onward. For Eliade, however, who has us regard primitive cultures on their own terms and to attend to the spiritual failings of modern society, it is civilization—the progressively rational and decentralized society—that is contra humanness.

This qualitative criticism of civilization has a particular tie to Eliade's Romanian mentor, Nae Ionescu. Ionescu was fiercely antagonistic toward the rationalism of the European Enlightenment and Western political Liberalism. For Ionescu these modes of thought were alien to Romania's cultural roots and undermined revelation and the authority of the state and church over the individual. These views of Ionescu are used by Ivan Strenski to criticize Eliade's own hope for culture. Strenski says that the culture Eliade favors is retrogressive and ideologically nationalistic and, thus, runs counter to individual freedom and cultural progress.[95] But Eliade is not an uncritical disciple of Ionescu. Eliade is far more appreciative of modern culture and its thought than Ionescu.[96] Though in many ways decrepit, modern culture makes its own creative contributions to world culture and manifests the activity of the sacred through these contributions, according to Eliade.

Another Romanian who influenced Eliade's view of culture was the philosopher-poet Lucian Blaga (1895–1961). Blaga felt that what lay behind the creation of culture was an unconscious, unknowable, transcendent "spirit" (the "Great Anonym"). This spirit expresses itself through cultural creations. Each individual culture acquires its distinct "style" according to how the "Great Anonym" happens to express itself. Culture, for Blaga, has a metaphysical base and is largely the product of the unconscious. In its concern for the creation of meaning, culture contrasts with civilization, whose purpose is to insure human security, comfort, and self-preservation. Culture arose as humans first inquired into matters of ultimate concern.

Influenced by Blaga, Eliade, however, sees structural continuities between cultures more than Blaga does; and, more importantly, the metaphysical impulse behind culture is not unknowable. This creative impulse enters historical existence as hierophanies. Thus human activity, science, reason, and concrete life are valued. So contrary to what Stresnki claims, Eliade's view of culture does not encourage antirationalism, antiscience, or antihistory.[97] The culture–civilization distinction is great enough in Eliade to merit a dichotomy, but to ignore the ways in which they paradoxically interrelate is to fundamentally misconstrue Eliade's view. Eliade does not dispense with civilization; he reinvests it with value by giving it a metaphysical impulse and setting it within a human–cosmos homology.

To help clarify what Eliade means by transforming civilization to new levels of value, we can turn to the typology ''Christ the Transformer of Culture'' as identified by the ethicist H. Richard Niebuhr in his classic *Christ and Culture*.[98] ''Christ'' in Niebuhr's typology would equal Eliade's ''culture,'' and Niebuhr's ''culture'' Eliade's ''civilization.'' When Niebuhr says Christ transforms culture he means that God is active in history yet always in judgment of it. God through Christ converts or transforms culture to values beyond the present human order but not in complete refutation of it. As for Eliade, what needs ''transformation'' is a spiritually vapid Western civilization. Cultural creators are not to reject Western culture and its religious-cultural traditions but, through its hermeneutical skills, are to learn from other cultural universes and synthesize their contributions with those of the West. That which ''judges'' the present human order, for Eliade, is two-fold: the ''sacred,'' which at once constantly elevates and limits human existence, and history itself; the ''terror of history'' will condemn historicism unless historicism restores the viability of a mythopoetic consciousness. The ''goal,'' the model toward which culture should aspire, is the archetype of the new humanism—a goal yet unrealized but always beckoning. In the same way that a Christian, according to Niebuhr's model, does not reject culture entirely but selectively appropriates values from the prevailing culture, so the person aspiring to a new humanism is similarly selective. Pastiche, kitsch culture—historically shallow, fadish, cultural creations—are rejected. Eliade would include in this cultural category parapsychology, synthetic new age religions, abstract artistic expressionism, pop art, and other such examples falling between high art and folk creations. Only those values and expressions not subject to the rise and tide of cultural fashions are suitable for cultural renewal. Eliade's article ''Cultural Fashions and History of Religions'' demonstrates well how hermeneutics can cut through cultural fashions and expose their mythic undercurrents.[99] Because Eliade's culture of a new humanism values classical forms and requires persons of power to define and shape these standards, is it regarded as elitist.

The New Humanism and Cultural Elitism

In Plato's *Republic,* Glaucon and Socrates discuss the best way to transform society with the minimum amount of change. Socrates proposes a solution:

Unless either philosophers become kings in their countries or those who are now called kings and rulers come to be sufficiently inspired with a genuine desire for wisdom; unless, that is to say, political power and philosophy meet together. . . . there is no other way of happiness either for the state or for the individual (3:18).[100]

Philosophers who become king will desire all wisdom. Justice will come as they search for and implement the beautiful and the good, and they will rule through the wisdom of their counsel, not through the force of their arms.

A SOCIAL CLASS ELITISM

The new humanism will come through the efforts of such a ruler. That is, to transform culture on a global scale the new humanism requires individuals with sufficient power to sway and order history. These will not be despots but persons of high morals and cultural sophistication. In order to trace the inspiration behind this view of leadership for Eliade's new humanism, we need to look at his early years in Romania.

As I have shown throughout, many of the roots to Eliade's thought and his vision for a new humanism are found from his time in Romania. Here, as a way to de-isolate Romania from European culture and to inspire Romania's own creative geniuses, Eliade wedded European and Oriental thought with the peasant, folk traditions of Romania and called for political leaders and intellectual elites to define the new Romania based on this inner–outer cultural–spiritual resource pool. Although the pastoral and agricultural peoples knew how to survive history's terrors, they were not in a position to shape the future of Romania. It would have to be the artists, teachers, writers, and, those whom we call the philosopher-kings who carried Romanianism forward. These were the ones who had the capacity to create in the realm of values, to produce oeuvres of art and thought, and to implement these values for the enlightenment of the masses. To "create" meant for them the achieving of an "inner equilibrium," the "harmonization of man with his soul."[101] Eliade, therefore, supported, for a period, the monarchy of King Carol and the Legionnaires when he thought they might empower indigenous religious values at the political level. And though Eliade rejected Hitlerism and fascist dictatorship for its lack of humanness and concern for the inner spiritual life, he did come to think, like his mentor, Nae Ionescu, that a dictatorship and not a democracy best suited Romania.[102] This dictator, while stern, would rule by "right not by might," in Gerhard Lenski's words.[103] He would rule by setting a moral and intellectual example and would generate culture-creating institutions. Eliade repeatedly advocated in the 1930s the establishment of such institutions through which the people might rise to higher ideals in achieving a new humanity, a "new man," a spiritual, revolutionary ideal of no single ideology.[104]

The hope for Romania would come through political savants, but it would require the creative contributions of the young generation, those not having served in the first World War, those unattached to the nostalgias of a bygone antebellum era. The young generation in Eliade's eyes constituted an elitist class of its own.

It was in his assortment of writings from his "Spiritual Itinerary" and in his many feuilletons from between 1927 and 1928, that Eliade challenged the youth to create and to make for themselves "oeuvres." These youth were to cultivate spiritual values, possess a critical spirit, and formulate syntheses. These aims were to be achieved not only individually but collectively, and it was through a symposium called "Criterion" that we have one of the clearest examples of how such a collective renewal of culture should come about.

Shortly after Eliade had returned from India in 1931, a symposium of young intellectuals called "Criterion" (The Criterian Association for Arts, Literature, and Philosophy) was formed during the fall of 1932 under the inspiration of the American-educated Petru Comarnescu. It would survive with popularity amidst great controversy for a couple of years until forced to disband under political pressures in 1933/34. Criterion sought to engage the Romanian youth and the general public in critical discussions of contemporary cultural, political, and religious subjects. In one of its public advertisements it stated its purpose as presenting "a critical orientation of the public to the problems of the times, from the viewpoint of the young generation."[105] In one of his articles in *Cuvântul* in 1932 Eliade stated that "It [Criterion] is a matter of a translation from an individual, isolated, and 'original' plane of manifestation, to one of collective activity, of intellectual cooperation, of living and working together." And what they were to cooperate in was in the creation of a *culture*, a Romanian yet critically cosmopolitan culture. They discussed topics as diverse as Marx, Lenin, Freud, Charlie Chaplin, Mussolini, Gandhi, Romanticism, Orthodoxy, among others. Eliade recalls one of the more moving and respected speeches was on Charlie Chaplin by Mihail Sebastian, a Jew. Sebastian spoke as "a Jew about the Jew, Charlie Chaplin." It was, Eliade recalled, "one of the most moving and intelligent lectures I have ever had the opportunity to hear."[106] These lectures were intended to enlighten and transform popular culture by pluralizing the public conscience and stimulating its critical capacities. There was nothing ideological or exclusivistic about Criterion's program (though it was accused, paradoxically, of being Communist and fascist in sympathy[107]). Instead Criterion was to emphasize the "primacy of the spiritual" over the political. What Criterion and the young generation were to do for Romania during its political-cultural crises, Eliade's new humanism through a "creative hermeneutics" would similarly do to renew a languishing and wayward Western culture. Criterion pluralized and synthesized meaning as a creative act, and in this same fashion so does Eliade's new humanism.

Based upon what I have said of the new humanism requiring a political and intellectual class for the transformation of culture, it would be easy to suppose that Eliade was somewhat of a political and social tactician. Despite forays into the public arena and occasional political-nationalistic declarations, Eliade never ceased being first and foremost a humanist with a strong distaste for party politics. But his views as a humanist do advocate a class elitism. Eliade once objected to an educational program aimed at the peasant class in Romania for "half-educating" the peasants out of their autochthonous, folkloric traditions.[108] Educating them, he felt, would taint and possibly erase Romania's archaic roots. Fundings for education, rather, should go to institutions of higher learning. For it is from these that the intellectuals will come to make history. Eliade directed his own writings toward the higher class and called other writers and artists to do likewise. But to address the higher class was not for the sole reason that the elite are in a better position to shape culture. There was also a philosophical reason. If, indeed, to create myth is a structure of human consciousness and this mythic creation articulates primordial archetypes, then it behooves the political and intellectual leaders of a new humanism to preserve an undefiled autochthonous base. In this way the autochthonous base, whose mythic mentality is the least unadulterated by civilization, could survive and remain "pure" and civilization would have its resources upon which to nurture itself against the "terror of history."

This notion of preserving the peasant foundation raises the larger issue of social, cultural, and religious impositions of one culture or point of view on another. The anthropologist Lévi-Strauss, knew the lamentable dilemma of the anthropologist who wants to preserve pristine cultures and avoid setting up a global "monoculture" while, as a scientist, feeling compelled to probe these very cultures for understanding the human condition.[109] So in not wanting to half-educate the peasants, Eliade was not just seeking to maintain a cultural hierarchy. More fundamentally, he was facing the issue in his own backyard of how much should one tarnish and adulterate that which is most closely primal, most closely attuned to the impulses of nature. Moreover, in keeping the pristine, Eliade raised the issue of who, as far as living freely is concerned, is more capable of living in the world anyway, the cultural and political sophisticates subject to the pressures of historicism or the peasants in their cosmic religiosity.[110] Just because the sophisticates of culture may be able to depict more loftily—through art, literature, philosophy, etc.—the struggles, ambiguities, and demands of life, that does not mean they are any better in dealing with these than subordinate and less advantaged groups and classes.[111]

So far I have spoken of an elite group of people—intelectualls and politicians of the philosopher-king type—who are regarded as being in the best position to bring about a new humanism for modern culture. They are thought to have the sophistication *and* power to disseminate their views and to carry out the reforms necessary for transforming culture. We can refer to the aggregate of this group as a "collective elite." But the term "collective elite" can apply to the individual as well. During his early years in Romania, Eliade encouraged the young people to realize their "personality" and "destiny." These terms refer to an individual's singular responsibility to create her or his own unique collective character of plural experiences, of broad knowledge, and self-defining deeds in becoming an authentic person. Eliade would shift from saying that "personality" and "destiny" could only come through one's individual Herculean efforts to recognizing that other forces are at work which assist the individual in their realization. In either case, for a person to achieve her or his "personality" and "destiny" she or he must do so by creating "syntheses," that is, reducing by integration the plurality of facts and values to which one is exposed to essential structures that cohere these facts and values. Eliade's *Patterns in Comparative Religion* is a reduction-by-integration of the many ways in which the sacred has been seen to manifest itself across space and time. This act, though, of creating "syntheses" is itself the domain of trained or gifted individuals, a kind of person who can both cognitively and intuitively appropriate and assimilate a diversity of elements into a harmonious and functional whole. Such individuals, by their ability to integrate a great diversity of material, constitute an elite group.

Eliade's view of "collectivity" must be distinguished from the view, as held by Nae Ionescu, that there are no individuals only "collectivities." This position, often equated with fascism, subordinates the individual to the collective whole, where the nation, for instance, becomes a "collective individual." Eliade does not subordinate the individual to the state or to the masses. For him "collectivity" refers to the individual as a symbol. An individual is a collective or "total person" in that he or she is made up of biological, psychological, emotional, and spiritual characteristics. And as a symbol, an individual refracts a host of simultaneously harmonious, competing, and contradictory images and meanings. As symbol, the human is, by nature, collective. In sum, the new humanism requires an elite collectivity and individuals who cultivate their capacity for collective experience.

AN ELITISM OF HISTORICAL CONSCIOUSNESS

In his article, "Religion, Art, and the Elite," the philosopher Nicholas Wolterstorff defines the "cultural elite" as those who cultivate a taste for "high art."[112] What makes art "high art" is when a work of art demonstrates a "historical self-consciousness." That is, the work and the artist have an appreciation for history, *all* history, from the evocative masks of primal cultures to the refined Renaissance works of Jan van Eyck. This historical pool constitutes a "cultural deposit" for thematic, conceptual, and stylistic inspiration. The artist is inspired not for imitation, but is inspired by the spirit of the precendents "suggest[ing]" themselves through the artist's work. As such, for the artist drawing on a rich cultural deposit, current social trends and fads become irrelevant in determining the value and function of the work. The artist, rather, "transcend[s]" and is "independent" of the flux in cultural taste, choosing instead to "abide" in those styles, values, tastes, and ideals which are thought to have a worth beyond any "social function" the artist's work might or might not have.

If this view is what is meant by "high art," it is not coincidental that Eliade criticized Western art and literature for having lost its historical consciousness to the fleeting tastes of modern culture. What Wolterstorff defines as "historical self-consciousness" is, for Eliade, the consciousness of the mythic mind. The Romanian sculptor Constantin Brancusi and the Jewish artist Marc Chagall are two prototypical examples of an artistic elite for a new humanism.[113]

But it is not enough to have "historical self-consciousness," a mythic view of history. To be of that cultural class that shapes a new humanism, one must also be in the position to shape history and universal culture. We get an indication of such a class in Bruce Lincoln's *Myth, Cosmos, and Society,* in which he describes the "priests" of society—the administrators of myth—as giving stability and social legitimacy to society by enveloping society with a cosmic, mythic vision. What makes their enveloping vision persuasive and effective is the priests' ability to "synthesize" a plurality of meanings and values for society as a whole. Lincoln comments:

> The fantastic persuasive power—the real genius—of such a system is its potential for synthesis. One feels that there was absolutely nothing that might not be satisfactorily subsumed within the pattern of homologic thought, which sought to integrate all existence within one encompassing structure. When members of the priestly class successfully propagated at least a superficial understanding of this powerful system of religious ideology through all social strata, two major results followed. First, people of all classes felt the cosmos to be an intelligible and reassuring entity, a place in which death was but temporary and every destruction was followed by a restoration. Second, people of all classes felt society to be legitimate, and also reassuring: stable, eternal, well-founded, and rightful. What is more, this sentiment contributed dramatically to the *actual* stability of society.[114]

The capacity for myth, or an "ideology," to authenticate a structure and provide its members at all levels of society with an encompassing vision of meaning, parallels the way in which the new humanism would seem to work in Eliade's culture of a "planetary consciousness." But the implied conservatism of this vision need not mean that myth must be conservative, that it simply authenticates and preserves the status quo. Or to put it differently, myth does not always create a cosmos, at least at the societal level. It can also create chaos. Competing myths or reinterpretations of the prevailing hegemonic myth(s) can lead to socio-political change, as Bruce Lincoln demonstrates in his subsequent book, *Discourse and the Construction of Society*. He identifies three ways in which myth can be used or created for encouraging socio-political change: 1) competing myths can contest the authority or credibility of a given myth, reducing it to the status of history or legend and thereby depriving it of its capacity to continually construct social forms, 2) one can invest history, legend, or even a fable with authority and credibility and thus elevate it to the status of myth, 3) by advancing novel lines of interpretation for an established myth or by modifying details in the narration of the myth thereby changing the nature of the sentiments it evokes.[115] In other words, though, for Eliade, myth principally creates a cosmos, order, myth has within itself the potential to reform and to be reformed. We find Eliade using this potential in myth when he challenged the authoritarian royal dictatorship of King Carol II and supported the spiritual-political ideals of the Legionnaires: the myth of Romanianism, in which the intellectual and peasant classes conjoined for a "new man," was to overturn a nonindigenous monarchy and the hegemonic myth of an outdated, pre-war Romanianism. In Eliade's novel *The Old Man and the Bureaucrats*, we get a literary example of how myth and memory subvert the machinations of a heavy-handed police state. Although myth for a new humanism authenticates society and its social structures by setting them within an encompassing framework of meaning, in pluralistic and politically and socially unjust contexts, myth equally has the capacity for stimulating socio-political reform for not only a culturally creative new humanism but a just one as well.

Despite the fact that disenfranchised peoples and their myths can find a voice in Eliade's new humanism, there is still the element of elitism in the new humanism. Elitism, however, need not be negative, since it does not necessarily mean the suppression of one group by another; how it is used defines its value. What I want to point out here, though, is an elitist supposition in Eliade's view of who is in the position to shape culture. For Eliade, the individuals who have the time, resources, and competency to create culture— to write the books, to think the thoughts, to found the museums, to govern society (in other words, the traditional priestly and warrior classes)—are regarded more highly over those who, presumably for lack of the above reasons, cannot: the assembly-line worker, the civil servant, the manager (in effect, the commoners). I am simplifying each's ability "to create" culture, of course. The view, however, that the masses somehow do not make history but must learn to escape it sidesteps the thorny question so poignantly posed in Tolstoy's *War and Peace:* who determines history, the Napoleons and their schemes or the minute affairs of the Russian and French people? Hegelian views of history in Marxism may not found history on archetypes in need of repetition, but Marxism realizes that history is shaped from the bottom up. It relocates the locus of power and the formation of an ideology from the divine archetypes to the masses.[116] Eliade's new humanism, in contrast, has the locus of power and the formation of ideology or myth at the top, among the intellectuals and philosopher-kings. Such an arrangement may follow the natural order of things, but to give principal weight to the elite discounts the ability of the common people or the powerless to be cultural innovators for the rest of society. Elitism fails to take seriously the significance—for good or for ill—of popular culture, usually the product of the "degradation" and "manipulation" of high culture.[117]

Eliade's elitism, aside from being top-heavy, is also strongly masculine in orientation. In Eliade's early Romanian years "culture," "personality," "destiny," and the ability—physical and intellectual—to realize these are associated with the "masculine." The life of the spirit is the domain of the male psyche and the initiatory feats to achieve it requires the will of the male hero who breaks from the entrapments of nature and society. The "feminine," consequently, is associated with "nature," dependence, and "society." In Eliade's later life we find other examples of this masculine orientation. Almost all his literature, from before his exile from Romania to the years afterward, reflects the male/spirit–female/nature dichotomy; though there are cases where a woman represents the spirit and enables the man to discover it, as in the short story, "With the Gypsy Girls." And in his scholarly interpretations, feminists have found Eliade in his three-volume opus *A History of Religious Ideas*[118] to prefer male symbols of power and in his studies on initiation to associate male with spirit and female with nature.[119] While feminists might make an issue of Eliade's male elitism, he cannot be so easily labled as chauvinistic. His attention to a nature–cosmos–human homology, to human authenticity found in being *and* becoming, and to symbols of androgyny as representative of a whole human being, demonstrate the other side to the masculine orientation. In fact, we might say that to create culture is itself both a male and female activity. From the Latin *cultura* and its past participle *colere,* culture is to cultivate, care for, and till—the labors of men and women.

As I have shown, the new humanism has a pronounced elitism, whether at the individual, national, or global level. According to Eliade, to be a human being is to be a cultural being. But it also means one is required to create culture, since humanness is more than a given but a creation. Cultural creativity, for Eliade, is informed by a mythic consciousness. To create culture is to invest society with meaning and counter cheap imitative life. It is to place the transcience of historical life on transtemporal models and direct society towards the good. But insofar as Eliade relies on a willing society to follow the examples of the intellectuals and the philosopher-kings, it is doubtful Eliade's view of culture and of human nature is realistic enough to guide society to a new humanism.[120]

Humans at the Center

Every exile is a Ulysses traveling toward Ithaca. Every real existence reproduces the *Odyssey*. The path toward Ithaca, toward the center.[121]

In the memorial address for Mircea Eliade on April 28, 1986, Charles Long said that the "center" for Eliade was *homo religiosus;* all of life was but a series of initiations leading toward the real.[122] Indeed, Eliade's anthropology of the sacred (the human as *homo religiosus*) does center and cohere his life oeuvre. In addition, it justifies his methodology and delimits his interpretations of religious data. Without the postulate *homo religiosus,* the raison d'etre of Eliade's life opus would be missing.

Nevertheless, even though the postulate *homo religiosus* may constitute a "center" in Eliade, it does not satisfy the goal toward which the thrust of his life work aimed, that of a new humanism. Although the original condition of *homo religiosus* cannot be regained—since it presupposes a prehistorical consciousness—upon its structure Eliade could still envision the possibility of attaining a new humanity. So to qualify Long, I again claim that the new humanism is the *Urpflanze,* the archetypal plant, the "center," of Eliade's life and of his scholarly and literary oeuvre.

But, to be true to a morphology and to the way Eliade conceives of the center, one must acknowledge not *one* center but many, for, to borrow the phrase of Joseph Kitagawa, "the world has many centers."[123] Conceivably, then, one could propose another form or concept as an archetype of the new humanism other than the one I have chosen here, the archetype of the center. That other forms could equally be proposed, I again suggest a morphological approach to Eliade. That is, the archetype of the center is but one "center" among many "centers," a morphology of "centers."

In considering the archetype of the center, I am more interested in the function of the center than I am in its composition. In other words, the symbol predominates, not the referents of the symbol. And as a symbol, the center empowers and orients. To put the symbol within the framework of the new humanism, therefore, the center pluralizes experience, aids in the interpretation of that experience, and founds that experience upon the reality of existence itself. To nominalize the above verbs, the new humanism is a pluralistic, hermeneutical, and ontological vantage point. Moreover, because the center is both a coveted destination and a founded condition, symbolizing place and no place, the new humanism is a state of being and a goal after which one aspires.

The Currency of the Center in Eliade

Without doubt, the symbol of the center dominates as one of the more important symbols in Eliade. It is, perhaps, a truly universal symbol in the history of religions.[124] In a jointly authored encyclopedia article with Lawrence Sullivan, Eliade writes that the symbol of the center is "that place where all essential modes of being come together; where communication and even passage among them is possible."[125] And in concluding the article they say:

> [T]he symbolism of the center, with great consistency of meaning, applies to the center of the universe, the center of the residential unity, the center of the village, the home, the ritual space, the human physiology mystically conceived, and the art of spiritual concentration. On every plane, the significance of the symbol of the center of the world underlies the fact that at the heart of existence lies an experience and mode of being entirely different from the ordinary world centered on it.[126]

Because it powerfully concentrates experience, the symbol of the center effectively empowers and transforms those who enter its sphere of influence. The center also orients one toward a reference point; it focuses attention, converges power, and, in distinction to the periphery, valorizes the subject(s) in its domain. These characteristics make the center a supreme interpretive, universalizing, and valorizing construct.

First mentioned in 1936 in the introduction to the publication of his dissertation on yoga, the symbol of the center comprises a complex set of meanings for Eliade.[127] The center is that concentration of the sacred in a hierophany; it establishes a point of orientation (an *orientatio*) as a sacred center amidst a profane periphery; it constructs a world axis (an *axis mundi*), reflects an image of the world (an *imago mundi*), and contemporizes one in "that time" (*in illo tempore*), the time of "beginnings." A cosmogony is recreated at the founding of any center, as in marking off a territory, constructing a house, building a temple or an altar, or in the installation of a ruler. The center also constitutes a yogi's cosmos–home–body (*Cosmos-Maison-Corps humain*) homology, a cosmicization of the individual. A mandala, a symbolic, visual representation of the cosmos usually of concentric circles or squares, clearly articulates a center and the difficult, labyrinthian route that one must follow to reach the power of the center. Undertaking this path toward the center naturally associates the mandala, and hence the center, with initiation, a prominent motif in Eliade. Not to be mistaken as a tranquil haven, life at the center is often quite explosive, harrowing, dark, threatening as it holds within itself multiform and often contradictory forces of a *coincidentia oppositorium*. Whether at the center or progressing toward it, the stay or the journey is frequently perilous.

Given the continuity between Eliade's scholarship and his life and literature, we naturally find reflections of the symbol of the center in Eliade's own life, and in the life experiences of his fictional characters. In his interview with Claude-Henri Rocquet, Eliade mentions having several times come face to face with his true self at the center. In his literature we find the center symbolized by the bordello in "With the Gypsy Girls," the air-raid shelter in "Twelve Thousand Head of Cattle,"[128] the mythical paradise of shambala and yogic ecstasis in "The Secret of Dr. Honingberger."[129] The examples could go on. The symbol of the center, in short, is no abstract history of religions symbol. Eliade experiences it in his life and weaves it into his fiction.

Before I tie the center to Eliade's new humanism, I must first address two critics of Eliade's use of this symbol. I refer to Jonathan Z. Smith's comments in his *Map Is Not Territory* (1978) and in his book on ritual, *To Take Place* (1987), and to those of Gregory Alles in Alles' article, "Surface, Space, and Intention: The Parthenon and the Kandariya Mahadeva" (1988).[130] Smith is one of Eliade's most astute critics. He defines religion as a second-order reality and holds that sacred space is created through a political imagination; that is, it is power and in the exercise of power that a given space is deemed henceforth sacred space. Alles is an historian of religion versed in Indian and Greek culture. His critique raises a point pertinent to a modern, scientific view of space. I shall refer to Smith's critique as the "Anthropological Critique" and to that raised by Alles as the "Spatial Critique." Both critiques, I believe, have a limited interpretation of the "center" and, therefore, do not restrain the symbol from having universal applicability.

The Anthropological Critique

In *Map Is Not Territory* Smith queries on several points regarding Eliade's use and interpretation of the symbol of the center. Smith asks if Eliade gives too much attention to the center as a locative symbol and not enough to its existential, "interiority" quality, as illustrated in the Eastern religions. Since Eliade minimizes interiority, Smith, therefore, attends to Eliade's locative interpretations. For instance, Smith thinks Eliade's interpretation of the Babylonian term *Dur-an-ki* is incorrect. Meaning the "navel of the earth," Eliade takes it to mean a bond between heaven and earth and as the place where creation began for the Babylonians. Smith says that "navel" here means not conjunction, as Eliade interprets it, but disjunction, a scar signifying the separation of heaven from earth.[131] Continuing with Babylonian examples,[132] Smith says the Babylonian creation myth *Enumma Elish* is not a celebration and recollection of a cosmogony, a world creation, but of a creation of a building, specifically of Marduk's Temple. Lastly, in Smith's list of queries into Eliade's interpretation of the center, Smith feels Eliade gives too much attention to the center and not enough to the periphery. These queries cover only a page, but they get full theoretical treatment in Smith's analysis of ritual space in *To Take Place*.

In his opening chapter, Smith lays the foundation to his anthropological approach. He aims to counter the view that sacred space relies on the founding of a cosmology. The scholar most associated with this view is Eliade, and one of the principal examples Eliade uses to prove his point is an ethnographic transcription by B. Spencer and F. J. Gillen of an Australian myth. Eliade uses this myth as told by Spencer-Gillen to demonstrate that humans cannot live long in a state of chaos and meaninglessness but must live in a world of order and open to the transcendent, hence, near or at the center. To critique Eliade Smith does a textual reconstruction of the Spencer-Gillen account to show that Eliade has misinterpreted and misused the account to support his own theory.

The myth, according to Eliade's paraphrase and reading of the Spencer-Gillen account,[133] goes as follows: the ancestors of the Tjilpa, an aboriginal tribe, had a sacred pole (*Kauwa-auwa*) that they carried wherever they went. In whatever direction the pole pointed, the ancestors proceeded to travel in that direction. The pole was thought to be the pole the creator god Numbakulla ascended in mythical "dream time" after having created the world. So, says Eliade, the pole symbolized an *axis mundi,* an axis that connected heaven to earth. As long as the pole remained unbroken and they remained near the pole, the Tjilpa were connected to the transcendent. They had access to Numbakulla.

One day, continues Eliade, the pole broke. To the Tjilpa, this breakage constituted a rupture of the Tjilpa's connection to heaven. With their connection to Numbakulla severed, the Tjilpa lost that which centered them in chaos and which linked them to the god who had created the world and defined them as human beings. Without a center and without meaning the Tjilpa ancestors laid down and died. That they gave up after their pole had been broken proves, says Eliade, that humans must live near the center. For without a cosmos, a linkage to the transcendent and a sense of order, humans fall into chaos and "die."

Taking this myth, Smith returns to the Spencer-Gillen account to see how well it matches with Eliade's own reading. I will not recount Smith's reading.[134] But because Spencer and Gillen made a couple of revisions of their own original account, Smith must do his own creative filling in of their accounts of an oral tradition regarding an "event" that was not witnessed by Spencer-Gillen or their informant, but which is said to have occurred in the Australian "dream time." In other words, ultimately, we have four "blind" parties describing a mythical elephant.

The fundamental distinction between Smith and Eliade is Smith's assertion that human's essential nature is firstly *homo faber*. That is, humans, in the order of things, first fashion their tools, domesticate the landscape, and construct their world and only later do they designate certain actions and certain places as special, different, sacred, as having religious meaning. Humans do not inherently require the need to establish and understand their place within the cosmos. Meaning is a later imposition, being principally done for establishing power relations. So when Smith looks at the Australian myth, he interprets the Tjilpa's wanderings and death as reflecting serendipitous human action and social dynamics and not the presence of any inherent religious cosmology. To Smith (as he interprets Spencer-Gillen), there is no concept of the center among the Tjilpa ancestors, nor is there an ontology of sacralized space. The sacred pole (*kauwa*) does not connect the Tjilpa to Numbakulla, whose name, according to Smith, is actually a generic term for "god" and does not denote a singular creator God; any creator designation given to Numbakulla is a Christian imposition, a "pious fraud."[135] Instead, the pole ties the Tjilpa to their mythical ancestors, a people who emerged from the terrestial subterranean regions to create their world. Creation is attached to humans and the earth, not to a divine being. Once the mystical ancestors emerged from below the ground, they wandered across the topography "marking off" and "mapping out" a territory—a space—as they went. Wherever the ancestors "happened" to trek that place would be designated by their descendants, the Tjilpa, as sacred. The Tjilpa would "memorialize" space at various points so as not to forget where the ancestors once roamed. Place, and hence ritual, became sacred through memory, not by patterning ritual action after any divine models. The stress for the Tjilpa is not on cosmos, but on *anthropos*. Space and human activity do not refer to transcendence but to the terrestial and chthonic. Any symbolic significance attached to the pole, therefore, lies in its connection to the ancestral past. For the pole to break, subsequently, meant a "rupture" not with heaven but with the mythic ancestors, and the embarrassment of having lost their connection to their ancestors, to those who founded the Tjilpa people, caused the Tjilpa to lose face before other tribes. The humiliation and disillusion plus the fatigue of wandering too much were enough to cause the Tjilpa to lie down and die.

Smith shifts the locus of authority from cosmogony—the pole as cosmic axis—to anthropology—the pole as a kind of memorabilia of the sacred past. According to Smith, the ancestors did not "create" space, there being no deliberateness to their wanderings. They simply wandered by whim and happenstance across the topography. Territory was not "created" but "marked off." And, Smith reasons, without a divine being willing creation there can be no cosmogony. Without a cosmogony there can be no cosmology of a cosmic axis, no *axis mundi*. Without an *axis mundi* there can be no geographic, locative center connecting heaven to earth. And without a symbol of the "center of the world" among the Tjilpa, one suspects Eliade's comparative typology of the center.

For Smith, humans construct sacred place. It is not founded upon any cosmogony. Through human construction, which Smith calls "objectification," the Tjilpa remembered, preserved, and made sacred, by memorializing, the grounds upon which their mythic ancestors "happened" to have walked. Following the position of Lévi-Strauss, Smith says *place* is sacred. The accident, the result, is sacred, not the essence, the impulse behind choosing one place over against another. Contrary to Eliade, for whom sacred space is founded or "created," Smith, á la Lévi-Strauss, says sacred space is where things are *in their place,* where they *happen* to be. A king raises a temple where he *happens* to have set camp. A sacred or mythic impulse does not inform and motivate the king's reasons for constructing the temple at a given place. Sacred and profane space are not divided according to a presupposed ontology.[136] Any center that might exist is secondarily ontological and religious. It is firstly (presupposing the human as *homo faber*) a "tool," a "power center." The king constructs because it is within his political interests. And the construction orients, defines boundaries, and acquires meaning as a religious center only in time, in its attachment to other objects already designated religious, and through memory. While Smith does not necessarily deny the concept of the center, he says after denying the cosmological notion of the center among the Tjilpa (and in ancient Near Eastern materials, from which Eliade gets foundational support for his cosmological symbol of the center) that:

> Without examining each and every instance, it cannot be claimed that the pattern of the "Center" is a fantasy, but it is clearly far from a universal (or even dominant) pattern of symbolization. At the very least, the burden of proof has shifted to those who will claim that a particular cultural construction represents a "Center." The "Center" is not a secure pattern to which data may be brought as illustrative; it is a dubious notion that will have to be established anew on the basis of detailed comparative endeavors.[137]

I would like to address Smith's critique on two fronts. First, although a cosmological notion of the center as a transcendent model may or may not exist or be the most accurate reading of the Tjilpa account, this does not mean the symbol of the center cannot be said to exist among the Tjilpa. The center can be located on anthropological grounds as well. In Eliade, the symbol need not be limited to cosmology. Second, Smith does not discredit the foundational support to Eliade's reasons for looking for a locative cosmological center among the Tjilpa in the first place. The Near Eastern materials upon which Eliade relies can be said to have a cosmological center.

In Smith's critique of the center among the Tjilpa, Smith fails to give attention to the "interiority" nature of the center. Although he acknowledges that Eliade deals with the interiority character of the symbol, Smith dismisses Eliade's use of interiority since it appears to be nothing more than a minor element in Eliade's use of the symbol.[138] But in failing to take it seriously in Eliade, Smith neglects an important point in Eliade's theory of symbols, namely, that people participate in symbolic behavior even on the unconscious level. That the metaphysical phrase the "center of the world" does not appear in the vocabulary of the primitives, does not mean the concept is not there. Though their vocabulary might not have it, their behavior indicates its presence, says Eliade.[139] Regarding the symbol of the center Eliade says:

> every human being tends, *even unconsciously,* toward the Centre, and towards his own centre, where he can find integral reality—sacredness. This desire, so deeply rooted in man, to find himself at the very heart of the real—at the Centre of the World, the place of communication with Heaven—explains the ubiquitous use of "Centres of the World" [emphasis added].[140]

The ancestors in Smith's exegesis of the Tjilpa myth who just "happen" to walk in this direction, and "happen" to stop here, and "happen" to consecrate this place, are not only without deliberate actions—a fact Smith stresses, they are also depicted as having no unconscious motivations as well. Smith does take the liberty to say that the Tjilpa "objectified" their topography. He does not seem willing, however, to allow for unconscious motivations among the mythic ancestors and the Tjilpa in their movement toward a need for founding a center. In his essay, "Cosmogonic Myth and 'Sacred History,'" Eliade refers to the Australian mythical ancestors as ones who "acted and thought like humans . . . [changing] *at will* into a particular species of animal" [emphasis added].[141] The ancestors are not walking automatons. They make choices. "To choose" is an essential element in a hierophany; one rock is chosen as a manifestation of the sacred over another.[142] Putting aside divine beings, sacred geographical landmarks, and *axis mundis,* an anthropological orientation does not disallow existential experiences. Humans *sense* that some places differ from others. A person is more alive, more real, qualitatively different at different places. What comes to mind is an incident in Carlos Castaneda's *The Teachings of Don Juan: A Yaqui Way of Knowledge*. One evening, Don Juan asked Castaneda to find a "place" on an empty porch where he would feel most at ease and then to sleep there. For almost the whole evening Castaneda moved and shifted around trying to find that "place" where he could feel most "centered." Near daylight he found it, and he finally could fall asleep ("die"?).[143] We find evidence of a similar inner sense of interiority among the Aranda aborigines in their longing for and trek toward home. "Longing for home—this is the motive which leads most of the weary ancestors of legend back to the place whence they originated," says the anthropologist T. G. H. Strehlow.[144] A death-sick Ulamba chief plods on for many miles singing, "High in the heavens shines the afternoon sun: His heart is filled with yearning to turn home" as he returns toward home for his final sleep.[145] The point is, the experience of the center need not be disqualified as an ontological force simply because a cosmogony is not posited. For the Aranda to sense an existential pull toward home—toward the "center," wherever home might be—demonstrates that the symbol of the center can exist on anthropological grounds as well. One cannot seperate space or landscape from the sensual and existential experience of it.

I do not purport to refute Smith's interpretation. But if he can postulate that the Tjilpa simply and merely wandered the territory, happening here and happening there with no predilection toward any place, then he must equally allow for the possibility that the Tjilpa *sensed* a difference between places, and chose accordingly. The aborigines are not without the capacity to transcend self for orienting themselves in their environment.[146]

In regards to the cosmological, locative quality of the symbol, Smith says it cannot be deduced to exist among the Tjilpa based on Near Eastern materials because, first, one cannot find a sacred cosmic mountain in the ancient Near Eastern world. So to infer that the sacred pole is a cosmic axis because it replicates a cosmic mountain, is unsound. And second, the Tjilpa do not deliberately "build" but arbitrarily "mark off," "trace," space. And if there is no deliberate "building," no construction, there is, then, no cosmogony, and without a cosmogony, there can be no cosmology of the center.

As to the first point, that there is no cosmic mountain in the ancient Mediterranean worldview is a matter of interpretation. To defend his position Smith refers to the recent conclusions of R. J. Clifford in *The Cosmic Mountain in Canaan and the Old Testament*.[147] Smith quotes Clifford saying, "The term 'cosmic mountain,' as it has been used in the study of Ancient Near Eastern religion, has been based in large measure on an assumed Mesopotamian *Weltberg*. . . . The *Weltberg*, as it has been understood by an earlier generation of scholars, does not exist.''[148] The Judaic scholar and philologist Jon Levenson, however, also draws on Clifford to demonstrate, contrarily, the presence of a cosmic mountain in ancient Israel and its attachment to the Israelite temple, Israel's locative spiritual center. And to make the connection from mountain to temple Levenson relies on Eliade.[149] Levenson says of Clifford's study, and serving to clarify the above quote, ''In the case of the cosmic mountain, it should be noted at the outset that the term 'cosmic' can be misleading. Clifford's point is not that the cosmos is envisioned in ancient Canaan as a mountain, but rather that a mountain is given characteristics and potencies of cosmic, that is, of an infinite and universal scope.''[150] Smith too narrowly restricts Eliade's views on the cosmic mountain, and so finds Eliade's interpretations inappropriate and misleading. Levenson is less literal than Smith, and thus can make the connections.[151]

Smith's second reason for critiquing why the Tjilpa's sacred pole cannot be deduced from Near Eastern materials as a locative symbol of the center, is that in the Near East cosmogony is ''intentional and constructivist.'' Cosmogony involves the deliberate building of temples, palaces, houses, and cities. The Tjilpa ancestors, in contrast, did not construct or build at all. They only emerged out of the ground and arbitrarily proceeded to ''mark off'' and ''map out'' the landscape.[152] So, Smith concludes, if Eliade interprets the wandering of the ancestors based on a Near Eastern cosmogony pattern, then Eliade builds his argument on an invalid association. The sacred pole of the Tjilpa cannot be a cosmological locative center since there is no cosmogony upon which it can be founded.

I have already pointed out how we cannot turn the ancestors and the Tjilpa into mere automatons, as wanderers with no deliberateness to their activities and movements. But is it right for Smith to say that since the ancestors did not build or construct they, therefore, did not create, did not act out a cosmogony? Is Smith's bias toward the human as maker (*homo faber*) limiting him in his usage of the verb ''to create'' to acts of building and construction? Cannot ''marking off'' and ''mapping out'' a topography also be a creative activity?

Cannot a cosmogony mean to give order to, to shape, and to define boundaries? Need it solely involve ''building'' and ''construction,'' terms which Smith takes etymological and philosophical pains to restrict in usage?[153] The Genesis account of creation involves bringing order out of chaos, parting the land from the seas, separating the heavens from the earth, and putting the animals in their respective domains. It is widely accepted that the Genesis myth is not *creatio ex nihilo* (creation out of nothing); it is more like ''creation without opposition'' in the subjugation of chaos. Says Jon Levenson, ''the confinement of chaos rather than its elimination is the essence of creation.''

And later, "Creation means making chaos into order. . . ."[154] Eliade echos this when he says:

> These chthonian beings [the Australian (Aranda) ancestors], commonly designated totemic ancestors, began to wander on the surface of the earth and *to modify the land,* giving the Central Australian landscape its actual physical features. Such works constitute properly speaking a cosmogony; the ancestors *did not create the earth, but they gave form to* [emphases added] a preexistent *materia prima.* And the anthropogony repeats the cosmogony.[155]

To "give form to," therefore, is an anthropological manner of creation. And by extension, to give order to is to constitute a center. Says Eliade, "any orientation implies acquiring a fixed point," and "the discovery or projection of a fixed point—the center—*is equivalent to* the creation of the world."[156] In short, to give form to what was once undifferentiated, relative space is a creative activity. The "center" is not just a "complex ideology of building—a matter of temples, palaces, and the like," as Smith claims.[157] Instead it is that location and state of being which grounds a person and a community. It at once orients them in their present habitable world as well as opening them up to the transcendent world of spiritual values, which are the product of divine beings or of the mystical ancestors. In this sense the junction of religion, for Eliade, is anthropological in intent.[158]

The Spatial Critique

Like Smith, Gregory Alles challenges Eliade's claims concerning the universality of the symbol of the center and its cosmological presuppositions. Alles believes that the center, when defined as that which focuses a person's orientation, is inappropriate in certain cases. He cites the Greek Parthenon as a structure whose architecture disperses instead of focuses attention. Alles sums up his critique as follows:

> It has been clear for years that Eliade's peculiar categories—the center, *axis mundi, imago mundi*—are helpful in some contexts (e.g., India) but totally inadequate in others (e.g., Greece). . . . Categories of orientation and cosmic imitation are appropriate when religion cultivates a kind of power that focuses on a hidden, radiating point that generates manifest reality. But when religion concerns a different kind of power—for example, a power that does not orient because it prefers the space of the "Cartesian grid" to masses with their centers, a power that does not seek to generate the cosmos but to govern the ordered interaction of society—to impose the received categories on physical form is misleading, and worse.[159]

The "Cartesian grid" of which Alles speaks derives from the theories of the philosopher-mathematician René Descartes. Descartes held that the physical world is a great machine of fragmented and unrelated parts, and humans experience it this way with each part existing independently from the other.[160] It is the task of analytical geometry to organize these unrelated parts into mathematical and geometrical patterns.[161]

With the physical world intrinsically fragmented there is no self-evident, privileged center of orientation. Any place will do. Place becomes relative. By refering to the Cartesian view of space, Alles says that architecturally and by "intention" the Parthenon has no "privileged point . . . [of] unity"[162]; there is no center. Instead, the monolith itself, not any point within it, constitutes a unity, a unity of "unbridled multiplicity." And instead of intending to attract attention to itself, the architectural "intention" of the Parthenon *disperses* attention *away from* itself. In contrast to the Parthenon is the Hindu temple of Kandariya at Khajuraho. Whereas in the former space has no implicit and explicit organization, in the latter space is meant to order and center. In the former the symbol of the center fails, in the latter it works.

The problem with Alles' critique is that he does not take into consideration Eliade's view that many centers can exist simultaneously. Says Eliade, "we must not envisage this symbolism of the Centre with the geometrical implications that it has to a Western scientific mind."[163] Eliade goes on to say that "all Oriental civilizations" recognized an unlimited number of centers. That Eliade mentions only "Oriental civilizations" need not obstruct us, for Alles' own Cartesian geometry is far removed from the ancient Greek worldview, which accepted an ordered and unified cosmos.[164] Furthermore, the Greek worldview would be closer to the Oriental worldview than to the mechanistic worldview of Newton and Descartes. If the Oriental–Greek parallel is held, then it is possible to tie Eliade's coexistence of many centers to Alles' "Cartesian grid." If the Parthenon fragments space into multiple points of reference and consequently disperses attention, this does not mean the symbol of the center cannot apply. Fragmented and dispersed space merely contains many centers rather than just one, and all these centers together constitute the whole of the Parthenon. And when placed in relation to other monuments in ancient Greece, the Parthenon itself is but one center among many. It both attracts attention and disperses it. The notion of many centers is an example of how mythical space belies geometrical space. For what may be impossible geometrically, is possible in the realm of myths and symbols.

But we need not solely rely on the normative and humanistic disciplines to speak of a coherence between the part and the whole and among wholes. We find modern science itself moving away from Cartesian dualisms. The physicist David Bohm at Birkbeck College, University of London, demonstrates the presence of internal coherences within perceived external incoherences.[165] Recent empirical studies in the nature of chaos find that even chaos can have degrees of both intrinsic and extrinsic order.[166] Alles' critique, therefore, is not very substantive when we posit that what on the surface seems fragmented and unrelated can—as seen through experiment and as constructed by the imagination—be of many centers wholistically conceived. In short, it depends upon the inclination of a person's imagination whether she or he will visualize coherence and unity or incoherence and disunity amongst many centers.

In the end, Smith and Alles focus on very specific interpretations of Eliade's symbolism of the center. Although Eliade emphasizes the locative dimension of the symbol, the center as a symbol is far more flexible than is usually recognized. The center centers and decenters, unifies and disperses, all within a greater unity. The symbol itself has many centers. Hence a morphology of the center coordinates with Eliade's morphology of sacred forms.

The New Humanism as a Pluralistic Vantage Point

As one deepens oneself in the myths and symbols of one's religio-cultural tradition one universalizes one's worldview. As I mentioned, by definition a symbol holds together a multiplicity of meanings; hence a symbol centers. There are many centers within every symbol, and every center, itself a symbol, has the potential to appropriate all other centers. The worship experience of a polytheist shares in the worship experience of a monotheist, and vice versa; there is a structural continuity between the two. The religion of ancient Israel contains such a syncretistic interrelationship between monotheism and polytheism. Otherwise there would have been no need for Israel's fierce polemics against its polytheistic neighbors.[167] The religious experience of a Muslim can center the Muslim within her or his own tradition while sharing in a Christian's, Buddhist's, primitive's, or any other's experience. Naturally, the particular tradition shapes the *value* of the experience, and not all experiences are duplicated. The point is, there is structural continuity between religious experiences across space and time, and it is such structural continuity which allows a religious traditon to communicate with other religious traditions and be compared with them.[168] After deepening himself in the Christian contemplative tradition, the Trappist monk Thomas Merton could plumb the riches of Buddhism and say "yes" to a unity within all opposites.[169] Because of their ability to transcend forms, mystics are often the best ecumenists.[170] It is usually the experiential path to the sacred which more readily universalizes an adherent's experience than the doctrines and rituals given to defining the path. Moreover, not only at the experiential level is a universal centering possible. An adherent of a religion can universalize her or his tradition by tackling shared ethical concerns among peoples of all faiths, such as those involving war, hunger, ecology, disease, etc. The new humanism can occur as much through ethics as it can through the recognition of common archetypes among diverse religio-cultural experiences.

As a Hermeneutical Vantage Point

As a symbolic "place" of orientation, the symbol of the center acts as a vantage point from which to interpret the surrounding world. But by the fact that a symbol limits what it symbolizes, a person's own symbolic vantage point is inescapably "fixed," relative. However one may extend one's experience and imagination, one is still limited to the bodily and historical place one occupies. One remains as one center among many other meaningful centers, as on the periphery of other perspectives and experiences. But if humans are *homo hermeticus,* then one continuously seeks to extend one's center of meaning into other domains of knowledge and experience. The whole hermeneutical enterprise from Schleiermacher to Heidegger, Gadamer, and Ricoeur, attends to clarifying how the imagination is to extend itself and interpret the "texts" of other peoples' world of meaning. As one's universe is enlarged, one is better able to situate oneself in the local and global community. From one's own center of value, then, from one's hermeneutical vantage point, one deepens and enriches one's self knowledge[171] and one's knowledge of other people and of other places. Hence in the continuous reach of the imagination, humans occupy a place and no particular place. Imaginatively, humans transcend their own physical place into other spatial and temporal domains while rooted in a paricular context, place. Whether it is a Native American or a Zen Buddhist who lives within the spatially full present or a Christian who imagines and yearns for a better life ahead, the imagination canvases its universe in an ongoing attempt to orient itself within it.

It is in the nature of Eliade's creative hermeneutics to deprovincialize one's limited yet expansive center. To learn about the Tibetan Buddhist, the Taoist in Taiwan, or the Guajiro in Venezuela, is not to treat them from a distance or imperialistically absorb them into one's own mental universe. Instead one listens to them as an equal, and through creative conversations, integrates their world with one's own. The phenomenological and comparative enterprise and inter-religious dialogue explicitly deal with such cross-cultural exchanges.[172] Aside from its aim to enlarge one's world of meaning, Eliade's creative hermeneutics also serves to set up momentary centers of meaning until new information or better interpretive skills are forthcoming. In the human quest for meaning, there are empty spaces in the historical record and spaces momentarily (and in some cases, perpetually) mysterious or meaningless. Hypotheses and leaps of faith are created to fill in such gaps. Obviously for a Zen practitioner, where the desire for mindlessness and emptiness supersedes any desire for rational explanations or a coherent belief system, meaninglessness and gaps in knowledge are not a problem—the mind and its constructs are the problem. But for those who do resort to a systematic and ongoing discovery for meaning, Eliade's creative hermeneutics is for the human on journey, *homo viator*. One establishes meaning as one proceeds through life.

Following upon the example of the Zen practitioner, the hermeneutical vantage point that we occupy does, however, have its limits. Jonathan Z. Smith says that to change "place," i.e., one's frame of reference, is to change to a new set of orientating symbols.[173] To convert from one frame of reference to another (as in a religious conversion or in a shift of the scholarly imagination), is to shift from a place now one's center to another center once on the periphery. The periphery, then, has a value all its own if one is indeed willing to convert to it and make it one's center. Zen mindlessness may appear meaningless to a rationally dominant person. But to convert to the Zen perspective, the person takes on a new center of value with new orientating symbols, symbols now fed by new images and perceptions. The former perspective—the world as a rational, logical universe—is replaced by one that discounts the primacy of the rational and the logical. Another example is when the secular or the profane—the ostensibly irreligious and meaningless profane—proves to be more just than the supposed religious or sacred center. The church often perpetuates the grossest injustices; mystics can be calloused to human suffering. The center one occupies, therefore, is defined, limited, and potentially reformed by other centers along one's periphery.

While hermeneutics plays a key role in Eliade's vision for the history of religions, it does not occupy such a prominent place for other historians of religion, such as Ugo Bianchi, Jonathan Z. Smith, Ursula King, and Gregory Alles, among others. Indeed, hermeneutics is undergoing a decentering, a shift to the periphery, as a disciplinary orientation in the history of religions. Eliade centered hermeneutics because he saw it as the West's best tool for appropriating Eastern and archaic worlds of meaning. Now that detached scientism and historicism wane and interdependency and interrelatedness between disciplines, the natural sciences, and human sciences wax,[174] hermeneutics need not command the center position it once demanded. Modernity decentralizes, making hermeneutics become one center among others. Nevertheless, the new humanism, as a "total hermeneutics," can be expanded to include the social, economic, and political, as well as the religious, in defining what constitutes the human being. Socio-economic-political expressions may articulate camouflaged "religious" myths. But if we bring these expressions into the center—where they are now peripheral to *homo reli-*

giosus—we can understand humans more completely and concretely ameliorate the world in which humanity lives. Neither sociology, nor politics, culture, economics, science, or religion can remain independent of each other. Together they unite and interrelate with human person as the center of value.[175] We can avoid, then, what the elderly Indian woman, Toona Devi of the Harijan village, said of the Indian Congress Party in recent elections, "They worship the Ganges, but they don't worship the village by the Ganges."[176] The human as *homo religiosus* never ceases being *human*.

As an Ontological Vantage Point

The symbol of the center also constitutes an ontological vantage point. For to be at the center is to encounter being, however defined. Here one fully learns what it means to *be*. It is a "place" of completeness, unity, and totality, than of perfection. To be at the center is comparable to the yogi's ecstasy, the Zen *sartori,* the Christian's mystical union with God, or to an I–Thou intimacy with the material, animal, and human world. Even transhuman experiences found in love and death, perennial themes in Eliade's literature, reveal an ontology. In mystical love and at death one completely integrates the spirit world; all contraries are collapsed. The distinctions between the sexes are erased; the two merge into an androgynous whole. In short, at the center one knows oneself, is known, and knows the nature of reality.

Arriving at the center, in every case, occurs through repeated initiations, whether the ordeals are especially arduous or not. But whatever the initiation, unless a person believes in the *potential* of a center for establishing ontological value and transformation, to speak of the center existentially loses significance. Though the experience of the center has a religious value for Eliade, the content of what is "seen" at the center went undefined. Eliade was especially guarded in describing his own experiences at the center. Each person, subsequently, gives her or his own value to and description of what is found at the center. As for its relevance to the new humanism, the new humanism seeks and is gained through the achievement of such centers of inspiration, intuition, unity, wholeness, and manifold plurality where all contradictions are harmoniously united.

As Changing and Being Changed

So far the center has been designated as a sacred place in opposition to the chaotic periphery of the profane. Jonathan Z. Smith said Eliade prefers the center to the periphery. For Smith the periphery constitutes exile. Smith defines exile as:

to be cut off from the land, from the blessing, from the ancestors, from history, from life, from creation, from reality, from the deity. It is to enter into a new temporal period, palpably different from that which has been before. It is to descend into chaos. . . . [and] to return from exile is to be re-created and reborn.[177]

For the ancient Israelites the destruction of the Temple meant the loss of their center and a plunge into exile. With the Temple destroyed, the people were forced to shift from a locative, cosmological center to a "new, utopian religious situation . . . [of] an anthropological view-point."[178] Here again Smith identifies the center as a locative place of orientation that loses value once that which identifies the center, in this case the Temple, is destroyed or damaged, hence, loses its capacity to give meaning. So as a locative reference of meaning the Temple as a center proved of limited value.

I have already discussed how in Eliade the symbol of the center is not as locative and cosmological as Smith makes it out to be. Eliade, however, does prefer the center to the periphery, as Smith states. Eliade's fascination with the sacred and his own geographical and existential exile from his native Romania contribute to this preference. But we should not easily conclude that Eliade undervalued and ignored the periphery and its chaos. To choose one prominent example, the attention and importance Eliade gives to initiation indicates how humans existentially are always at the periphery. Only through a repeated series of intiations does the human proceed to the center, death being the complete liberation toward the center.

Not only is the periphery not ignored, it is also not purely negative in value. Chaos and crises are stimulants to creativty. Eliade's *A History of Religious Ideas* traces the creative evolutions and revolutions in humanity's religious history as they occurred at periods of intellectual and spiritual disturbance. Moreover, it is mainly in chaos that humans most yearn to transcend themselves and their historical condition. So the playwright Angel D. Pandele (A.D.P.), in Eliade's novella "Nineteen Roses," explains why his play must be difficult, even shocking:

> As you have seen very well, the reader *must* be shocked, startled, made indignant. Only after that can *metanoia* . . . take place—the "overturning," the awakening, the reintegration. I believe you've understood that in this chaos rich in potentialities, certain individuals can achieve self-realization even now, immediately, in the midst of the general decomposition; they are not obliged, like all the others, to wait for a new Creation in order to regain the plenitude. . . .[179]

Similar to the effect of a Zen koan, one's rational, comfortable world can be shocked, jarred into a chaos of sorts, thus awakening the individual to new and profound insights, even *sartori,* "enlightenment." The playwright Pandele recognized this potential for his play when he said the reader must be "shocked," and out of this momentary "chaos" a "self-realization" can occur in certain individuals. Crises are potentially rich for transformation. Chaos (the periphery) is potentially as creative as order (the center).

The line that separates the crisis-laden periphery from the center is not always so clearly defined. The center is no mere place of tranquility. Great turbulence and darkness can exist at the center, as so many mystical experiences readily attest. And whenever the sacred breaks through into historical existence space and time are no longer the same; they are thrown into paradoxical confusion. Similarly, rituals charge space and time with eruptive energy, compounded by the clash of multiple interpretations given to the ritual. The center contains various *coincidentia oppositorium.* Whether through ritual, or myth, or both, the center reveals the potential for the way of evil over the way of good, the way of destruction over the way of creation, and that all interpretations ultimately remain ambiguous. Just as the cosmological center axis joins heaven, earth, and hell, so enthroned rulers or elevated gods are as subject to plunge toward hell and malevolency as to ascend toward heaven and benevolency. Much depends on the will of the ruler or god or on the intepretation given to them. The center is at once a powerful yet fragile place. If we were to set aside the cosmological axis and choose, as Smith prefers us to do, the anthropological plane, we find that the potential for order or chaos equally exists. Should a people forget their myths, their tradition, they would settle into chaos; they rupture their connection to the ways of their fathers and mothers and to the paradigmatic and etiological stories. The potential for order and continuity or for chaos and discontinuity balances gingerly upon the scales of memory. The center, subsequently, implies disjunction as much as it implies conjunction. The fact that we are *compelled* to remember in order that our tradition may survive suggests a disjunction between the past and the present. All historical and spatial dualisms imply disjunction.

The above points suffice to show that every person is "an exile on the road toward Ithaca." The new humanism occurs through the process of changing one's present awareness and mode of being. And this transformation initially occurs nowhere but at the periphery, in exile from the center. Even if we should achieve a center (short of heaven, *Moksha,* nirvana, etc.), we must not be so naive as to think that suffering will cease for us. For it is at the center where the most painful facts of existence are usually most readily confronted.

Notes

1. Sergiu Al-George, "India in the Cultural Destiny of Mircea Eliade," *The Mankind Quarterly* 25,1/2 (1984), 123.

2. Kaufmann, *Discovering the Mind*, p. 54.

3. Martin Heidegger, *Being and Time*, trans. John Macquarrie and Edward Robinson (New York: Harper & Row, 1962), pp. 311ff.

4. Al-George, "India," pp. 123–24.

5. Ibid., p. 121.

6. I am here disagreeing with Sergiu Al-George, Ivan Strenski, and Matei Calinescu, whom Strenski refers to, who set the beginning of authenticity in Eliade's life from Eliade's Indian experiences onward. See Al-George, "India," pp. 115–16; Strenski, *Four Theories*, pp. 85–86.

7. Mircea Eliade, *Autobiography* 1:6–7.

8. Ibid, p. 6.

9. Ricketts, *Romanian Roots*, pp. 62–69, 196ff. This desire to engage the authentic, to reveal the "true," got Eliade into trouble when he wrote his impressions of his conversations with R. P. Ernesto Buonaiuti and Vittorio Macchioro for *Cuvântul*. Eliade was so sincere in his reportage that he wrote up unquotable comments which ended up getting Buonaiuti and Macchioro in trouble with the Italian authorities. Eliade, *Autobiography*, 1:127.

10. The term is similar to W. Dilthey's *Erlebnis* ("experience"). See Ricketts, *Romanian Roots*, p. 105.

11. Ibid., pp. 97, 583–85. Today, Romanian writers describe *Trăirism* as an irrational, pro-fascist philosophical current fathered by Ionescu and fostered by the periodicals *Cuvântul* and *Gandirea*. Ibid., p. 1237 n. 44.

12. Ibid., pp. 96–97.

13. Ibid., pp. 99–100.

14. Eliade, *Autobiography*, 1:133; see also, Ricketts, *Romanian Roots*, pp. 585 et passim.

15. The decision was also made by default, for he had failed at the life of a "saint." Eliade, *Autobiography*, 1:199–200.

16. Virgil Ierunca, "Littérature et fantastique," in *L'Herne: Mircea Eliade*, ed. Constantin Tacou (Paris: Editions de L'Herne, 1978), pp. 322–26; see also Ierunca and Spaltmann in Joseph M. Kitagawa and Charles Long, ed. *Myths and Symbols: Studies in Honor of Mircea Eliade* (Chicago: University of Chicago Press, 1969).

17. Ierunca, "Littérature," p. 324 et passim.

18. Eliade, *Autobiography*, 1:173.

19. This "liberation in history" got its deeper treatment in his 1937, 1954–58 works on yoga. See Ricketts, *Romanian Roots*, pp. 518, 820; Eliade, *Yoga: Immortality and Freedom*, pp. 40–41. Eliade also found in the works of the Christian mystic Meister Eckhart and his disciple Nicholas of Cusa this presence of miracle in the ordinary affairs of life. Through the freedom and self-limitation of the sacred, the sacred enters

and charges history. The sacred is at the same time absolutely free and self-limiting; it is the paradox of Nicholas of Cusa's *coincidentia oppositorium*.

20. Mircea Eliade, *No Souvenirs: Journal, 1957–1969,* trans. Fred H. Johnson (San Francisco: Harper & Row, 1977), p. 8.

21. See ritual as a form of authentication in Eliade, *Cosmos and History,* pp. 21f.

22. Ricketts, *Romanian Roots,* p. 983.

23. Ricketts, *Romanian Roots,* p. 210; Eliade, "With the Gypsy Girls," in *Tales of the Sacred and the Supernatural,* pp. 63–108.

24. Ricketts, *Romanian Roots,* p. 1055; Eliade, *Autobiography,* 1:316ff; idem, *Mademoiselle Christina* (Paris: L'Herne, 1978).

25. Ricketts, *Romanian Roots,* pp. 1097ff.; and Eliade, *Autobiography,* 2:85.

26. Eliade refers to a distinction between purely party politics, a politics without the spiritual, concerned with materialistic gains, and guided by the masses, and a spiritual politics in which the intellectuals provide the guiding moral and spiritual principles for the masses. See Ricketts, *Romanian Roots,* p. 889.

27. When I say they were not responsible, I mean here a lack of accountability to their stated aims of liberating Romania from corrupt leaders. The Legionary, under Horia Sima in 1938 and later in 1940, when they gained governmental standing under Ion Antonescu, became as tyrannical as the government of King Carol II during the years 1938–1939. But the Legionary oath of personal sacrifice did command a sense of reponsibility among the Legionary, at least in the earlier years of 1936–1937. For whenever they carried out a violent act, as in the assassination of Miahil Stelescu, a former commandant of their group, they turned themselves in to pay for the consequences of their acts. Eliade was impressed at the time with this willingness to accept responsibility. He compared it to a Christian asceticism. See Ricketts, *Romanian Roots,* pp. 919–20, 924.

28. Ibid., pp. 1027–29.

29. Heidegger, *Being and Time,* pp. 317–23.

30. Richard Schmitt, *Martin Heidegger on Being Human* (New York: Random House, 1969), p. 250.

31. Culianu says the nontemporality of Eliade's authentic self enables one's limited condition to be universalized. This extension beyond imposed limits constitutes the distinction between "miracle" and "facts," "miracle" (the divine) being that which reveals itself in *contact* with (not, in *contrast* to) "facts," with humanity. See Culianu, *Mircea Eliade,* pp. 42–43.

32. Heidegger, *Being and Time,* p. 320.

33. Schmitt, *Martin Heidegger,* p. 250.

34. Ibid. Schmitt would disagree with Richard Rorty who resists drawing tangents between a person's scholarship and any moral breaches that he or she might have committed. See Rorty's "Taking Philosophy Seriously," review of *Heidegger et le Nazisme* by Victor Farrias, in *The New Republic* (April 11, 1988), 31–34.

35. Ricketts, *Romanian Roots,* p. 908.

36. In correspondence in 1933 with the Legionary Mihai Polihroniade, Eliade voices his displeasure at the expulsion of Moses Gaster and Lazar Saineanu, two

Jewish intellectuals. Eliade also was critical of his mentor's—Nae Ionescu—anti-Semitism and religious views of the Orthodox Church and of the Jews. Eliade is commended by the Jew Ion Calugaru for Eliade's "love for oppressed races." And Eliade is never found saying in print any anti-Semitic propoganda. See Ricketts, *Romanian Roots,* pp. 908–9.

Even the Romanian Radu Ioanid in his *The Sword of the Archangel: Fascist Ideology in Romania,* who ties Eliade to the Legionary and to fascism (pp. 11, 80), does not show any conclusive evidence attesting to anti-Semitism in Eliade. Ioanid quotes a 1934 article of Eliade's in which Eliade challenges the presence of too many minorities in positions of command. But even this quote is inconclusive in evidencing anti-Semitism and even seems to say the opposite: "We are going to relieve them [minorities in governmental positions] by competition, by our forces, by administrative laws if necessary. . . . [The Jews] may consider themselves persecuted, because that helps them to survive. . . . *We don't need intransigence and intolerance,* which are *vices foreign to our structure* [emphasis mine]." See Ioanid, *The Sword of the Archangel,* trans. Peter Heinegg (New York: East European Monographs, Boulder, Co. Distributed by Columbia University Press, 1990) p. 125.

37. Ibid., p. 82.

38. On the characteristics of Romanian facism, its mysticism, and anti-intellectualism See Ibid., pp. 20–23, 81, 139ff. Eliade did not react against Dostoevski, André Gide, Eugene Ionesco, Malraux, Brancusi, among others, who were regarded by fascists as being democratic and humanistic, hence enemies of the state. Ibid., p. 107.

39. Ricketts, *Romanian Roots,* p. 548.

40. Ibid.

41. Clifford Geertz, *The Interpretation of Cultures* (New York: Basic Books, 1973), pp. 98, 106.

42. Eliade was detained for his associations with Nae Ionescu and the Iron Guard and for failing to sign a statement that would discredit the Legionary, many of whom were his friends. Though not a Legionary himself and not favoring the political ambitions of the Legionary, Eliade nevertheless could not betray those suffering for causes he himself believed in—Romanianism and spiritual values. Eliade's detention was not severe, but that he was detained demonstrated his alienation from the Romania then shaping up. He knew he was a persona non grata. See Ricketts, *Romanian Roots,* p. 1401 n. 150 on Eliade not being a Legionary. On Eliade's detention and unwillingness to sign see, Ricketts, *Romanian Roots,* pp. 1078ff., and Eliade, *Autobiography,* 2:62–76.

It is curious that in Radu Ioanid's roster of people who were advocates or members of the Legionary, see *The Sword of the Archangel,* pp. 288–93, he does not list Eliade.

43. Eliade, *Journal IV: 1979–1985.* Read the epilogue by Wendy Doniger O'Flaherty on the significance that writing and books held for Eliade.

44. See his chapter 4 in *The Myth of the Eternal Return,* pp. 139–162.

45. Strenski, *Four Theories,* pp. 197, 198.

46. Honko, *Science of Religion,* pp. xxi–xxiii.

47. Ricketts, *Romanian Roots,* pp. 58–59.

48. Ibid., p. 59.

49. Charles Long, "Freedom, Otherness, and Religion: Theologies Opaque," in *Significations,* pp. 185–99, 194.

50. Ninian Smart, "Beyond Eliade: The Future of Theory in Religion," *Numen* 25 (1978), 183.

51. Even though in Buddhism suffering constitutes the essential condition of humanity and of the entire universe, it is still possible to speak of *willing suffering* as part of the transformative process toward authenticity. By willing to face her or his own personal contribution toward the universal state of suffering, the Buddhist heightens her or his awareness of suffering and, in doing so, becomes prey to the trauma of seeing how tragic is his or her condition and how culpable are his or her thoughts and actions toward the increase of suffering. But by undergoing this pain, the Buddhist eventually will break through to a state of actually diminishing the amount of personal and universal suffering, since the person is now more aware of how he or she contributes toward it. It is this willingness to undertake this epistemological, ontological, and soteriological process of transformation, however risky and painful, that I mean by the Buddhist "willing suffering."

52. John Caputo speaks of a "radical hermeneutics" that operates in meaninglessness and suffering yet without seeking to resolve them. Radical hermeneutics is not for finding meaning but for helping us grope our way through meaninglessness. John D. Caputo, *Radical Hermeneutics* (Bloomington, IN: Indiana University Press, 1987), pp. 271ff.

53. Eliade, *Autobiography,* 1:261.

54. Heidegger, *Being and Time,* p. 313.

55. One such example was in his writing of his epic novel, *The Forbidden Forest.* Struggling with the character Ileana, Eliade was awakened to her symbolic significance as the Angel of Death. This meaning was there all along, but only in time and in the process of narration did her meaning emerge for Eliade's discovery. See Mac Linscott Ricketts, "Mircea Eliade and the Writing of *Noaptea de Sânziene,*" *Journal of American Romanian Christian Literary Studies* 1 (Spring 1980), 45–56.

56. Eliade, *Occultism, Witchcraft, and Cultural Fashions,* pp.45–46.

57. Eliade, *The Sacred and the Profane,* pp. 32–33.

58. In the process thought of Whitehead every entity is in the process of change and experience. "God-relatedness is constitutive of every occasion of experience"; and "It is God who, by confronting the world with unrealized opportunities, opens up a space for freedom and self-creativity," say John Cobb and David Griffin in *Process Theology* (Philadelphia: Westminster Press, 1976), p. 29.

59. Eliade, *Youth Without Youth,* pp. 139–40. For a history of religions approach to Eliades' belief in the human race, see "Religious Symbolism and the Modern Man's Anxiety" Eliade, *Myths, Dreams, and Mysteries,* chapter 9.

60. Marjorie Greene, "Martin Heidegger," *The Encyclopedia of Philosophy* (New York: Macmillan Publishing, 1967), 3:460–61.

61. Smith, *Map Is Not Territory,* pp. 91–92.

62. Ibid., p. 94.

63. Jack B. Rogers and Forrest Baird, ed. *Introduction to Philosophy* (San Francisco: Harper & Row, 1981), pp. 109–13.

64. Kant, *The Philosophy of Kant,* p. 389.

65. Charles Hartshorne, "God and the Meaning of Life," in *On Nature,* ed. Leroy S. Rouner (Notre Dame, IN: Notre Dame University Press, 1984), p. 157.

66. Eliade, *Patterns in Comparative Religion,* p. 13.

67. Adolf E. Jensen, *Myth and Cult Among Primitive Peoples,* trans.Marianna Tax Choldin and Wolfgang Weissleder (Chicago: University of Chicago Press, 1951), p. 206.

68. See Raffaele Pettazzoni on the "Confession of Sins: An Attempted General Interpretation," in his *Essays on the History of Religions,* trans. H. J. Rose (Leiden: E. J. Brill, 1954).

69. I recognize the lack of the concept "individual" among primitives. In effect, to the primitive mind people are most free when they lose their "self" in imitating the archetypes. Here, though, I am supposing that a primitive person is acting not under duress but is exercising personal volition.

70. Walter Kaufmann says Kant's contribution to the development of the human mind has been a disaster. It was in Goethe that the mind received its greatest exemplar. Goethe in his own life incarnated the manifold and developmental potential of the mind. Again, it was through his creative productions that Goethe exemplified freedom more convincingly than Kant attempted to do in theory. Kaufmann, *Discovering the Mind,* pp. 42–56.

71. Eliade, *Yoga,* p. 364.

72. Hall and Ames, *Thinking Through Confucius,* pp. 17–18.

73. Ricketts, *Romanian Roots,* pp. 572–75.

74. Sullivan, *Icanchu's Drum,* p. 545.

75. Ricketts, *Romanian Roots,* p. 977.

76. Eliade, *Autobiography,* 1:224.

77. In 1936 Eliade had given up on Romanian democracy for its limp nationalism and structured mediocrity to choose instead dictatorship, with a model in the fascism of Mussolini, as the best route for Romanian nationalism and intellectual creativity. See Ricketts, *Romanian Roots,* pp. 902–3. Eliade was deluded by the exhuberant, charismatic, and one can say, sexual, vitality of a dictatorship. He failed to see, however—only later would he realize—that such vitality is, in reality, loveless, cold, and, hence, unconcerned with human expression. An interesting way of looking at this is found in Ioan P. Couliano's *Eros and Magic in the Renaissance,* in which he speaks of the great "manipulator" as the one who knows no love yet is able to command it from those he manipulates. Couliano goes on to speak of the "police state" versus the "magic-state" as two forms of the manipulator. The former destroys vitality and is structurally inflexible, and the latter has an excess of vitality and is most flexible. The "police state" manipulates through state ideology, and the "magician state," as well. But less by state ideology, the character of the nation's will in a "magician-state" is principally manipulated by modern advertising. See *Eros and Magic in the Renaissance,* trans. Margaret Cook (Chicago: University of Chicago Press), pp. xviii, 99–106.

78. Eliade, *Journal IV: 1979–1985,* p. 70.

79. On Heidegger's view of freedom at death see Merold Westphal, *God, Guilt, and Death* (Bloomington, IN: Indiana University Press, 1984), pp. 97–98, 99–100.

80. Rudy Rucker, *The Fourth Dimension: A Guided Tour of Higher Universes* (Boston: Houghton Mifflin, 1984), p. 193.

81. This argument is an implemetation of Einstein's theory of relativity: since there is no absolute space or time, one perspective in time and space is relative to another perspective in time and space. So the retrieved structures appear to change and, in fact, do change as our personal and cultural contexts change. Rucker, *The Fourth Dimension,* p. 150. See also Stephen Hawking, *A Brief History of Time* (New York: Bantam Books, 1988), pp. 21–22.

82. Eliade, *The Quest,* pp. 61–62. Compare this position with Bergson's philosophy of continuous novelty, paralleling Whitehead's process philosophy, in Henri Bergson, *The Creative Mind,* trans. Mabelle L. Andison (New York: The Philosophical Library, 1946), pp. 19–21. In contrast to Eliade, Bergson would say that the discoveries were *not there* beforehand. But matter's and humans' continual flux are always bringing in something totally new that never existed, or had been conceived of, before.

83. In Hindu cosmology it is to be free from samsara, endless reliving, and in Buddhism, from samsara as well and from the idea that there is any "self" at all.

84. There is, of course, the notion that God forgets human sin, casting it into the depths of the ocean.

85. Eliade never did articulate his ontology. See his *Ordeal by Labyrinth,* p. 189. In Romania it assumed a sacramental Orthodox lean. And though Eliade never departed from his Orthodoxy, as Joseph Kitagawa said in conversation with me, it would be misleading to confine it to that tradition. In fact, Eliade partook of a philosophical-phenomenological sensibility to all aesthetic and religious creations. I find the best description of Eliade's ontological orientation in James Fowler's final stage 6 of a "Universalizing Faith." See *Stages of Faith* (San Francisco: Harper & Row, 1981), pp. 200–201.

86. Eliade, *Quest,* p. 69.

87. Ibid., p. 115.

88. Ibid., p. 67.

89. Cioran, "Beginnings of a Friendship," pp. 413–14.

90. Eliade and Kitagawa, ed., *The History of Religions,* p. 109.

91. E. B. Tylor, *The Origins of Culture* (New York: Harper and Brothers, 1958), p. 1; see also pp. 26ff.

92. Bronislaw Malinowski, *A Scientific Theory of Culture And Other Essays* (Chapel Hill, NC: The University of North Carolina Press, 1944), pp. 36–40. Malinowski saw culture in three ways: 1) as a tribal microcosm, a functioning whole, 2) in the functioning of its customs, institutions, and beliefs which formed part of each culture, and 3) as a social heritage. See Audrey Richards, "The Concept of Culture in Malinowski's Work," in *Man and Culture,* ed. Raymond Firth (London: Routledge and Kegan Paul, 1957), p. 16.

93. Clifford Geertz, *The Interpretation of Cultures* (New York: Basic Books, 1973), p. 89. Derived from his "culture" definition, Geertz's definition of religion is also widely used. "[Religion is] a system of symbols which acts to establish power-ful, pervasive, and long-lasting moods and motivations in men by formulating concep-tions of a general order of existence and clothing these conceptions with such an aura of factuality that the moods and motivations seem uniquely realistic." See p. 90.

94. There are those in anthropology and the history of religions who see a greater cultural role for their disciplines. Among anthropologists George Marcus and Michael Fischer forsee anthropology affecting "administrative policy" and "social reform," alerting "the public to problems of society's victims and disadvantaged," and cri-tiquing Western epistemological assumptions. See *Anthropology as Cultural Critique* (Chicago: University of Chicago Press, 1986), pp. 113, 135, 137. Historians of reli-gion such as Bruce Lincoln, Lawrence Sullivan, Charles Long, Ioan Culianu, Wendy Doniger O'Flaherty, to name a few, see the history of religions encouraging general cultural reflection.

95. Strenski, *Four Theories,* pp. 211 et passim; also pp. 192–94.

96. Ricketts, *Romanian Roots,* p. 125. Eliade rejected the "traditionalists" Réne Guenon and Jules Evola (with whom Strenski associates Ionescu, Blaga, and Eliade) for their overly negative view of modern culture. Ricketts pp. 849–50; Strenski, *Four Theories,* pp. 92–97, 125.

97. Strenski, *Four Theories,* pp. 126ff.

98. Richard Niebuhr, *Christ and Culture* (New York: Harper & Row, 1951), pp. 33–38. Niebuhr relies on Malinowski's interpretation of culture. As a result, culture is defined by its functional purposes and so would not possess the spiritual impulse that Eliade places in culture.

99. Eliade, *Occultism, Witchcraft, and Cultural Fashions.*

100. *The Republic of Plato,* trans. Francis MacDonald Cornford (New York: Ox-ford University Press, 1965), pp. 178–79.

101. Ricketts, *Romanian Roots,* p. 897.

102. In his writings between 1934 and 1935 Eliade rejected fascism and commu-nism because both were foreign importations to Romania and did not practice the Romanian trait of *omenie,* "humanness." Moreover, they persecuted minorities and had a disregard for the sacred in their burning down of churches and destruction of religious iconography. Ricketts notes that though Eliade repeatedly rejected fascism and Hitlerism, journalists nevertheless insisted he was fascist because he strongly condemned communism. Ricketts, *Romanian Roots,* pp. 895–97.

103. Gerhard E. Lenski, *Power and Privilege* (Chapel Hill, NC: The University of North Carolina Press, 1984), pp. 51–56.

104. The term "new man" was used by revolutionists of both the right and the left, Iron Guardists and communists. See Ricketts, *Romanian Roots,* pp. 599–601.

105. From an English translation provided for me by Mac Linscott Ricketts of his article "Criterion" in *Die Mitte der Welt,* ed. Hans Peter Duerr (Frankfurt: Suhrkamp, 1984), p. 197.

106. Mircea Eliade, *Autobiography,* 1:234.

107. At one point, in 1932, after Criterion gave symposiums on Lenin and Jews, the Union of National Romanian Christian Students (UNSCR) accused Criterion of cultivating values alien to the nation of Romania. Criterion responded by providing an official statement in which it defined itself as "an association of intellectuals grouped on an exclusively cultural terrain, without a political character. . . ." Duerr, *Die Mitte,* p. 204. But after government clamp-downs on right-wing leaders and newspapers, including *Cuvântul,* during 1933/34, Criterion began to break apart, in large part because of political differences among its members. The "primacy of the spiritual" did not, apparently, override politics altogether. Ibid., pp. 212–14.

108. Ricketts, *Romanian Roots,* pp. 620–22.

109. Claude Lévi-Strauss, *Tristes Tropiques,* trans. John and Doreen Weightman (London: Jonathan Cape 1973), pp. 37–38.

110. See Eliade's treatment of peasant religiosity in Eliade, *Zalmoxis, The Vanishing God,* trans. Willard R. Trask (Chicago: University of Chicago Press, 1972), pp. 253ff.; and in Stefan's admiration for the peasants obliviousness to history in Eliade's *The Forbidden Forest,* pp. 242–43.

111. Hauser, *The Sociology of Art,* p. 559.

112. Nicholas Wolterstorff, "Art, Religion, and the Elite: Reflections on a Passage from André Malraux," in *Art, Creativity and the Sacred* (New York: Crossroad, 1985), pp. 262–73.

113. See Eliade on Brancusi and Chagall in Eliade, *Symbolism, the Sacred and the Arts,* pp. 90ff, 99ff.

114. Bruce Lincoln, *Myth, Cosmos, and Society* (Cambridge, MA: Harvard University Press, 1986), p. 170.

115. Lincoln, *Discourse and the Construction of Society,* p. 25.

116. T. B. Bottomore, *Classes in Modern Society* (New York: Vantage Books, 1966), pp. 82ff.

117. See Michel de Certeau's comments on how culture that is passed down by the elites ends up being manipulated by the populace for their own consumption and use. Certeau, *The Practice of the Everyday,* pp. 31–32.

118. Carol P. Christ, "Mircea Eliade and the Feminist Paradigm Shift: Toward a Feminist Critical Approach to the History of Religion." A paper presented at the Annual American Academy of Religion Conference. Chicago, Illinois, 1988.

119. Valerie Saiving, "Androcentrism in Religious Studies," *Journal of Religion* 56 (1976), 184ff.

120. The writings of Reinhold Niebuhr, *Moral Man and Immoral Society* (New York: Charles Scribner's Sons, 1960); and idem, *The Nature and Destiny of Man,* vols. 1-2 (New York: Charles Scribner's Sons, 1964), highlight the naivete of seeking to achieve justice in society only through the enlightenment of people.

121. Eliade, *No Souvenirs,* p. 84.

122. Charles Long, *Criterion: Newsletter of the University of Chicago* (Fall 1986).

123. Kitagawa, *The History of Religions: Understanding Human Experience,* pp. 161f.

124. Ioan Culianu, "Mircea Eliade at the Crossroad of Anthropology," *Neue Zeitschrift für Systematische Theologie* 27,2 (1985), 128. I will look at Jonathon Z. Smith more closely later, but Smith says that this symbol is not necessarily universal. See Jonathan Z. Smith, *To Take Place* (Chicago: University of Chicago Press, 1987), p. 17.

125. Mircea Eliade and Lawrence Sullivan, "The Centre of the World," *The Encyclopedia of Religion*, 3:166.

126. Ibid., 3:171.

127. It was in his 1936 article, "Cosmical Homology and Yoga," that Eliade elaborated on the concept. He associated the yogi's focused, centered breathing with a cosmic axis. The notion of "axis" was first developed by Paul Mus in *Barabudur*, on the Buddhist temple in Indonesia. Eliade got the notion of "axis" from Mus. See Ricketts, *Romanian Roots*, p. 822.

128. Mircea Eliade, "Twelve Thousand Head of Cattle," in Eliade and Mihai Niculescu, *Fantastic Tales*, ed. and trans. Eric Tappe (London: Dillons, 1969).

129. Mircea Eliade, *Two Strange Tales* (Boston: Shambhala Press, 1986).

130. Gregory Alles, "Surface, Space, and Intention: The Parthenon and the Kandariya Mahadeva," *History of Religions*, 28, 1 (August 1988), 1–37.

131. The difference between Eliade and Smith is more than a difference of interpretation, but one of a pre- and post-Kantian view of reality, respectively.

132. To stick with Babylonian examples is not without reason, for, as I will note, Smith questions Eliade's comparative enterprise of the symbol of the center on a purportedly faulty analysis of cosmic mountains in the ancient Near East by the Pan-Babylonian school. See Smith, *To Take Place*, p. 122, n. 3.

133. For the places where Eliade refers to it see Smith, *To Take Place*, p. 122 n. 1, 2.

134. For Smith's reading and digression from Eliade's reading of the myth see Smith, *To Take Place*, pp. 6ff, 125 n. 19.

135. Ibid., pp. 4–5, 124 nn. 11, 15. After referring to Eliade's discovery of the pattern of the center among the "Oriental civilizations of Mesopotamia, India, China, etc.," among shamans, and among "tertiary, nomadic, hunting, and pastoral cultures of the Americas, northern and central Asia, and Africa," Smith says, p. 14, "But in both his earliest and latest discussions of the topic, the Tjilpa and their pole remain the *sole* example for the presence of the pattern of the "Center" among *truly* [emphasis mine on truly] 'primitive' peoples." One wonders who is "truly" primitive for Smith. Smith speaks of "pious fraud" among the Tjilpa when he suggests that a creator God designation is given to the Tjilpa's generic name for God, Numbakulla. Yet even with this pious intrusion, the Tjilpa remain for Smith "truly" primitive. It seems he is speaking out of both sides of his mouth. On the one hand the Tjilpa are true primitives, but on the other they are tainted. How are the Tjilpa, then, that different from the other primal cultures that Eliade refers to to show evidence of the symbol of the center? Smith limits the possibility of the universality of the symbol by limiting the ethnological pool to the Tjilpa.

136. Ibid., pp. 22–23; see also Smith, *Map Is Not Territory*, p. 92 n. 23.

137. Smith, *To Take Place*, p. 17.

138. It is curious that while Smith says in his *Map Is Not Territory*, p. 98, "Has not the illuminating category of the 'center' been too narrowly discussed in literalistic terms of geographical symbolism?," he does little, in his own argument, to correct this imbalance.

139. Mircea Eliade, "Centre du Monde, Temple, Maison," *Le Symbolisme Cosmique des Monuments Religieux*, ed. Giuseppe Tucci (Serie Orientale Roma, 14, Roma: Is. M.E.O., 1957), p. 61.

140. Eliade, *Images and Symbols*, p. 54.

141. Eliade, *Quest*, p. 84.

142. Eliade, *Patterns*, p. 13.

143. Carlos Castaneda, *The Teachings of Don Juan: A Yaqui Way of Knowledge* (New York: Simon & Schuster, 1968), pp. 32–39.

144. T. G. H. Strehlow, *Aranda Traditions* (Melbourne: Melbourne University Press, 1947), p. 32.

145. Ibid., p. 32. Moreover, this attachment to "home" does not come by simply taking place, as if it is something the Aranda make happen. The aborigines do not "own" the land. It is more that the land "owns them." See the cultural geographer David Sopher's essay "The Landscape of Home: Myth, Experience, Social Meaning" in *The Interpretation of Ordinary Landscapes*. D. W. Meinig, ed. (NY: Oxford University Press, 1979), p. 132.

146. W. E. H. Stanner, "The Dreaming," in Lessa and Vogt, ed., in *Reader in Comparative Religion*, 2d. ed., pp. 162, 165.

147. R. J. Clifford, *The Cosmic Mountain in Canaan and the Old Testament* (Cambridge, MA: Harvard Semitic Monographs, 4. 1972), p. 2.

148. Cited in Smith, *To Take Place*, p. 16.

149. Jon D. Levenson, *Sinai and Zion* (San Francisco: Harper & Row, 1985), pp. 111f., 114–15.

150. Levenson refers to four characteristics of the cosmic mountain that Clifford delineates: it is 1) "the meeting place of the gods," 2) "the battleground of conflicting natural forces," 3) the "meeting place of heaven and earth," and 4) "the place where effective decrees are issued." Ibid., p. 111.

151. Says Levenson, p. 114, "Even if Eliade is in error on some of his examples and even if he has overstated the degree of parallelism in general, it is still dangerous to ignore the evidence that he adduces, in a discussion of the cosmic mountain as a theological concept in ancient Israel."

152. Smith, *To Take Place*, pp. 15, 17, 18.

153. Smith, *To Take Place*, pp. 21–22.

154. Levenson, *Creation and the Persistence of Evil*, pp. 7–8, 17, 22, and his chapter "Creation Without Opposition: Psalm 104."

155. Eliade, *The Quest*, pp. 84–85.

156. Eliade, *Occultism*, p. 22, with emphasis mine.

157. Smith, *To Take Place*, p. 15.

158. Smith restricts Eliade's view of religion to the transcendent, divine, vertical plane. He ignores the anthropological, horizontal element. See Smith, *To Take Place,* pp. 2, 122 n. 2.

But note the function of religion for Eliade, to which Smith refers but does not quote. ". . . the principal function of religion, [is] that of maintaining an 'opening' toward a world which is superhuman, the world of axiomatic spiritual values. These values are 'transcendent' in the sense that they are considered revealed by divine beings *or* mythical ancestors. They therefore constitute absolute values, paradigms for all human activity. The function of religion is to awaken and sustain the consciousness of another world, of a 'beyond,' *whether* it be the divine world *or the world of mythical ancestors.* This other world represents a superhuman 'transcendent' plane, that of absolute realities [emphasis mine]." Mircea Eliade, "Structures and Changes in the History of Religion," in *City Invincible,* Carl H. Kraeling and Robert M. Adams, eds. (Chicago: University of Chicago Press, 1960), p. 366. Also see my reference to Brian K. Smith's definition of religion.

159. Alles, "Surface, Space, and Intention," p. 36.

160. René Descartes, *Essential Works of Descartes,* trans. Lowell Bair (New York: Bantam Books, 1961), pp. 89–107.

161. Gary Zukav, *The Dancing Wu Li Masters: An Overview of the New Physics* (New York: William Morrow, 1979), pp. 48, 50, 148, 322–26.

162. Alles, "Surface, Space, and Intention," p. 22.

163. Eliade, *Images and Symbols,* p. 39.

164. Stephen Toulmin, *The Return to Cosmology* (Los Angeles: University of California Press, 1982), pp. 224, 238.

165. Zukav, pp. 323–26.

166. Modern researches into chaos are finding more order in nature than was previously supposed. There may be randomness, but there is regularity in randomness. See James Gleick's *Chaos: Making a New Science* (New York: Viking-Penguin Books, 1987). Even if we accept a chaos that is purely random, we could refer to coherence as the coexistence of chaos and order, a *coincidentia oppositorium.*

167. "The proof of the idea that 'pagan' religion struck a responsive chord in Israelite consciousness is the fact that the prophets continually polemicized against a syncretism of the two," says Jon Levenson. And continuing, "Syncretisms do not form between things that have nothing in common. The prophetic assertions that YHWH and Baal are totally different must not be taken at face value. They must be seen within the rhetorical intents of interreligious polemic." Levenson *Sinai and Zion,* pp. 109–111.

168. See Jonathan Z. Smith's keen defense on needing to get rid of the "imposition of the extra-historical categories of uniqueness." To claim that an experience or a phenomenon is wholly unique or "wholly other"—such as a conception of the divine or the sacred—prevents it from being compared with any other experience or phenomenon regarded as different. For in being so unique, it disallows the setting up of any correspondences, in which case it remains unknowable to the investigating mind.

Smith obviously refers to the problem as it exists for the academe or for when it takes place on the anthropological plane, since mystics or anyone who holds to the reality of the divine and any primordium would say that indeed there are realities beyond human inquiry, beyond the human capacity to "know" them. Nevertheless, Smith wants to avoid theological and intellectual apologetics, and the setting up of any "wholly others" does nothing but delimit an apologetic, an over-and-against stance. Jonathan Z. Smith, *Drudgery Divine: On the Comparison of Early Christianities and the Religions of Late Antiquity* (Chicago: University of Chicago Press, 1990), pp. 36ff., 42–43.

169. Thomas Merton, *Conjectures of a Guilty Bystander* (Garden City, NY: Doubleday & Co., 1966), p. 128.

170. Evelyn Underhill defines the goal of the mystic as a "closer reading of Truth; to an apprehension of the divine unifying principle behind appearance." *The Essentials of Mysticism* (New York: E.P. Dutton, 1920), p. 7.

171. It is germane to Eliade's hermeneutics that it leads to a discovery of the self ("la réalisation de soi"), according to Adrian Marino. Marino, *L'Hermeneutique de Mircea Eliade,* p. 279.

172. One of the first principles in interfaith dialogue is to recognize one's own position as one center among many. Leonard Swidler states that there should be three goals in interfaith and "interideological" dialogue: 1) "to know oneself ever more profoundly," 2) "to know the other ever more authentically," 3) "to live ever more fully accordingly." See Leonard Swidler, ed. *Toward a Universal Theology of Religion* (Maryknoll, NY: Orbis Books, 1987), pp. 14–16, 26.

173. Smith, *Map Is Not Territory,* p. 143.

174. Stephen Toulmin says that scientists are now forced to integrate the world of nature and the world of humanity. They are having to think morally. No longer is there a "pure" science. For to be in the world of nature, Toulmin concludes, "means making sense of the relations that human beings and other living things have toward the overall patterns of nature in ways that give us some sense of their proper relations to one another, to ourselves, and to the whole." See Toulmin, *The Return to Cosmology,* pp. 257, 272.

175. Charles Long speaks of positioning the human person at the center of religious studies. *Significations,* p. 74. Eliade would speak of placing humanistic concerns not just at the center of religious studies but at the center of the natural sciences as well.

176. "Indians Resume Voting in Disillusioned Mood," *The Christian Science Monitor* (June 12, 1991), 2.

177. Smith, *Map Is Not Territory,* p. 120.

178. Ibid., p. 128.

179. Eliade, *Youth Without Youth,* pp. 221–22.

6

The Challenges of the New Humanism

Now that I have eluciated several goals found in the new humanism, it is necessary to address the challenges a person must undergo in order to realize these goals. Eliade constantly referred to various challenges or ordeals which individuals and cultures must face as they progress toward their respective destinies. Both humans and culture are in a constant process of becoming. Through continued creativity and an endless series of initiations, their development expands to include broader universes of meaning, thus lessening individual and cultural alienation, fragmentation, and meaninglessness. This being opened to, and founded upon, greater panoramas of meaning is what Eliade meant by "transcendence." Transcendence does not mean being dissociated from history. For it is possible to speak of transcendence as intrinsically connected to the social and political dimensions, as found in Chinese thought.[1] Rather, for Eliade, transcendence pertains to cosmic structures of meaning which exist independent from changing, irreversible history, by essence but not by fact; these structures of meaning can only be known *in* history. It is through inevitable and self-imposed challenges, then, that humans and culture uncover these structures of meaning. Life is lived within the boundary between immanence and transcendence, death and life, ignorance and knowledge, sterility and creativity, analysis and synthesis, the particular and the universal, the isolated and the whole. The challenges humans face throughout life force one to stress one side against the other. We can stress life over death, transcendence to immanence, the universal to the particular, meaning over meaninglessness, or vice versa. Yet the dialectic remains. For similar to the Chinese yin/yang interconnection, within each pole exists the active presence of the other: in death we can find life, and in every choice of life there is the death of something else.

Like the goals of the new humanism, the challenges in the new humanism are themselves archetypes. They exist throughout Eliade's oeuvre in numerous

169

variations. And along with the other archetypes, they contribute to the morphology of the new humanism. I isolate three archetypes in this section: the challenge that humans be creative; the challenge that humans be initiated, and the challenge that the new humanism proceed scientifically. By creative we find that the new humanism is a meaning-giving hermeneutics and aesthetics which follows a recurring pattern: from sacrifice comes new life. In that humans must be initiated, the new humanism involves an ongoing series of ordeals and transformations that open one to a larger but still limited number of universes and communities of meaning. In the sense that it proceed scientifically, the new humanism incorporates both the natural and human sciences for establishing a human–cosmos homology.

Humans as Creative

Existence must coincide with [the act of] creation. "To be" must mean a continuous creation, an uninterrupted process of self-transcending, an enrichment of universal life with new and living forms, with new and fertile gestures. We are insofar as our life is an organism, . . . survival means to be continually creating yourself [Eliade, *Oceanografie*, 1933].[2]

"To Create" as Consubstantial with the Human Experience

I have already spoken in part on creativity. Here, though, I want to focus more on the dynamics involved in the creative process. For Eliade, to encourage the coming to a new humanism historians of religion and individuals must create.[3] According to Eliade, they must create "syntheses" of culture and "personality." In other words, they must produce oeuvres and make of their life an oeuvre. To create "syntheses" or oeuvres means accumulating a plurality of existential experiences and integrating them into a meaning-giving whole.[4] Out of such a structural synthesis one can be endlessly creative; one simply elaborates upon these structures into numerous and various contexts.

Synthesis is a natural element of creativity, since for Eliade every creation recounts the primordial creation of the cosmos, a time of totality, wholeness, and completeness. Creation of any kind, therefore, recovers this primordial totality. Creation not only distinguishes humans from the animals; it also patterns our life and labors after the divine creative activity. Thus all creative acts are valorized. They are put within a larger sphere of meaning and they share in the fecund power of the cosmos itself. To create, then, as an archetype within the morphology of the new humanism, is to invest human activity with meaning and with an ongoing inspiration to perpetuate new life.

The creative ambitions of alchemy, a long fascination with Eliade, is a good example for demonstrating how creativity is capable of modifying the human and world condition. Alchemists believed that humans constitute part of the sacred *materia prima*. If the alchemists could discover the secret—the "philosopher's stone"—to the world's own creative process, they could turn base *materia prima* into its perfected form, gold, a spiritual symbol for immortality. By this procedure of transmutation, and on the assumption that humans are consubstantial with *materia prima,* humans could themselves become "perfected," immortal. By collaborating with nature's own creative process through mining and smelting, human creativity assists the cosmos in its progress toward its sacred destiny. So in the manner that the new humanism mines religio-cultural ores through a "creative hermeneutics" for transforming the human and cultural condition, can it be regarded as a form of alchemy. Indeed, giving hermeneutics a creative motivation was a distinctly Eliadean contribution to hermeneutical theory.[5] In as much as humans more fully reintegrate themselves into the creative processes of the cosmos, do they overcome the terror of death and of "history," in effect, "become" immortal.

In his approach to creativity, Eliade is inspired by the alchemists. But he is equally inspired by Indian cosmogony with its separation of spirit, *purusha,* from *prakriti,* nature, by various archaic cosmologies, and by Christian, Jewish, and Muslim cosmologies of *creatio ex nihilo*. And his view of creating of one's life a "personality," is inspired by Romanticism, with its clearest model in Goethe. So like Eliade's views on freedom, the archetype of creation has a morphology of its own. In every case, though, creativity remains inseparably tied to the divine creative acts *in illo tempore*. Whether it be artistic, literary, scholary, or material constructions, the act of creation, for Eliade, has mythological significance.[6] Creativity has a sacred character. It repeats a cosmos–human homology. As humans create, so is the world created anew. And conversely, as the world creates, so are humans created for repeatedly new beginnings.[7]

As symbols possess a dialectic, so for every creation there is equally a destruction, or a sacrifice. Whether it be creation out of chaos or Indian recreations, creativity involves bringing the old state or world to a close and starting anew. From sacrifice and death there is rebirth, and on it continues. In that the old dies and a new condition arises, creativity is initiatory in character. The new humanism, consequently, requires a repeated series of sacrifices, of deaths, so as to reemerge with new sources for synthesis. Despite his races against time, which betrayed a fear of closure, Eliade remained confident in humans' and the cosmos' potential to endlessly renew themselves.[8]

Immolation and the Divine Cosmic Impulse

If, according to Eliade, any creative activity is to repeat the initial creative act of the gods "in the beginning," then humans can give value to many diverse types of creative acts, since the gods and mythical heros themselves created in various ways, by differentiating water from land, by sacrifice, by sexual union, by initiating cosmic forces, etc.[9]

One of the prevalent themes in creative activity is immolation, sacrifice, whether it occurs through the sacrifice of a god or in a god's own self-emptying, termed *kenosis*. One could even speak of transmigration as a sacrifice, since to be ultimately liberated, one must undergo repeated rebirths and sufferings. In regards to immolation Eliade says:

> It is important to grasp the significance of the novelty presented by the idea that creation is effected by immolation or self-immolation. Previous mythologies know only of a creation *ex nihilo* or from some primordial substance fashioned by God. The making of the blood sacrifice into a condition of creation— cosmogony as well as anthropogeny—reinforces not only the homologies between man and the cosmos, . . . but also introduces the idea that life can only be engendered from another life that has been immolated.[10]

We can apply the view that sacrfice brings new life to the way in which Eliade refers to the hermeneutical processs. An interpreter of religious materials must descend into history's religio-cultural expressions, including its monstrous and brutal ones, in order to *experience* the world of the other. In so doing the interpreter risks losing her or his identity and faith in humanity, especially when barbaric human expressions are plumbed, whose apparent meaninglessness and whose horror can so overwhelm one. Eliade often spoke of experiencing such anxiety whenever he plunged into the worlds of witches, sorcerers, bloody ritual sacrifices, and the like. Nevertheless, if the *total* human condition is to be understood, and since the barbaric are *human* expressions, then the hermeneute must descend into its depths. Eliade's "creative hermeneutics" for a new humanism becomes a form of self-immolation. This immolation is initiatory in that it requires one to die to the old self (or to old assumptions) and assume a new one (new or revised assumptions). The hermeneutical process, in short, especially as seen by Eliade, is never indifferent to, or unaffected by, the subject encountered. To get at the meaning of any phenomenon under study, we find that Eliade's hermeneutics, especially as a "creative hermeneutics," involves a certain methodological immolation of its own, since it sacrifices empiricism and historicism and partial explanations for the irreducibly religious and the total phenomenon. To create for Eliade is to render it whole.

But need analysis, with its breakdown of the subject into isolated and logical parts, be uncreative and unhelpful in drawing out a phenomenon's spiritual meaning? The theologian David Tracy says, "Creativity in interpretation is not opposed to explanation and method."[11] Since the history of religions as a field of study describes as well as interprets, it can occupy a middle ground between the social sciences and the normative disciplines. Hermeneutics, as the process of interpreting through discovery, combines the two approaches. Yet if creativity comes through various sacrifices, then even Eliade's own position on the irreducibility of religion must, occasionally, be "sacrificed." To interpret the meaning of a millenial cult, for instance, as the desire of a people to recapture paradise, can minimize or overlook the fact that there are some people who are indeed suffering from or pointing to, or both, some urgent political, social, economic, or cultural deprivations. In like manner, reductionism, too, needs to be "sacrificed" on occasion. A phenomenon must be taken for what it is. A religious millenial cult is inescapably a *religious* phenomenon. To fail to take a millenial cult as religious, one avoids its religious, existential, apocalyptic messages. Society may indeed be suffering from a loss of meaning and a breakdown of moral values. Similarly, to reduce religious belief and practice to an "opium" is to fail to note their ability to inspire and bring about social and political change. So if the hermeneutics of the new humanism aims to conjoin the methodological temperaments of the historical-scientific (reduction) with the phenomenological (integration), each, at times, must be willing to sacrifice its absolutes in order for this paradoxical merger to occur.

The sacrifice involved in the "creative hermeneutics" equally applies to provincial and confessional cultural and religious orientations. Such immolations can encourage a hermeneutical ethic. In a review of Tzvetan Todorov's *The Conquest of America: The Question of the Other* (1984), the Meso-American historian of religion, Davíd Carrasco, notes how the fifteenth-century Spanish conquistadores shaped the perceptual framework of the Meso-Americans for the West. The conquistadores undertook not only a religious, political, and military conquest in the name of Spain (the "modern world") but a hermeneutical conquest as well. Unwilling to interpret the Aztec's worldview and its rites and social practices except through a Catholic and Renaissance hegemonic hermeneutics, the conquistadores slaughtered those whom they were unable (and unwilling) to typologize into their worldview. The conquistatores would return home to define Spain's "others" as less civilized and less human than the European.

Among the colonizing Spaniards who went to Mexico, it was Diego Duran and the Franciscan Bernardino de Sahagún who exemplified a hermeneutics and an ethics worthy of a new humanism, says Carrasco.[12] Though Carrasco does not acknowledge as favorably the hermeneutical contributions of Bartolomé de las Casas, one could also mention las Casas' interpretation of Aztec sacrifice and its implications for his own Catholic belief as an example of the hermeneutics of the new humanism in action.[13] The above were willing and patient enough to incorporate the world of the Aztecs into their own worldview and sacrifice their Spanish-Catholic hegemony for a creative, religious hybrid. The problematics of hybrid acculturation are great. But the creative motif of the new humanism is enough to stress the necessity for sacrifice as a prerequisite to a liberating and creative hermeneutics.[14]

Culture and Personality

To create is to combat sterility, the epitome of death and evil for Eliade. In his first published novel, *Isabel și Apele Diavolului* (*Isabel and the Devil's Waters*) (1930),[15] a ''doctor'' of Oriental art resists believing in the devil, who for him is the symbol and ''creator'' of sterility. Even though he periodically succeeds in disbelieving in the devil, he is never free from the threat of sterility. Sterility, personified in the devil, threatens the doctor's productivity as a scholar and his own existence, since sterility also means death. In the same way that the fear of sterility overhung Eliade's literary character, so did the fear of becoming sterile symbolize evil for Eliade.[16] All despairs, complexes, political authoritarianisms, materialisms, religious beliefs and behaviors which threaten to deprive an individual or culture from creating were regarded as evil. He could, therefore, comment, as he did in 1949 for Romanian exiles, that cultural creativity is a form of political action. To ''create culture'' is the exiles' ''political mission.''[17] Sterility and all sterilizing structures are antithetical to the supreme divine act, the supreme regenerative force.

So in order to overcome evil one must create works which share in the eternal, in the sacred cosmos, and which do not debase the purpose of human existence to the level of mere survival. Though Eliade saw the salvation of culture through acts of creation, a Zoroastrian form of overcoming evil with greater good, he also knew that creativity occurs through more than human ability. Despite human action, creative moments happen, like the sacred which erupts into the world thus transforming human existence. Transformative, creative movements frequently come without calculated human procedures. Instead, they burst forth when all necessary elements converge at the fullness of time. With this idea in mind, one understands why Eliade saw the creative potential in initiatory ordeals and in existential encounters with the ''others.'' For at periods of crisis and disturbance, creative possibilities are at their highest. Says Eliade:

> We don't live in a world of angels or spirits or in a purely animal world either. We are "between." And I believe that confronting the revelation of this mystery always leads to an act of creation. I believe that the human spirit is at its most creative when faced with great ordeals.[18]

Thus said, the parallel with Zoroaster must now be modified. If human existence is defined as the ability and need to create, then one would not want to eliminate or deplete all evils and sufferings from human life, as Zoroastrianism and Zoroastrian-based religions (Judaism, Christianity, Islam) would have it. For suffering is the arena for much creativity. In the same way that antihuman and antisacred forces can suppress creativity, so can pure goodness and pure sacredness suppress creativity. A sublime, unperturbed, beatific, nonparadoxical existence is unappealing to Eliade. Like the philosopher Lessing, if God offered truth in one hand and paradox and thirst for truth in the other, Eliade would choose the latter. It is not only a matter of preference. For it is in the nature of both the divine and the human to deny a one-sided existence: the gods create and destroy, good exists with the bad, and so on.

As various cultural, individual, and methodological sacrifices are undertaken and creative breakthroughs of value happen, individuals and cultures move toward establishing "syntheses" and distinct "personalities." Out of such "syntheses" of values a new humanism will be created. Although creativity is born out of sacrifice, creativity is always full of hope. For creative acts repeat a cosmogony, an already established and repeatable precedent. What humans do, therefore, falls within the realm of the possible. And since the endtime, the *Endzeit,* is another "beginning," eschatology becomes cosmogony, and imagining *new* beginnings becomes possible. Images of future renewal and creative possibilities motivate human activity forward. Hence humans are free to overcome historical determinism and shape their destiny. Present actions have transformative potential. This kind of renewal of history based on future projected paradigms differentiates Christianity's renewal of history from the archaic view. The latter repeats *past* eternal models, while the former repeats models *forseen* in the eternity yet to come. As I have shown, both models, the mythical past and the mythical future, repeat archetypal models for acquiring meaning in "history."

Intuition in the Paradox of Creativity

As creativity is being stimulated by various crises, so is creativity stimulated when it operates in the paradox between the analytic and the poetic, the two principal modes of human thought. Eliade's creative genius resided in his ability to operate with equal ease in both the artistic ("nocturnal") and rational ("diurnal") sides of his brain. He was a preeminent religious scholar and professional writer, and frequently remarked that hermeneutical insights into religious behavior came to him in the playful abandon of writing literature. The pull from both sides of his creative genius often caused him to lament the dilemma of having to live in two different worlds. Nevertheless, he found that creativity is most full in the "between" of the artistic and the scientific modes. Because of the dual worlds, each reveals their hermeneutical and revelatory potential. The new humanism arises within the paradox of mystical, intuitional creativity and scientific, analytical creativity. Each is equally valued as an instrument of knowledge, and the worlds they uncover are also equally respectable in aiding in the understanding of *homo religiosus*.

But in giving equal value to these two modes of thought the new humanism comes into a great deal of controversy. For the two realms are usually taken as opposites in their assumptions, interpretations, and use of data. The artistic sees the material firstly as a *human* document; thus it acknowledges the human interpreter as subjectively participating in some degree in the material under study. Moreover, the full range of human life—the unconscious, dreams, intuition, imagination, emotions, etc.—enters into the interpretive process and the realm of what is considered "observable" material. The scientific stance principally acknowledges the material as objective "fact," largely independent of the interpreter, and has empirical testing overriding nonverifiable interpretations. For Eliade, the new humanism in its "creative hermeneutics" seeks to make use of both modes of thought through a type of intuitional "science." Though Eliade could not create in both realms simultaneously, he found, as in the writing of his novel *Şarpele*, that both the artistic and the scientific, can work together in the interpretive and creative process. The scholarly world need not divorce literature from science, the artistic from the analytic. For in the apprehension of form, in the formulation of hypotheses, and in the exploration of an idea in all its details are ways in which analysis and art conjoin as creative enterprises.[19] The analytic looks at the mechanics—language, semiotics, neurology, psychology—which give rise to the artistic (or religious) experience and which enable it to be communicated to others. And it is because of such analytical mechanics that we can speak of "history" as an avenue through which an artistic or religious experience can operate through and be passed on to a community, a society, a tradition. The artistic dimension, conversely, given to immediacy, spontaneity, and unconventionality, prizes the subjective experience over the potentially sterilizing mechanics. But if the artistic and analytic conjoin, they are to do so dialectically and in balance, since raw experience without the mechanics of transmission has no history and mechanics without spontaneous, emotive experience sterilizes and kills.[20] While Eliade's "creative hermeneutics," sub-

sequently, can be faulted for not attending enough to the mechanics of interpretation and communication, it at least suggests that hermeneutics is not just a
science of *how* interpretations are made, but is a creative "tool" for articulat-
ing the "hidden" experiences in symbols and myths. Through language (philology) and erudition (history), hermeneutics interprets the existential experiences and then, through the ability of language to transmit, model, and
universalize experience, gives voice to these meaningful and potentially transformative experiences for contemporary culture.[21] Speaking of the religious
creativity of the historian of religions, Eliade says:

> Religious creativity implies helping others to see things; it implies the establish-
> ment of a repeatable model that can be acted out in the lives of others. If a purely
> mystical experience is involved, it is buried there; it is not communicated and
> does not become a model which can be meaningfully imitated; it is a purely
> ecstatic experience. . . . Only language can make the mystical experience into
> the religiously creative one.[22]

It is through language, then, the "all-embracing" ability of language, that
will "bring men together in the universal community."[23] For Eliade, the goal
is to draw forth and translate for contemporary consciousness the creative
contributions of other peoples' religious and cultural experiences. It is less
important to attend to the institutional and political processes by which these
contributions have come down to us. In this respect we find here a marked
contrast between him and Jonathan Z. Smith. Smith's Judaic scholarship
predisposes him to focus on tradition, on the institutional and political ways in
which religious experiences have been transmitted as religion.[24] For Eliade,
whose primary area of scholarly expertise is on the religions of South Asia,
principally Hinduism, the artistic and philosophical weighs heavier than the
analytical and empirical.

Nevertheless, to attempt a balance between the artistic and the analytical
modes of thought does not settle the challenge of holding them parodoxically
together. Sorin Alexandrescu notes in his essay "Mircea Eliade: La narrazione
contro il significato," that the dual nature of Eliade's creative process contains
a contradiction.[25] Alexandrescu says that in Eliade's "scientific" writings the
creative process purports to uncover hidden worlds of meaning in past and
distant places and in modern quotidian life. In his literary writings, however,
Eliade creates worlds devoid of meaning or whose meaning is hopelessly
opaque. The former moves toward meaning and the latter hides it. Eliade
seems to overreach and underestimate humans' ability to creatively interpret
and uncover other worlds of meaning, a point noted earlier in this study. Or is
the contradiction, as Alexandrescu says, an indication of the incompatibility
between the scientific and artistic realms? Science clarifies, isolates, reduces.

Art enriches, pluralizes, and "complicates" mystery. Thus the problem is one of the limits to both the analytic and the artistic modes of thought and discovery.[26] Alexandrescu is right to note the contradiction. As long as Eliade characterizes creativity metaphysically and wholistically and modern science regards creativity as empirical and atomistic the contradiction will remain for many scholars.

To sum our discussion on creativity, we find that for Eliade humans must continually create in order to give the world meaning and to escape all kinds of sterilizing structures and behaviors. If anything, the new humanism highlights the essentialness of creativity to being human.

Humans and Initiation

> The supreme rite of initiation is to enter a labyrinth and return from it, and yet every life, even the least eventful, can be taken as a journey through a labyrinth. The suffering and trials undergone by Ulysses were fabulous, and yet any man's return home has the value of Ulysses' return to Ithaca.[27]

To be human is to be initiated. To be a creative human is to be initiated. Human existence is constituted as a series of ongoing transformations. Simple biological development from childhood to adulthood demonstrates this. In addition, there appears to be an inherent need in humans to enter into social and "transhuman" relations and to go beyond human limits and their contingencies. According to Eliade, because of the mythic rupture of human existence from its divine condition "in the beginning," humans desire, consciously or unconsciously, to recapture that earlier, preconditioned mode of being. It is by means of a series of ordeals and their initiations, or "rites of passage," that humans approximate that desire for freedom, completeness, and unity. And since crises and longings never cease, initiations continue. Every quest, every death, every rebirth, every mystery, every ordeal, whether social or personal, is an initiation to another mode of existence. So to achieve a new humanism, initiations are expected. Taking Eliade's view of initiation in mind, as humans undergo ontological transformations into other universes of meaning they will begin to approach a new humanism. And as a universal hermeneutics of an existential kind, the new humanism will contain its own existential, methodological, and social challenges or ordeals.

The Nature and Presence of "Initiation" in Eliade

Eliade defines initiation as that which changes a person's religious and social status, or in philosophical terms, as an existential transformation to a new ontological level.[28] Through diverse ordeals initiates are tested and ritually and symbolically "killed" to be restored to new life. Once reborn the individual comes into a knowledge of the sacred; he or she learns of a tradition's gods, mythical ancestors, and its rites and myths. The individual learns how the world and his or her community works and about culture and its spiritual values. In coming into the realm of spiritual values, the person becomes a human being, since now he or she is understood in relation to the gods and the eternal models and repeats the very initiatory ordeals that the god or mythical hero did once before: Christians are initiated in baptism as Christ was so baptized; the female Apache initiate repeats and appropriates the creative activity of Changing Woman, the mythical creator of the world. Needless to say, among primitive communities, the rite of initiation is of great importance. It determines whether a person is to survive at all—as a tribal member, as a human being, and in life after death.

Eliade breaks down initiation into three general types,[29] (1) initiation at puberty: every male and female in the community undergoes this "rite of passage" from childishness and ignorance to adulthood and knowledge; in turn he or she becomes an accepted member of the community; (2) initiations for entering a secret society: a person is initiated into an exclusive confraternity; most of these secret societies are for males; (3) initiations into a mystical vocation, as in becoming a shaman: the chief feature distinguishing this third type from 2, besides its personal nature, is the fact that the initiate must have had an ecstatic experience. Sometimes the shaman is chosen by the group or is felt called to the vocation in a dream or after having survived a life-threatening sickness. There is also alchemical initiation, but it takes place on a different plane. The motif here regards the initiatory death and rebirth of *Terra Mater* herself. In expunging minerals and smelting them into pure metals (into coveted gold) matter itself is initiated.[30] It too, as with humans, is "killed" to be reborn, transformed, to a new, refined state. It must be added that whenever an initiation occurs individuals are given access to some "secret" knowledge, such as how to transmute metals, how to hunt, on the doctrines of a mystery religion, in the ways of a fraternity, etc. Furthermore, initiation always involves the "total" person. It affects the person as a social, religious, psychological, and cognitive being.

The above types are found in primitive societies and in the classical and modern religions. Though no longer undertaken at the conscious level, initiatory longings, quests, and ordeals also survive in the modern conscience—evidenced in novels, poetry, the cinema, travel, the arts, and in the popularity that all such quests hold in the public's attention. However explicitly or implicitly manifested, initiation is a religious quest for transcendence and transformation. As persons are initiated they acquire an increase of knowledge into the nature of things and become members of the community of the initiated.

The interpretations that Eliade brings to initiatory rites evince an aggressive, ascetic, and domineering nature. This temperament is largely due to the antagonism he sets up between nature and spirit. In her article on androcentrism in religious studies, Valerie Saiving notes that in Eliade's *Rites and Symbols of Initiation* there is an emphasis upon a "masculine," power-oriented interpretation given to male and female initiation rites.[31] Saiving says that female initiations do not have as their primary function the asceticizing of the initiate from her baser, natural impulses. The initiatory ordeal is not to conquer "nature" for the more preferred "spirit," as male initiates are supposed to do. Female rites, instead, prepare women to embrace "nature" in an accepting and relational way. Because of their biological role in the giving of life, women are to nurture their biological and symbolic tie to birth and fecundity.[32] Moreover, as the historian Caroline Walker Bynum notes among medieval women saints, the initiatory process for women tends to be more gradual, unlike male initiations, which are defined by their radical ruptures from the community and their previous stage of development.[33] Though I think Saiving overstates Eliade's negative attitude toward nature, Eliade does indeed place a high value on asceticsm and on the mastery of "nature" in becoming fully human.

If Eliade's new humanism is to integrate wholistically the panorama of human experience, then the new humanism must appropriate the female model of initiation. The new humanism needs to place a greater emphasis on community, for instance. Collaborative efforts and interpretations—characteristics of community—as found in the stimulating work of David Hall and Roger Ames, *Thinking Through Confucius,* will mark the progress of the new humanism.

> We have . . . sought through our collaboration to complement the individual
> virtues of the sinologue and the philosopher by combining both sorts of exper-
> tise. . . . [T]he intellectual engagement permitted by this collaboration has
> required a continual examination of the insights emerging from the thought of
> each of the two principals. This sort of engagement guaranteed that the deter-
> minations of the meanings of concepts and the character of arguments, along
> with the conclusions drawn therefrom, were always codeterminations.[34]

In Elide we find traces of collaborative effort. His participation and confidence in the symposium Criterion and that he argued for a history of religions of an interdisciplinary kind, are two examples. But in that he shaped a discipline without nurturing any disciples, contrary to his predecessor Joachim Wach,[35] and demonstrated a Faustian drive for knowledge and a personal synthesis of global reach, Eliade is a lone, path-breaking giant upon whose shoulders we stand. But he is hardly a model for a collaborative humanism, a humanism in which oeuvres are less the product of single individuals but of a community of scholars and writers. The female model of initiation with its assertions of human frailty, individual limitations, and allowance for gradual maturation warns of overextending one's reach—intellectual, hermeneutical—in one's yearning for transcendence.

A Continuous Ontological Transformation

In its goal for a universal consciousness, the new humanism implies a continual modification of the hermeneute's self-understanding and mode of being in the world. This modification assumes a willingness to be so changed in the face of the spiritual-cultural values of other religio-cultural traditions. An unalterable, detached objectivism, therefore, is disallowed. The "creative hermeneutics" requires an engagement with the spiritual world of the "other," even if that might imply being "converted" to the "other's" views. This does not mean one approaches other religious, cultural traditions with a tabula rasa. One cannot be dissociated from one's individual presence as a unique human being. Nor does encounter mean a complete transformation to the "other." Eliade did not encourage the "Western" mentality to be sacrificed for the archaic or Oriental. He did not wish it for himself, nor could he have accomplished it had he wished it. Continual ontological transformations, rather, mean a sort of reflexive *épochē*. As we "bracket," hold in abeyance, our own outlook we reflect back upon our experience once we have encountered and dialogued with the "others."[36]

To undergo ontological transformations increases one's intuitional capacity, believed Eliade. It is difficult to say to what extent Eliade felt that one needed to have experienced the sacred to understand religious phemomena. In his Romanian writings Eliade concurred with Rudolf Otto that an experience with the "wholly other" was necessary for a true intuition into the nature of things. But in the sense that Eliade posited *homo religiosus* and his phenomenology was ontologically based, not being purely a discriptive phenomenology, we can say that for Eliade the "authentic" understanding of spiritual creations comes through an initiation into intuition. Phenomenology is itself an initiatory move.[37] As stated earlier, this experience and receptivity to the sacred need not mean affirming any defined set of beliefs. Nor does it imply that the object under study is "unique" and thus immune from comparative relations. And the scholar's own act of comparison is still an activity of the imagination, in which differences are manipulated for creative and progressive ends.[38] Existential experiences, ontological transformations, simply add the spiritual dimension to the academic, "scientific" study of religion.

Transformations of one's ontology need not be confined to the individual and private realm of experience. Transformations of one's being and self-understanding can have social implications as well. More practiced at the individual level than at the cultural, the Buddhist doctrine of *anatta,* for instance, speaks of an interconnection between all sentient and nonsentient life and formulates an ethic of compassion and environmental concern. Says Steven Collins:

> On the social level, it [*anatta*] has been able to legitimate a full and positive involvement with the "conventional" world of society, providing a rubric for those who appear to themselves as individuals under which they might feel both a justifiable moral concern for themselves, and also a non-ascetic, "non-heroic" altruistic concern for others (at least in aspiration).[39]

At the cultural level, one can mention changes in a culture's ecological consciousness. People see the good of society and the value of a human being as less answered by theories of scientific, evolutionary progress than by a greater regard for and intimacy with the local and global landscape. Ontological modifications in the new humanism seek nothing less than ongoing modifications in what it means to be and act as a human being in relation to the self, the socio-political-cultural aggregate, and to the created order.

A Larger Religious and Cultural Universe

After an initiate successfully completes his or her initiation, the person enters the community of the initiated. Once an outsider of less maturity and spiritual knowledge, the initiate is now mature and informed; she or he has become an adult and an equal among the members of the group. The person is part of a larger community. "Other peoples' myths" become one's own, sometimes becoming appropriated as "metamyths," a myth upon a myth.[40] One's "center" enlarges to include and relate with other "centers." Structurally, the rites, ethics, kinships, and social order based on these myths are now "found" in one's own rituals and ethical, familial, and societal arrangements.[41]

To encounter and appropriate other cultures and universes of meaning largely depends on the degree to which individuals or communities allow themselves to be initiated. Communities, sacred institutions, secret societies, academies, "esoteric truths," often have less than permeable boundaries; they are difficult to enter. C. J. Bleeker shares an anecdote of how Rudolf Otto learned of such uncrossable boundaries when visiting a Hindu temple in Madras, India:

> Standing, at the entrance of the temple, he detected far away in the holy of holies a white object. It proved to be the temple-cow, ruminating in serene quiet and great dignity. Attracted by its mysterious appearance, Rudolf Otto intended to

cross the sacred but forbidden threshold. At the same moment, a temple-bell was loudly rung, warning him not to profane the sanctuary by his unholy feet. His travelling companion who relates this story writes that, at that moment, a smile flitted across the face of the author of the famous study on the Holy, because he understood that nothwithstanding [sic] all his knowledge of the subject, he was not allowed to enter this Hindu holy place.[42]

In other words, humans and societies are limited, in their capacity to extend into other domains. So is a hermeneutics limited in its ability to extend the interpreter's range of experiences. A person, by default, is limited to certain religio-cultural experiences and is kept from others. Eliade himself failed at integrating himself into both the "historical" and "eternal" India. Because of such limits the new humanism is unable to be truly universal. Even a "creative hermeneutics" cannot permeate certain enclaves of meaning and devotion. The "female" model of initiation is again suitable at this point. For by recognizing one's inability to overcome and master, one must instead soberly accept one's real and imposed limits.

Conversely, when one is initiated into other religious and cultural universes, one is less able to be loyal to any single group or position. Not to be loyal to any single position is one element that separates the history of religions from the normative disciplines, such as theology, ethics, and philosophy. Seen negatively, not to have a particular loyalty, a norm, one has less chance of rising in status within a single community; one remains only intermittently committed to the structure. Moreover, in being non-normative, the place upon which one stands becomes no single place. One risks having no place on which to orient oneself and to evaluate positions that conflict with one's own. Positively, larger universes of meaning mitigate any relative positions one might hold. One notices the "opacity" of one's reality, as Charles Long puts it.[43] Furthermore, to come into larger cultural universes places one into, again in the words of Long, an "extraregional hierophany"[44]—one is rooted to, and finds meaning in, no single place. Long speaks of Buddhism and Christianity as "extraregional hierophanies." Negatively or positvely, the decentralization of the the new humanism has its trade-offs.

On another plane, initiation as suffering opens one to other worlds of meaning. The experience of suffering facilitates a hermeneutical interconnection. One who knows suffering can connect with the suffering of one's "others." Citing Charles Long once again:

> The theologians of opacity [James Cone, Vine Deloria, Jr.] with their emphasis on suffering and oppression [sic] force one to deal with the actuality of the suffering itself, and with that human act whereby one human being or community forces another person or community to undergo an ordeal for the salvation of one or both.[45]

On the sheer human plane of suffering, to experience suffering allows one to share in the sufferings and tragedies of other peoples and contexts. In the process, one "understands" these in a way mere cognitive understanding could not at all or alone.

Existential and Methodological Challenges

To accomplish the new humanism, in sum, an individual or a community must undertake several existential challenges. First, one must find a workable epistemological, hermeneutical, and ethical center. If, according to Eliade, the new humanism is a spiritual orientation in which an individual remains on the periphery or the boundary of various religions and cultures, then one must find some place upon which to stand, however momentary and unproven one's position. Second, a universal hermeneutics of an experiential kind requires the interpreter to face all human acts, even the more barbaric human acts, and attempt to find meaning in them. Facing and experiencing the darker side of human history is an existential challenge, for one risks loosing one's own identity and ability to rise out of such despair. In the course of interpreting the range of human experiences, the hermeneute descends to hell and ascends to heaven but must finally rest on earth. Many religious phenomena demand a response; they do not wait for new facts or allow for a detached aloofness. Third, the quest for a new humanism is an especially lonely one. As Eliade conceives them, all quests are lonely and individual. However collaborative and communitarian the new humanism is and needs to be, Eliade places the onus on the individual to make of her or his life a creation, a "personality."

Among the methodological challenges for accomplishing a new humanism we find, first, the difficulty of orchestrating an interdisciplinary and methodological syncretism. No single method has proven serviceable for integrating the range of disciplines, and the two principal orientations to religious data defined by Eliade, the historical and the phenomenological, are as much a factor of the scholar's temperament as they are suitable approaches for particular interpretations. Second, the new humanism must balance the paradox between the artistic and scientific modes of knowledge. Third, the new humanism valorizes mythic consciousness as "history" in its own right. One's methodology, consequently, must acknowledge an existential meaning in history. Fourth, once one elucidates the historical form of a phenomenon, one integrates it within the diversity of all such forms from other cultures and times. The new humanism as a morphology reduces through integration.

In the end, each historian of religions must evaluate the initiatory challenges she or he is willing to undertake for the sake of a new humanism, if she or he is willing to undertake them at all. Whether to pursue a new humanism or not, most students of religion and every historian of religion cannot circumvent the challenges and contributions Eliade has brought to the history of religions. In other words, all succeeding historians of religion to Eliade must be initiated through Eliade if one is ever to go "beyond Eliade."

The New Humanism: A Science

This "machine age" must go, and be replaced at last by the "scientific age"; we must prepare a new culture, the first to be deliberately based upon science, upon humanized science,—the New Humanism.—George Sarton[46]

Curiously, before we can characterize the new humanism in any other way, Eliade's new humanism is first of all a "science," albeit a "philosophical science." The new humanism is concerned with "facts," the mysteries of nature, the formulation of hypotheses, the advancements of experimental sciences, the "perfectibility of humankind," and the resolution of the anxiety of death, of finitude. It is a *philosophical* science in that it asks for meaning, decries reductionism, valorizes intuition as an instrument of knowledge, allows for nonempirical realities, posits a priori structures to the human mind, and is wholistic—parts are understood in relation to the whole.

In its "scientific" mode, the etiology of the term "new humanism" comes from the late Harvard science historian George Sarton, who proposed it in his *Introduction to the History of Science* (1927) and then elaborated on it in his *The History of Science and the New Humanism* (1931).[47] During his early school days, Eliade was very interested in scientific investigations. He studied chemistry, botany, zoology, and biology, and conducted researches of empirical nature. He read Sarton when Sarton's books were first published and wrote several reviews of Sarton's work. Eliade's first article published in America, "Botanical Knowledge in Ancient India (1931), came out in Sarton's journal, *Isis*.[48] Eliade shared Sarton's enthusiasm for renewing science from the mechanization and positivism to which it has succumbed. Sarton called for a wholistic science that would include philology, history, and aesthetics while remaining true to the "disinterestedness" of the scientific method. Nevertheless, such a science was to be only the frame for Sarton's new humanism, not its core. "We cannot live on truth alone," said Sarton. "We need beauty, love, and grace as much as truth."[49] Sarton's program for a new humanism strove for disciplinary synthesis, a universal history, philological and epistemological concreteness, and for the good of human, cultural development.[50] Eliade's own vision for a new humanism would subsequently follow a similiar program once he had read Sarton. In a review in the Romanian paper *Cuvântul* in 1928 of Sarton's *Introduction to the History of Science,* Eliade gives his own interpretation of the significance of a history of science for culture:

> The *purpose* would be the apprehension of the *unity* of science, which has been manifested variously and without order, in time. Around this concept there could be developed a *new humanism,* a series of methods which would investigate and valorize man not as understood by a humanism based on philology, but as viewed from the evolution of science.[51]

Eliade would also see the new humanism coming through a history of medicine. In contrast to Eliade, however, Sarton categorically separated religion, the mystical life, from science and did not see scientific discovery as an ontology founded on a human need to create.[52]

Because for Eliade the new humanism is an ontological expression of human creativity, and has, therefore, a mythic significance, as a "science" the new humanism constitutes a mythic-scientific wholism. It is not just concerned with history, as is Sarton's new humanism. Eliade's new humanism is a history based on the mythologic—on meaning, on the "spirit" (*Geist*), on unity, on the cosmos, on creativity.[53]

As a mythic science, the new humanism is concerned with facts—but with the meaning of those facts for human existence; with hypotheses—but with how those hypotheses can help humans be freely creative; with nature—not for manipulating it, but that nature may be deciphered and collaborated with; with origins—but cosmogonic "origins"; with the perfectability of humans—but upon the impulse of the "spirit" and the perfection of humans through regeneration and "new births," not through endless evolution. The wholism in Eliade's "science" is found in the striving for "syntheses," and the whole, the cosmos, is the final limit that evaluates all provincialisms, be they individual, methodological, or cultural. As an archetype within the new humanism, the mythic science challenges students of religion to incorporate the discoveries of modern-day science with religion in as much as science contributes toward enriching human freedom, creativity, and meaning—in short, toward establishing a cosmos. (Technological exploitations of nature, while not directly addressed by Eliade, do have an effect on one's and a culture's hermeneutics, specifically their hermeneutics of landscape. Archaic traditions would, naturally, be the more "advanced" than Western technological culture in this hermeneutics, as they would also be in their ecological regard.) Methodologically, a mythic science interprets religio-cultural facts through hypotheses, *èpoche,* and critical-poetic intuition. Similar to the natural sciences' own process of development, the new humanism comes through repeated discoveries.

For Eliade, science will best serve humanity if it regains its spiritual impulse, its wholistic, humanistic, metaphysical base. Eliade was persuaded of science's fundamentally religious character after his researches into alchemy. While most of modern-day science is radically opposed to Eliade's position, there are indications of scientists returning to a cosmological and humanistic orientation.[54] Stephen Hawking, one of the most brilliant and promising scientists of our day and most capable for unraveling the mysteries of the heavens, concludes his recent *A Brief History of Time* (1988) with the hope for a unified scientific theory combining the hard sciences with philosophy. With great brashness he says:

> if we do discover a complete theory, it should in time be understandable in broad principle by everyone, not just a few scientists. Then we shall all, philosophers, scientists, and just ordinary people, be able to take part in the discussion of the question of why it is that we and the universe exist. If we find the answer to that, it would be the ultimate triumph of human reason—for then we would know the mind of God.[55]

The mythic science of the new humanism, though, is less concerned with "why" the universe was created than it is in saying, *"now that* it is created, *therefore* . . . a new humanism."

Notes

1. Tu Wei-Ming rejects the notion that transcendence necessarily implies radical otherness, some "wholly other," a viewpoint coming from a Christian perspective. In regards to transcendence in the neo-Confucian tradition, Tu Wei-Ming says, "within the symbolic resources of the Neo-Confucian tradition, the authentic possibility exists for developing a transcendent leverage which can serve as the ultimate basis for an intellectual community . . . structurally independent of the political order and functionally inseparable from the lived experiences of society and politics. Despite the difficulty of conceptualizing transcendence as radical otherness, the Confucian commitment to ultimate self-transformation necessarily involves a transcendent dimension." The transcendent dimension is the "Heavenly endowned nature" that calls us to surpass our experience here and now. *Confucian Thought,* pp. 136–37. For a more refined and etymological discussion of transcendence (as *t'ien,* "heaven") in Chinese thought see Hall and Ames, *Thinking Through Confucius,* pp. 204–8. They labor to state that for Confucius, the cosmos "creates" *t'ien* as much as *t'ien* "creates" the cosmos. On this account one can compare Eliade's view of "destiny" with the Chinese anthropomorphic view of *t'ien.* See Hall and Ames, p. 206.

In that the Chinese views of transcendence is structurally distinct from the social and political order, it parallels Eliade's notion of the "irreducibility of the sacred." But that the sacred is known and functions in the immanental world demonstrates the inseparability of the transcendent from lived reality.

2. Cited in Ricketts, *Romanian Roots,* p. 588.

3. One of the clearest statements I have found on Eliade's view of cultural creativity and the history of religions is his article, "The Sacred in the Secular World," *Cultural Hermeneutics* 1 (1973), 101–13. See especially the relevant sections, "Religious Creativity and the Historian of Religions," "Religious Creativity and Language," and "Religious Creativity and the Secularized World."

4. Mircea Eliade, *The Quest,* p. 61; Ricketts, *Romanian Roots,* pp. 162 et passim, 211 et passim.

5. Adrian Marino, *L'Hermeneutique de Mircea Eliade,* pp. 278, 331.

6. I do not wish to imply that Eliade's scholarly works were created myths, as some critics have alleged. There is a difference between modeling "after" and creating "as." Eliade modeled all of his works—scholarly and literary—*after* the cosmogonic model, but only his literature can be said to be mythopoetic, *as* myth. See Eliade's article, "Literary Imagination and Religious Structure," in *Symbolism, the Sacred, and the Arts,* pp. 171–77.

7. It would be interesting to compare Eliade's view of creativity with the Chinese. I have already mentioned some relations, but more nuanced relations are needed. Again refer to Hall and Ames *Thinking Through Confucius,* as a place to begin.

8. On the motif of death and rebirth, dying and rising, and of how rebirth and rising need not exist in order for there still to be a positive outcome to death and dying, see Jonathan Z. Smith's discussion of this point as it is found in the differences between the Christian groups of the First Century C. E. Smith, *Drudgery Divine,* pp. 124–29.

9. For Buddhists, naturally, in their doctrine of nonconditioned origination, there is no specific beginning to the universe.

10. Eliade, *The Forge and The Crucible,* p. 31.

11. David Tracy, "Is a Hermeneutics of Religion Possible?", p. 125.

12. Davíd Carrasco, "Review of *The Conquest of America: The Question of the Other,* by Tzvetan Todorov," *History of Religions* 28,2 (November 1988), 151–60.

13. Todorov, *The Conquest of America: The Question of the Other,* trans. Richard Howard (New York: Harper & Row, 1984), pp. 188–90.

14. See my chapter 2 above on the three ways Eliade saw hermeneutics as creative.

15. Ricketts, *Romanian Roots,* p. 415.

16. Though the "doctor" character parallels Eliade, Eliade said he never believed in the devil nor been obsessed with sin. The "problem of evil" has also been of little interest to him. See *Eliade: Autobiography,* p. 168. Because Eliade continuously spoke of liberating initiatory ordeals and always fought against personal frailties and outside forces that threatened his drive to create, Eliade was not so indifferent to evil as he lets on. He was not preoccupied with evil in the moral sense, but the "terror of history" was forever an "evil" for him.

17. Mircea Eliade, *Journal I: 1945–1955,* pp. 88–89.

18. Eliade, *Ordeal by Labyrinth,* p. 125.

19. See Robert Grudin's Chapter on "Analysis" and its section on "Analysis and Invention." Grudin, *The Grace of Great Things: Creativity and Innovation* (New York: Ticknor & Fields, 1990), pp. 40–41. On art formulating hypotheses, Grudin

The Challenges of the New Humanism 189

mentions the example of an author testing the resiliency of an idea, as Joseph Conrad did when he explored the implications of "lost honor" in *Lord Jim,* and as Plato's dialogues which tested the notions of "temperance," "virtue," and "justice."

20. On the above discussion see Hauser, *The Sociology of Art,* pp. 37–39, 332–33.

21. I found the collaborative work of Hall and Ames, *Thinking Through Confucius,* to be an excellent example of the "creative hermeneutics" of which Eliade speaks. Hall's and Ames' work, refreshingly, is more methodologically and analytically up front. See their opening "Apologia."

22. Eliade, "The Sacred in the Secular World," p. 109.

23. Ibid.

24. Says Smith, *Imagining Religion,* p. xiii: "For there is no primordium—it is all history. There is no 'other,'—it is all 'what we seen in Europe every day.'" And on his view of myth Smith says, "myths are best approached as 'common stories,' as pieces of prosaic discourse rather than as multivalent, condensed, highly symbolic speech. In short, I hold that there is *no privilege* to myth or other religious materials. They must be understood primarily as texts in context, specific acts of communication between specified individuals, at specific points in time and space, about specifiable subjects."

25. Sorin Alexandrescu, "Mircea Eliade, la narrazione contro il significato," in *Mircea Eliade e l'Italia,* eds. Marin Mincu and Roberto Scagno (Milan: Jaca Book, 1987), p. 311.

26. See Hauser, *The Sociology of Art,* p. 38; and Grudin, *The Grace of Great Things,* pp. 42–45.

27. Eliade, *Patterns in Comparative Religion,* p. 382.

28. Eliade, *Quest,* p. 112; idem, *Rites and Symbols of Initiation* (New York: Harper & Row, 1958), p. x; and idem, "L'initiation et le monde moderne," in *Initiation,* ed. C. J. Bleeker (Leiden: E.J. Brill, 1965), p. 1.

29. These types are further broken down into seven patterns of ordeals to which initiates are generally subjected: 1) the separation of a young boy from his mother, 2) inflicting a symbolic death through mutilation (circumcision, self- and other-inflicted tortures), 3) embryological and gynecological patterns, as in return-to-the-womb symbolisms, 4) an individual withdrawing into the wilderness, 5) overcoming evil or natural and animal forces through magic, 6) shamanistic mystical death through descent or ascent into the subterranean or heavenly regions, respectively, 7) or ordeals inconceivable on the level of human experience, that is, of transcendent experiences available only to the spiritual person, as in enlightenment or mystical experiences. Eliade, *Rites and Symbols,* pp. 64–67, 130.

30. Eliade, *Forge and Crucible,* pp. 149–51; idem, *Rites and Symbols,* pp. 123–24.

31. Saiving, "Androcentrism in Religious Studies, pp. 177–97.

32. Ibid, pp. 190–92. Challenging the "nature-spirit" dualism is the basis for feminist critiques of male aggressiveness and dominance. On the history of this dualism and its impact on sexism, racism, and ecological exploitation see Rosemary Radford Reuther, *New Women/New Earth* (New York: Seabury/ Press, 1975).

33. Carol Walker Bynum, *Holy Feast and Holy Fast* (Los Angeles: University of California Press, 1987), p. 25. See also her dicussions on the nature/body/female–

spirit/mind/male dualisms. She says that for medieval women these dualisms were not as important as they were to men. But women knew how to exploit them as a form of power over men, pp. 294–96.

34. Hall and Ames, *Thinking Through Confucius,* pp. 2, 3.

35. In a conversation with we, Paul Wheatley, of the Committee on Social Thought at the University of Chicago and colleague of Eliade, said that Eliade failed to cultivate a group of disciples or students who would carry on and extend his thought. Wach, contrarily, was very "hands-on" and deliberate in guiding his students into specific areas of interest. Though Eliade may not have been as determined a mentor, one cannot deny his influence upon his students, on the many who came into his sphere, and upon the history of religions as it existed at Chicago and throughout the world.

36. Charles Long, "Archaism and Hermeneutics," in *The History of Religions: Essays on the Problem of Understanding,* ed. Joseph M. Kitagawa (Chicago: University of Chicago Press, 1967), p. 80.

37. He quotes Husserl who spoke of phenomenology as the abolition of the natural man, the "preinitiatory condition." Eliade, *Journal I: 1945–1955,* p. 201. And Eliade says of the historian of religions, "So at some point the historian of religion must become a phenomenologist of religion, because he tries to find meaning." Eliade, "The Sacred in the Secular World," p. 106.

38. See Smith's chapter, "On Comparison" in *Drudgery Divine,* pp. 36–53 in which he discusses claims to "uniqueness" and the academic process of comparison.

39. Steven Collins, *Selfless Persons: Imagery and Thought in Therevada Buddhism* (Cambridge: Cambridge University Press, 1982), p. 195. In a recent conference, Collins spoke of the doctrine of anatta as not workable for society at large. Under the question "What would a no-self society look like?," Collins admits that anatta, in its implications, is only workable in "the *samgha,*" the community of Buddhist monks, *bhikkhus.* Collins, "What are the Buddhists *Doing* when they Deny the Self?," in "Deconstructing/Reconstructing the Philosophy of Religions: Diverging Rationalities: Problems and Possibilities of Comparison," The Divinity School, The University of Chicago, May 10–11, 1991.

40. Doniger O'Flaherty, *Other Peoples' Myths,* pp. 112–13.

41. See, for instance, Howard Eilberg-Schwartz's discussion of African initiatory rites and symbols and their connection to ancient Israelite practices of circumcision and views of ritual purity in *The Savage in Judaism: An Anthropology of Israelite Religion and Ancient Judaism* (Bloomington, IN: Indiana University Press, 1990).

42. Bleeker, "Some Introductory Remarks on the Significance of Initiation," in *Initiation,* p. 16.

43. Long, *Significations,* p. 193. The opacity of which Charles Long speaks modifies the transparent quality Eliade ascribes to symbols.

44. Charles Long, "Religions, Worlds, and Order: The Search for Utopian Unities," in *Pushing the Faith: Proselytism and Civility in a Pluralistic World,* eds. Martin E. Marty and Frederick E. Greenspahn (New York: Crossroad, 1988), p. 6

45. Long, *Significations,* p. 193.

46. George Sarton, *The History of Science and the New Humanism* (New York: George Braziller, 1931, 1956), p. 163.

47. Ricketts, *Romanian Roots,* p. 316.

48. Ibid., 1283 n. 107. In this article Eliade noted the distinctiveness of Oriental science. "[T]he concept of *science,* in the modern Western sense of the word, is not found in India. . . . Indian sciences are Oriental forms of knowledge, i.e., they are subordinate to a whole system of metaphysical, universal, and absolute knowledge," and further, "Indian science, philosophy, and religion cannot be expounded separately; they constitute an organic and natural whole; and if a detail is discussed without the preliminaries, the sense is lost." Ibid., p. 358.

49. Ibid., p. 161.

50. Ibid., pp. 136, 154–55, 158–59.

51. Ricketts, *Romanian Roots,* p. 316.

52. Sarton did say that if by religion is meant a desire to see unity and wholeness to life, then the pure scientist is intensely religious. Sarton, p. 116.

53. Structuralism also seeks to rectify the atomism and separation of the sciences—natural from the human—but it does so upon spatial, nontemporal arrangements, which is contrary to Eliade's historical consciousness.

54. Toulmin, *The Return to Cosmology,* pp. 262–74.
There is a science that has arisen within the past fifteen years, which ties human consciousness, the "mind," to the physical world. This science is centered around a collection of ideas called the "Anthropic Cosmological Principle." It is stated in the following way: "the Anthropic Principle deepens our scientific understanding of the link between inorganic and organic worlds and reveals an intimate connection between the large and small-scale structure of the Universe." See John D. Barrow and Frank J. Tipler, *The Anthropic Cosmological Principle* (New York: Oxford University Press, 1986), p. 4. The human mind, and as they speak of it, our ability to observe, is dependent upon the formation and age of the universe. Without getting into nature–culture debates, the above indicates an inextricable connection between the mental (hermeneutical) and the biological life and their connection to the larger cosmic world.

55. Hawking, *A Brief History of Time,* p. 175.

7

Conclusion

The purpose of this study was to arrange Eliade's oeuvre around the morphological structure of the new humanism. It was proposed that the new humanism is the primordial archetype of Eliade's work and life and that it has a morphological nature. Eliade wrote on a range of subjects, and his theories as to human religiosity were meant to grasp wholistically the nature and quality of individual and religio-cultural life. He also sought to lead cultures to deeper levels of meaning and creativity by having them persistently interact with their cultural "others." It was thought that through these interactions cultures would bring to the surface their own already-existing structures of meaning.

Summary of Intent

Because of the new humanism's salvific hopes and its preference for integration over reductionism, it is a spiritual and morphological vision. Although other morphological forms could be proposed, the above forms give an indication of the presuppositions, ambitions, and processes which inform the vision of a new humanism. The new huamanism is naturally pluralistic in expression and is meant to spawn further creative arrangements for organizing and interpreting religio-cultural life. So while a morphology cannot restrict the number and nature of its forms—though the considered subject will necessitate certain elements and parameters—it does require that a structure be attempted and that this structure be flexible, comprehensive, and serviceable enough to order and interpret the phenomenon. When I suggest, then, that the new humanism be taken morphologically and that it be the integrating principle of Eliade's work, I imply two things: first, a new humanism will not proceed by any single directive, along any single confessional trajectory, but will come through a network of interrelating structures. Second, the new humanism is the best interpretive guide for understanding and evaluating Eliade wholistically and for providing the context for broadening and balancing the more specialized studies on his life and thought.

Because of its morphological character, the new humanism will come about in the ensemble itself. As its structures creatively interact and integrate with each other, newer breakthroughs of meaning will happen. There is no perceived "omega point," no singularly defined *Endzeit,* no return to the "golden age." The new humanism constitutes, rather, a community of meaning and of mutually inclusive modes of being capable of modifying the quality of human life. A morphology is not limited to any single normative position. All it can do is expose and repeat certain archetypes essential to any wholistic proposal for humankind.

With the new humanism as the morphological center of Eliade's work, specialized studies of the man, whether as a historian of religions or as a writer, will be incomplete in their interpretation if they are not ultimately placed within Eliade's vision of a new humanism. This vision of a new humanism affords a very flexible interpretation of Eliade's thought, which many critics have too hastily and one-sidedly attempted to discredit. I realize that giving the new humanism this central position in Eliade's thought may trouble some scholars who want to conform Eliade to natural-science models or, similarly, who wish to dismiss him as too nonhistorical and nonrational and better left to artistic flights of fancy. But the purpose in setting the new humanism to the fore is to attest to the flexibility and dialectics of Eliade's thought. For in the same way that he sought to place human culture upon archetypal religious structures which at once unified and diversified humans, so the new humanism unifies Eliade while also maintaining the applicability of his thought for very specialized studies and interpretations.

Eliade cannot be dismissed by faulting his nonhistoricism, nonempiricism, political associations, *creative* approach, dual vocation, Platonism, androcentrism, etc. The morpholgical approach to Eliade is, I believe, the best way to evaluate him because it considers him on his own plane of reference. A morphology in the end is, as Jan de Vries was quoted as saying at the beginning of this study, an excellent medium by which to grasp a "creativity that sprouts and grows in sundry ways."

Naturally a morphology is not self-sufficient. Eliade understood this when he said it must be accompanied by ethnological history. His *A History of Religious Ideas* is the historical complement to his earlier *Patterns in Comparative Religion.* My own morphological study, therefore, is complemented by Mac Linscott Ricketts' historical study, *Mircea Eliade, The Romanian Years, 1907–1945* and by Eliade's autobiography and journal. In my morphological study and in the historical writings alike, the new humanism is central and flowers throughout.

Appraisal of Findings

It is difficult to synthesize the morphological forms or archetypes of the new humanism and their respective theses. Each form adds a certain dimension to the new humanism. The archetype of the "symbol" accents an incarnational, cosmic spirituality, and that of "myth" an emulative, transhistorical, communitarian humanism. As *"homo religiosus,"* the human being recognizes his or her thrist for meaning and transcendence. The archetype of "authenticity" signifies an ontology rooted in concrete history, in experiments and experiences. And though these experiences pass and change, it is in concreteness that the real is found. In the archetype of "freedom" the new humanism finds unlimited potential for creativity and meaning, since for the "spiritual" person there are other realities of meaning available within the historical. The new humanism has in the archetype of "culture" the intention of shaping history and valorizing it upon classical themes; the new humanism is not given to passing cultural moods. At the "center," the new humanism prizes concentrated space and time for their ability to empower, synthesize, and order existence. Yet because life is more often lived in exile or on the boundaries, one must live among many "centers" of value and in transition. The archetype of "creativity," which has us value what adds to life, instead of what maintains and narrows it; of "initiation," which is of constant growth and increases in awareness and communal life; and of "science," which seeks discovery, all encourage humans to be initiated and to create for the good of their own personhood and of the larger cultural world. From all of these archetypes a semblance of the primordial archetype of the new humanism can be constructed. It is found that the new humanism consists of meaning, experiments, ultimacy, community, and individual initiative. But if one word were chosen to synthesize the whole, it would be creativity. The metaphysics of the new humanism is a metaphysics of creativity, for in creating one engages in life yet also participates in the divine initiative.

Eliade encouraged an intensely experiential "being in the world." For him human life is to be lived fully, plurally, arduously, and creatively. We are not to try to escape concrete, historical existence, but to penetrate it deeply, so deeply that we face the real, the "reality" of freedom, meaning, order, power, etc. The real may not always be understandable, but it is never sterile. Eliade knew well by experience and from prolonged and impassioned thought the potentialities and pains of human existence. Eliade's work is validated in part in the way it gave him a self-confidence and a confidence in the cosmos in the face of the many personal, national, and global ordeals of the twentieth century. If he was too abstract in some of his interpretations of cultural and religious life, too nationalistic, too mystical in his hermeneutics, too socially and culturally elitist, too Orthodox, and too chauvinistic, there is in all cases an opposite side to him as well. So, for instance, although Eliade was guilty of cultural elitism, his attention to the now-silent voices of history, to folk traditions, to concrete existence, and to existential transformations through suffering (initiation) gave his thought a humbler rootage. A morphology does not prevent us making evaluative judgments, but it does require that those judgments take place in the full purview of the whole. Once done, the judgments are then more impartial, perceptive, and possibly instructive for one's own position.

Though Eliade's new humanism is versatile, it is not without its limitations. Eliade's attention to the problem of history and his valorization of hierophanies limits his morphology to a Christian orientation, since Christianity boasts the most historically involved incarnation of the "sacred." If the ability to survive and create in history is so highly prized in a religious creation, then the contributions of other religions are, though not ignored, diminished in significance. The importance, then, of compassion in Buddhism, obedience in Islam, law in Judaism, respect for life in Jainism, change and order in Confucionism, and justice in Christianity would be only side issues, to be interpreted within a phenomenology-of-history framework. It is shortsighted, therefore, to say that Eliade is unconcerned with history or that he is "anti-history" when in fact history—existential, chronological, sacred, and secular—is all-important to him, either in a positive or negative way. In a sense, if the new humanism is to be more universal, it is not *more* historical consciousness that is needed, but less. On the other hand, the dialectics of Eliade's history amplifies greatly the continuity between historical peoples and overcomes, to some degree, historical conditioning, as in a hierophany being structurally repeatable across space and time. The particular historical interpretations brought to a hierphany may not have a one-to-one correlation or possess any agreement on the "facts" surrounding the event. But insofar as the "sacred" as reflected in the cosmos has its consistencies, there will exist a spatial and temporal unity of "being in the world" among all historical peoples.

Another limitation is that the new humanism can only be so universal. Even granting the dialectic of hierophanies, an individual can be initiated into only so many "universes of meaning"; the simple limitations of the human condition confirm this. Eliade does, indeed, recognize limits to interpretation. His "creative hermeneutics" seeks to surpass these limits while recognizing that they exist. Nevertheless, the "creative hermeneutics" is impeded by the fact that humans are never unlimited and unconditioned, and they are resistant to undergoing certain initiations and to initiating others into their domain.

Eliade's concern for meaning, however, strikes with great intensity to the center of existential life. Eliade forces us to account for ourselves in the world. He does not excuse us from asking hard questions about the givenness of our being in the world. He pushes us to think of those bedrock values which inform our humanness and of what those values are to mean for us as human beings. His metaphysics of creativity goes beyond what most ordinary people are willing to consider when simply economic or physical survival is utmost in their minds. But he does make us see that we dare not remain preoccupied with base concerns or we will be engulfed by history. His dynamics between the microcosm and macrocosm invite us to engage with concrete realities but then to back away from them and appraise them within the panorama of ultimacy. Eliade is thoroughly existential, and his methodology does not attempt to escape that fact; what Eliade saw and learned and the way he learned it, he incorporated into his life. There are always conversions, initiations, contributions, insights, miracles to be made. Space and time are full for thought, action, freedom. Every place, every experience, every moment of time is potentially rich in meaning if we are willing to ask the hermeneutical question, "What does it mean?" Simply by asking it we call ourselves to accountability and to the possibility, henceforth, of transforming and being transformed.

BIBLIOGRAPHY

Primary Sources

BOOKS

Eliade, Mircea. "About Miracle and Event." In *Imagination and Meaning: The Scholarly and Literary Worlds of Mircea Eliade*. Ed. Norman J. Girardot and Mac Linscott Ricketts. New York: Seabury Press, 1982.

————. *Australian Religions: An Introduction*. Ithaca, NY: Cornell University Press, 1973.

————. "Comparative Religion: Its Past and Future." In *Knowledge and the Future of Man*. Ed. Walter J. Ong. New York: Holt, Rinehart and Winston, 1968.

————. *The Myth of the Eternal Return or, Cosmos and History*. Princeton, NJ: Princeton University Press, Bollingen Series 46, 1954.

———— and Mihai Niculescu. *Fantastic Tales*. Ed. and trans. Eric Tappe. London: Dillon's, 1969.

————. *The Forbidden Forest*. Trans. Mac Linscott Ricketts and Mary Park Stevenson. Notre Dame, IN: University of Notre Dame Press, 1978.

————. *The Forge and the Crucible*. Trans. Stephen Corrin. New York: Harper & Row, 1962.

————. *Fragments d'un journal*. Trans. Luc Badesco. Paris: Gallimard, 1973.

————. *Fragments d'un journal, II: 1970–1978*. Trans. C. Grigoresco. Paris: Gallimard, 1981.

————. *From Primitives to Zen: A Thematic Sourcebook of the History of Religions*. New York: Harper & Row, 1967.

————. *A History of Religious Ideas. Vol. 2: From Gautama Buddha to the Triumph of Christianity*. Trans. Willard R. Trask. Chicago: University of Chicago Press, 1982.

————. *A History of Religious Ideas. Vol. 3: From Muhammad to the Age of Reforms*, Trans. Alf Hiltebeitel and Diane Apostolos-Cappadona. Chicago: University of Chicago Press, 1985.

————. *A History of Religious Ideas. Vol.1: From The Stone Age to The Elusinian Mysteries*, Trans. Willard R. Trask. Chicago: University of Chicago Press, 1978.

————. "*Homo Faber* and *Homo Religiosus*." In *The History of Religions: Retrospect and Prospect*. Ed. Joseph M. Kitagawa. New York: Macmillan Publishing, 1985.

————. *Images and Symbols: Studies in Religious Symbolism*. Trans. Philip Mairet. New York: Sheed & Ward, 1969.

————. "L'initiation et le monde moderne." In *Initiation*. Ed. C. J. Bleeker. Leiden: E.J. Brill, 1965.

————. *Journal I: 1945–1955*. Trans. from the Romanian by Mac Linscott Ricketts. Chicago: University of Chicago Press, 1990.

————. *Journal III: 1970–1978*. Trans. from the French by Teresa Lavender Fagan. Chicago: University of Chicago Press, 1989.

————. *Journal IV: 1979–1985*. Trans. from the Romanian by Mac Linscott Ricketts. Chicago: University of Chicago Press, 1990.

————. "Methodological Remarks in the Study of Religious Symbolism." In *The History of Religions: Essays in Methodology*. Eds. Mircea Eliade and Joseph M. Kitagawa. Chicago: University of Chicago Press, 1959.

————. *Mademoiselle Christina*. Paris: L'Herne, 1978.

————. *Mircea Eliade: Autobiography. Vol. 2: Exile's Odyssey, 1937–1960*. Trans. Mac Linscott Ricketts. Chicago: The University of Chicago Press, 1988.

————. *Mircea Eliade: Autobiography. Vol. 1: Journey East, Journey West, 1907–1937*. Trans. Mac Linscott Ricketts. San Francisco: Harper & Row, 1981.

————. *Myth and Reality*. Trans. Willard R. Trask. New York: Harper & Row, 1963.

————. *Myths, Dreams, and Mysteries: The Encounter Between Contemporary Faiths and Archaic Realities*. Trans. Philip Mairet. New York: Harper & Row, 1960.

————. *No Souvenirs: Journal, 1957–1969*. Trans. Fred H. Johnson Jr. San Francisco: Harper & Row, 1977.

————. *Occultism, Witchcraft, and Cultural Fashions*. Chicago: University of Chicago Press, 1976.

————. *The Old Man and The Bureaucrats*. Trans. Mary Park Stevenson. Notre Dame, IN: University of Notre Dame Press, 1979.

————. *Ordeal by Labyrinth*. Trans. Derek Coltman. Chicago: The University of Chicago Press, 1982.

————. *Patanjali and Yoga*. Trans. Charles Lam Markmann. New York: Schocken Books, 1975.

————. *Patterns in Comparative Religion*. Trans. Rosemary Sheed. London: Sheed & Ward, 1958.

————. *The Quest: History and Meaning in Religion*. Chicago: University of Chicago Press, 1969.

————. *Rites and Symbols of Initiation: The Mysteries of Birth and Rebirth*. New York: Harper & Row, 1958.

————. *The Sacred and the Profane: The Nature of Religion*. New York: Harper & Row, 1957.

————. *Shamanism: Archaic Techniques of Ecstasy*. Trans. Willard R. Trask. Princeton, NJ: Princeton University Press, 1964.

————. "Structures and Changes in the History of Religion." In *City Invincible*. Eds. Carl H. Kraeling and Robert M. Adams. Chicago: University of Chicago Press, 1960.

————. *Symbolism, the Sacred, and the Arts*. Ed. Diane Apostolos-Cappadona. New York: Crossroad, 1985.

———. *Tales of the Sacred and the Supernatural*. Philadelphia: Westminster Press, 1981.

———. *The Two and the One*. Trans. J. M. Cohen. New York: Harper & Row, 1965.

———. *Two Strange Tales*. Boston: Shambhala Press 1986.

———. *Yoga: Immortality and Freedom*. Trans. Willard R. Trask. New York: Pantheon Books, Bollingen Foundation, 1958.

———. *Youth Without Youth and Other Novellas*. Ed. Matei Calinescu. Trans. Mac Linscott Ricketts. Columbus, OH: Ohio State University Press, 1988.

———. *Zalmoxis, The Vanishing God*. Trans. Willard R. Trask. Chicago: The University of Chicago Press, 1972.

ARTICLES

Eliade, Mircea. "Centre du Monde, Temple, Maison." In *Le Symbolisme Cosmique des Monuments Religieux*. Serie Orientale Roma, 14. Ed. Giuseppe Tucci. Rome, Is.M.E.D., 1957.

———. "Mircea Eliade," an interview with Delia O'Hara. *Chicago* (June 1986), 146–79.

———. "Oddest Graduate School in the United States." *University of Chicago Magazine* 57 (1965), 18–22.

———. "The Sacred in the Secular World." *Cultural Hermeneutics* 1 (1973), 101–13 (title of journal changed to *Philosophy and Social Criticism* in 1978).

Secondary Sources

BOOKS

Alexandrescu, Sorin. "Mircea Eliade: La narrazione contro il significato." In *Mircea Eliade e l'Italia*. Ed. Marin Mincu e Roberto Scagno. Milan: Jaca Book, 1987.

Albanese, Catherine L. *Nature Religion in America: From The Algonkian Indians to the New Age*. Chicago: University of Chicago Press, 1990.

Allen, Douglas. *Structure and Creativity in Religion: Hermeneutics in Mircea Eliade's Phenomenology and New Directions*. The Hague: Mouton Publishers, 1978.

Altizer, Thomas. *Mircea Eliade and the Dialectic of the Sacred*. Philadelphia: Westminster Press, 1963.

Altshuler, David and Linda Altshuler. "Judaism and Art." In *Art, Creativity and the Sacred*. Ed. Diane Apostolos-Cappadona. New York: Crossroad, 1985.

Aristotle, *Ethics, Book 1: Politics, Book 1*. Trans. W. D. Ross. Chicago: Henry Regenery Company, 1954.

Baird, Robert. *Category Formation and the History of Religions*. The Hague: Mouton, 1971.

The Bhagavad Gita. Trans. Juan Mascaro. New York: Penguin Books, 1962.

Balu, Ion. "Les debuts litteraires." In *L'Herne: Mircea Eliade*. Ed. Constantin Tacou. Paris: Editions de L'Herne, 1978.

Bantly, Francisca Cho. ed. *Deconstructing, Reconstructing the Philosophy of Religions*. Chicago: The Divinity School, 1990.

Barrow, John D. and Frank J. Tipler. *The Anthropic Cosmological Principle*. New York: Oxford University Press, 1986.

Bergson, Henri. *The Creative Mind*. Trans. Mabelle L. Andison. New York: The Philosophical Library, 1946.

Bianchi, Ugo. "Current Methodological Issues in the History of Religions." In *The History of Religions: Retrospect and Prospect*. Ed. Joseph M. Kitagawa. New York: Macmillan Publishing, 1985.

Bleeker, C. J. "Some Introductory Remarks on the Significance of Initiation." In *Initiation*. Ed. C. J. Bleeker. Leiden: E.J. Brill, 1965.

Bolle, Kees W. *The Freedom of Man in Myth*. Nashville, TN: Vanderbilt University Press, 1968.

Bottomore, T. B. *Classes in Modern Society*. New York: Vantage Books, 1966.

Browning, Don S. *Religious Thought and the Modern Psychologies*. Philadelphia: Fortress Press, 1987.

Buber, Martin. *I and Thou*. Trans. Ronald Gregor Smith. New York: Charles Scribner's Sons, 1958.

———. *Two Types of Faith*. Trans. Norman P. Goldhawk. New York: Harper & Row, 1961.

Burkhalter, Sheryl. "Summary Report II." In *Deconstructing-Reconstructing the Philosophy of Religions*. Ed. Francisca Cho Bantly. Chicago: The Divinity School, The University of Chicago, 1990.

Bynum, Carolyn Walker. *Holy Feast and Holy Fast*. Los Angeles: University of California Press, 1987.

Calinescu, Matei. *Faces of Modernity: Avant-Garde, Decadence, Kitsch*. Bloomington, IN: Indiana University Press, 1977.

———. "Introduction: The Fantastic and Its Interpretation in Mircea Eliade's Later Novellas." In *Youth Without Youth and Other Novellas*. Ed. Matei Calinescu. Trans. Mac Linscott Ricketts. Columbus, OH: Ohio State University Press, 1988.

———. "The Function of the Unreal: Reflections on Mircea Eliade's Short Fiction." In *Imagination and Meaning: The Scholarly and Literary Worlds of Mircea Eliade*. Ed. Norman J. Girardot and Mac Linscott Ricketts. New York: Seabury Press, 1982.

Caputo, John D. *Radical Hermeneutics*. Bloomington, IN: Indiana University Press, 1987.

Carrasco, David, and Jane Marie Swanberg, ed. *Waiting for the Dawn: Mircea Eliade in Perspective*. Boulder, CO: Westview Press, 1985.

Castaneda, Carlos. *The Teachings of Don Juan: A Yaqui Way of Knowledge*. New York: Simon & Schuster, 1968.

de Certeau, Michel. *The Practice of Everyday Life*. Trans. Steven Rendall. Berkeley: University of California Press, 1984.

Chagnon, Roland. "Religion Cosmique, foi Humaine et Christianisme chez Mircea

Eliade.'' In *Questions Actuelles sur la Foi*. Ed. T. Potuin and J. Richard. Montreal, Canada: Corporation des Editions Fides, 1984.

Cioran, E. M. ''Beginnings of a Friendship.'' In *Myths and Symbols: Studies in Honor of Mircea Eliade*. Ed. Joseph M. Kitagawa and Charles Long. Chicago: The University of Chicago Press, 1969.

Clifford, R. J. *The Cosmic Mountain in Canaan and the Old Testament*. Cambridge, MA: Harvard Semitic Monographs, 4, 1972.

Cobb, John and David Griffin. *Process Theology*. Philadelphia: Westminster Press, 1976.

Codrescu, Andrei. *The Disappearance of the Outside*. Reading, MA: Addison-Wesley Publishing, 1990.

Collins, Steven. *Selfless Persons: Imagery and Thought in Therevada Buddhism*. Cambridge: Cambridge University Press, 1982.

Cox, Harvey. *Many Mansions*. Boston: Beacon Press, 1988.

Csikszentmihalyi, Mihaly. *Beyond Boredom and Anxiety: The Experience of Play in Work and Games*. San Francisco: Jossey-Bass, 1975.

Culianu, Ioan P. *Eros and Magic in the Renaissance*. Trans. Margaret Cook. Chicago: University of Chicago Press, 1987.

————. *Mircea Eliade*. Assisi, Italia: Cittadella Editrice, 1977.

Descartes, René. *Essential Works of Descartes*. Trans. Lowell Bair. New York: Bantam Books, 1961.

Doty, William G. *Mythography*. University, AL: The University of Alabama Press, 1986.

Dudley, Guilford, III. *Religion on Trial: Mircea Eliade and His Critics*. Philadelphia: Temple University Press, 1977.

Dulles, Avery. *Models of Revelation*. Garden City, New York: Doubleday & Co., 1983.

Eilberg-Schwartz, Howard. *The Savage in Judaism: An Anthropology of Israelite Religion and Ancient Judaism*. Bloomington, IN: Indiana University Press, 1990.

Falaturi, Abdoldjavad. ''Experience of Time and History in Islam.'' In *We Believe in One God, The Experience of God in Christianity and Islam*. Eds. Annemarie Schimmel and Absoldjavad Falaturi. New York: A Crossroad Book, 1979.

Faruqi, Al Lois Ibsen. ''An Islamic Perspective on Symbolism in the Arts: New Thoughts on Figural Representation.'' In *Art, Creativity and the Sacred*. Ed. Diane Apostolos-Cappadona. New York: Crossroad, 1985.

Fingarette, Herbert. *Confucius—The Secular as Sacred*. New York: Harper Torchbooks, 1972.

Foucault, Michel. *The Order of Things*. New York: Vintage Books, 1970.

Fowler, James. *Stages of Faith*. San Francisco: Harper & Row, 1981.

Francoeur, Robert T. ''The Cosmic Piety of Teilhard de Chardin: A Study of the Divine Epiphany.'' In *Cosmic Piety: Modern Man and the Meaning of the Universe*. New York: P.J. Kennedy and Sons, 1965.

Frazier, Ian. *Great Plains*. New York: Farrar/Straus/Giroux, 1989.

Freud, Sigmund. *Collected Papers, Vol. IV*. London: The Hogarth Press, 1949.

————. *Civilization and Its Discontents*. Trans. Joan Riviere. Garden City, New York: Doubleday & Co., 1961.

Geertz, Clifford. *The Interpretation of Cultures*. New York: Basic Books, 1973.

Gleick, James. *Chaos: Making a New Science*. New York: Viking-Penguin Books, 1987.

Goethe, Johann Wolfgang von. *Italian Journey, 1786–1788*. Trans. W. H. Auden and Elizabeth Mayer. San Francisco: North Point Press, 1982.

————. *The Autobiography of Goethe. Truth and Poetry: From My Life*. Ed. Park Godwin. New York: Wiley and Putnam, 1846.

Greeley, Andrew M. *Unsecular Man: The Persistence of Religion*. New York: Schocken Books, 1985.

Grudin, Robert. *The Grace of Great Things: Creativity and Innovation*. New York: Ticknor & Fields, 1990.

Hall, David L. and Roger T. Ames. *Thinking Through Confucius*. Albany, New York: State University Press, 1987.

Hartshorne, Charles. "God and the Meaning of Life." In *On Nature*. Ed. Leroy S. Rouner. Notre Dame, IN: Notre Dame University Press, 1984.

Harvey, Van A. *A Handbook of Theological Terms*. New York: Macmillan Publishing, 1964.

Hauser, Arnold. *The Sociology of Art*. Trans. Kenneth J. Worthcott. Chicago: University of Chicago Press, 1982.

Hawking, Stephen. *A Brief History of Time*. New York: Bantam Books, 1988.

Heidegger, Martin. *Being and Time*. Trans. John Macquarrie and Edward Robinson. New York: Harper & Row, 1962.

Honko, Lauri, ed. *Science of Religion, Studies in Methodology*. The Hague: Mouton Publishers, 1979.

Ierunca, Virgil. "Littérature et fantastique." In *L'Herne: Mircea Eliade*. Ed. Constantin Tacou. Paris: Editions de L'Herne, 1978.

Ioanid, Radu. *The Sword of the Archangel: Fascist Ideology in Romania*. Trans. Peter Heinegg. New York: East European Monographs, Boulder. Distributed by Columbia University Press, 1990.

Jackson, Carl T. *The Oriental Religions and American Thought*. Westport, CT: Greenwood Press, 1981.

Jensen, Adolf E. *Myth and Cult Among Primitive Peoples*. Trans. Marianna Tax Choldin and Wolfgang Weissleder. Chicago: The University of Chicago Press, 1951.

Jung, C. G. *Critique of Psychoanalysis*. Trans. R. F. C. Hull. Princeton, NJ: Princeton University Press, Bollingen Series, 1975.

Kant, Immanuel. *The Philosophy of Kant*. Ed. Carl J. Friedrich. New York: Random House, 1977.

Kaufmann, Walter. *Discovering the Mind: Goethe, Kant, and Hegel*. New York: McGraw-Hill, 1980.

Kermode, Frank. *The Sense of an Ending*. New York: Oxford University Press, 1967.

King, Ursula. "Historical and Phenomenological Approaches." In *Contemporary Approaches to the Study of Religion*. Vol. 1. Ed. Frank Whaling. New York: Mouton Publishers, 1983.

Kitagawa, Joseph M., and Gregory Alles. "Afterword: The Dialectic of the Parts and the Whole. Reflections on the Past, Present, and Future of the History of Religions." In *The History of Religions: Retrospect and Prospect*. New York: Macmillan Publishing, 1985.

———. "The History of Religions in America." In *The History of Religions: Essays in Methodology*. Ed. Joseph M. Kitagawa and Mircea Eliade. Chicago: The University of Chicago Press, 1959.

———. "The History of Religions *(Religionswissenschaft)* Then and Now." In *The History of Religions: Retrospect and Prospect*. Ed. Joseph M. Kitagawa. New York: Macmillan Publishing, 1985.

———. *The History of Religions: Understanding Human Experience*. Atlanta, GA: Scholars Press, 1987.

———. *The Quest for Human Unity: A Religious History*. Minneapolis, MN: Fortress Press, 1990.

———, and Charles Long, ed. *Myth and Symbols: Studies in Honor of Mircea Eliade*. Chicago: University of Chicago Press, 1969.

Kolakowski, Leszek. *Modernity on Endless Trial*. Chicago: University of Chicago Press, 1990.

Kurzweil, Edith. *The Age of Structuralism: Lévi-Strauss to Foucault*. New York: Columbia University Press, 1980.

Leeuw, G. Van der. *Religion in Essence and Manifestation*. Vols. 1 & 2. Trans. J. E. Turner. New York: Harper & Row, 1963.

Lenski, Gerhard E. *Power and Privilege: A Theory of Social Stratification*. Chapel Hill, NC: The University of North Carolina Press, 1984.

Lessa, William A., and Evon Z. Vogt. *Reader in Comparative Religion: An Anthropological Approach,* 4th ed. New York: Harper & Row, 1979.

Levenson, Jon D. *Creation and the Persistence of Evil*. San Francisco: Harper & Row, 1988.

———. *Sinai and Zion*. San Francisco: Harper & Row, 1985.

Lévi-Strauss, Claude. *The Jealous Potter*. Trans. Benedicte Chorier. Chicago: The University of Chicago Press, 1988.

———. *Tristes Tropiques*. Trans. John and Doreen Weightman. London: Jonathan Cape Ltd., 1973.

Lincoln, Bruce. *Discourse and the Construction of Society*. New York: Oxford University Press, 1989.

———. *Myth, Cosmos, and Society*. Cambridge, MA: Harvard University Press, 1986.

Long, Charles H. "A Look at the Chicago Tradition in the History of Religions: Retrospect and Future." In *The History of Religions: Retrospect and Prospect*. Ed. Joseph M. Kitagawa. New York: Macmillan Publishing, 1985.

———. "Archaism and Hermeneutics." In *The History of Religions: Essays on the*

Problem of Understanding. Ed. Joseph M. Kitagawa, Chicago: The University of Chicago Press, 1967.

———. *Criterion: Newsletter of the University of Chicago* (Fall 1986).

———. "Religions, Worlds, and Order: The Search for Utopian Unities." In *Pushing the Faith: Proselytism and Civility in a Pluralistic World*. Ed. Martin E. Marty and Frederick E. Greenspahn. New York: Crossroad, 1988.

———. "The Significance for Modern Man of Mircea Eliade's Work." In *Cosmic Piety, Modern Man and the Meaning of the Universe*. New York: P.J. Kennedy and Sons, 1965.

———. *Significations*. Philadelphia: Fortress Press, 1986.

Lovin, Robin W., and Frank E. Reynolds. "In the Beginning." In *Cosmogony and Ethical Order*. Ed. Robin W. Lovin and Frank E. Reynolds. Chicago: University of Chicago Press, 1985.

Malinowski, Bronislaw. *A Scientific Theory of Culture and Other Essays*. Chapel Hill, NC: The University of North Carolina Press, 1944.

Marcus, George E., and Michael M. J. Fischer. *Anthropology as Cultural Critique: An Experimental Moment in the Human Sciences*. Chicago: The University of Chicago Press, 1986.

Marino, Adrian. *L'Hermeneutique de Mircea Eliade*. Trans. Jean Gouillard. Paris: Gallimard, 1981.

———. "Mircea Eliade's Hermeneutics." In *Imagination and Meaning: The Scholarly Worlds of Mircea Eliade*. Ed. Norman J. Girardot and Mac Linscott Ricketts. New York: Seabury Press, 1982.

Merton, Thomas. *Conjectures of a Guilty Bystander*. Garden City, New York: Doubleday & Co., 1966.

Mooney, James. *The Ghost Dance Religion and the Sioux Outbreak of 1980*. 1896. Rpt. Chicago: The University of Chicago Press, 1965.

Morris, Brian. *Anthropological Studies of Religion*. New York: Cambridge University Press, 1987.

Narayan, R. K. *The Guide*. London and Harmondsworth: Penguin Books, 1958.

Niebuhr, Reinhold. *Moral Man and Immoral Society*. New York: Charles Scribner's Sons, 1960.

———. *The Nature and Destiny of Man*. New York: Charles Scribner's Sons, 1964.

Niebuhr, H. Richard. *Christ and Culture*. New York: Harper & Row, 1951.

O'Flaherty, Wendy Doniger. *Other Peoples' Myths*. New York: Macmillan Publishing, 1988.

Ong, Walter J. *Interfaces of the Word*. Ithaca, New York: Cornell University Press, 1977.

Ortega y Gasset, José. *The Revolt of the Masses*. New York: Mentor Books, W.W. Norton & Company Inc., 1932.

Ortiz, Alfonso. *The Tewa World: Space, Time, and Becoming in a Pueblo Society*. Chicago: University of Chicago Press, 1969.

Otto, Rudolf. *The Idea of the Holy*. Trans. John W. Harvey. New York: Oxford University Press, 1958.

Oxtoby, Willard Gurdon. "Religionswissenschaft Revisited." In *Religions in Antiquity*. Ed. Jacob Neusner. Leiden: E.J. Brill, 1968.

Pagels, Elaine. *Adam, Eve, and the Serpent*. New York: Random House, 1988.

Panikkar, Raimundo. "Religious Pluralism: The Metaphysical Challenge." In *Religious Pluralism*. Ed. Leroy S. Rouner. Notre Dame, IN: University of Notre Dame Press, 1984.

Penner, Hans. H. "Myth and Ritual: A Wasteland or a Forest of Symbols?" In *On Method in the History of Religions*. Ed. James S. Helfer. Middletown, CT: Wesleyan University Press, 1968.

Pettazzoni, Raffaele. *Essays on the History of Religions*. Trans. H. J. Rose. Leiden: E.J. Brill, 1954.

Petterson, Olof, and Hans Akerberg. *Interpreting Religious Phenomena: Studies with Reference to the Phenomenology of Religion*. Stockholm, Sweden: Almquist and Wiksell International, 1981.

Plato, *The Republic of Plato*. Trans. Francis MacDonald Cornford. New York: Oxford University Press, 1965.

Preus, J. Samuel. *Explaining Religion*. New Haven, CT: Yale University Press, 1987.

Proudfoot, Wayne. *Religious Experience*. Los Angeles: University of California Press, 1985.

Reuther, Rosemary Radford. *New Women/New Earth*. New York: Seabury Press, 1975.

Richards, Audrey. "The Concept of Culture in Malinowski's Work." In *Man and Culture*. Ed. Raymond Firth London: Routledge and Kegan Paul, 1957.

Ricketts, Mac Linscott. *Mircea Eliade: The Romanian Roots, 1907–1945*. New York: Columbia University Press, East European Monographs, Boulder, CO, 1988.

Ricoeur, Paul. *Hermeneutics and the Human Sciences*. Trans. John B. Thompson. Cambridge: Cambridge University Press, 1981.

———. "The History of Religions and the Phenomenology of Time Consciousness." In *The History of Religions: Retrospect and Prospect*. Ed. Joseph M. Kitagawa. New York: Macmillan Publishing, 1985.

Ries, Julien. "Histoire des religions, phenomenologie et hermeneutique." In *L'Herne: Mircea Eliade*. Ed. Constantin Tacou. Paris: Editions de L'Herne, 1978.

———. et al., eds. *L'Expression du Sacre dans Les Grandes Religions*, Vol. 3. Louvain-La-Neuve: Centre D'Histoire des Religions, 1986.

Rogers, Jack B., and Forrest Baird, eds. *Introduction to Philosophy: A Case Study Approach*. San Francisco: Harper & Row, 1981.

Rucker, Rudy. *The Fourth Dimension: A Guided Tour of the Higher Universes*. Boston: Houghton Mifflin Co., 1984.

Sarton, George. *The History of Science and The New Humanism*. New York: George Braziller, 1956.

Sasaki, Ruth Fuller. "Zen: A Method for Religious Awakening." In *The World of Zen*. Ed. Nancy Wilson Ross. New York: Vintage Books, 1960.

Schmitt, Richard. *Martin Heidegger on Being Human*. New York: Random House, 1969.

Seung, T. K. *Structuralism and Hermeneutics*. New York: Columbia University Press, 1982.

Sharpe, Eric J. *Comparative Religion, A History*. 2d ed. La Salle, IL: Open Court, 1986.

Smart, Ninian. "The History of Religions and Its Conversation Partners." In *The History of Religions: Retrospect and Prospect*. Ed. Joseph M. Kitagawa. New York: Macmillan Publishing, 1985.

Smith, Jonathan Z. *Drudgery Divine: On the Comparison of Early Christianities and the Religions of Late Antiquity*. Chicago: University of Chicago Press, 1990.

———. *Imagining Religion*. Chicago: University of Chicago, 1978.

———. *Map Is Not Territory*. Leiden: E.J. Brill, 1978.

———. *To Take Place*. Chicago: University of Chicago Press, 1987.

Sopher, David. "The Landscape of Home: Myth, Experience, Social Meaning." In *The Interpretation of Ordinary Landscapes*. Ed. D. W. Meinig. New York: Oxford University Press, 1979.

Spiro, Melford. "Religion: Problems of Definition and Explanation." In *Anthropological Approaches to the Study of Religion*. London: Tavistock Publications Ltd., 1966.

Stanner, W. E. H. "The Dreaming." In *Reader in Comparative Religion: An Anthropological Approach*, 2d. Eds. Wm. A. Lessa and Evon Z. Vogt. New York: Harper & Row, 1965.

Steiner, Rudolf. *Goethe the Scientist*. Trans. Olin D. Wannamaker. New York: Anthroposophic Press, 1950.

Storr, Anthony, ed. *The Essential Jung*. Princeton, NJ: Princeton University Press, 1983.

Strehlow, T. G. H. *Aranda Traditions*. Melbourne: Melbourne University Press, 1947.

Strenski, Ivan. *Four Theories of Myth in the Twentieth Century*. Iowa City, IA: University of Iowa Press, 1987.

———. "Mircea Eliade, Some Theoretical Problems." In *The Theory of Myth: Six Studies*. Ed. Adrian Cunningham. London: Sheed & Ward, 1973.

Sullivan, Lawrence E. *Icanchu's Drum*. New York: Macmillan Publishing, 1988.

———. "Lévi-Strauss, Mythologic, and South American Religion." In *Anthropology and the Study of Religion*. Ed. Robert L. Moore and Frank E. Reynolds Chicago: Center for the Scientific Study of Religion, 1984.

Swidler, Leonard, ed. *Toward a Universal Theology of Religion*. Maryknoll, New York: Orbis Books, 1988.

Teilhard de Chardin, Pierre. *The Divine Milieu*. New York: Harper & Row, 1960.

Tillich, Paul. "The Significance of the History of Religions for the Systematic Theologian." In *The History of Religions: Essays on the Problem of Understanding*. Ed. Joseph M. Kitagawa. Chicago: The University of Chicago Press, 1967.

Todorov, Tzvetan. *The Conquest of America: The Question of the Other*. Trans. Richard Howard. New York: harper & Row.

———. *The Fantastic: A Structural Approach to a Literary Genre*. Trans. Richard Howard. Ithaca, New York: Cornell University Press, 1973.

Toulmin, Stephen. *The Return to Cosmology*. Los Angeles: University of California Press, 1982.

Tracy, David. "Is a Hermeneutics of Religion Possible?" In *Religious Pluralism*. Ed. Leroy S. Rouner. Notre Dame, IN: University of Notre Dame Press, 1984.

Tylor, E. B. *The Origins of Culture*. New York: Harper and Brothers, 1958.

Underhill, Evelyn. *The Essentials of Mysticism*. New York: E.P. Dutton, 1920.

Updike, John. *A Month of Sundays*. New York: Alfred H. Knopf, 1975.

Vries, Jan de. *The Study of Religion: A Historical Approach*. Trans. Kees W. Bolle. New York: Harcourt, Brace & World, 1967.

Wach, Joachim. *The Comparative Study of Religions*. Ed. Joseph M. Kitagawa, New York Columbia University Press, 1958.

———. *Introduction to the History of Religions*. Ed. Joseph M. Kitagawa and Gregory D. Alles. New York: Macmillan Publishing, 1988.

———. *Types of Religious Experience*. Chicago: The University of Chicago Press, 1951.

Wei-Ming, Tu. *Confucian Thought: Selfhood as Creative Transformation*. Albany, New York: State University of New York Press, 1985.

Westphal, Merold. *God, Guilt, and Death*. Bloomington, IN: Indiana University Press, 1984.

Whaling, Frank. Ed. *Contemporary Approaches to the Study of Religion*. Vol. 2. New York: Mouton Publishers, 1985.

Wolterstorff, Nicholas. "Art, Religion, and the Elite: Reflections on a Passage from André Malraux." In *Art, Creativity and the Sacred*. Ed. Diane Apostolos-Cappadona. New York: Crossroad, 1985.

Zukav, Gary. *The Dancing Wu Li Masters: An Overview of the New Physics*. New York: William Morrow, 1979.

ARTICLES

Al-George, Sergiu. "India in the Cultural Destiny of Mircea Eliade." *The Mankind Quarterly* 25, 1/2 (1984), 115–35.

Allen, Douglas, "Eliade and History." *Journal of Religion* 68 (October 1988), 545–65.

Alles, Gregory. "Surface, Space, and Intention: The Parthenon and the Kandariya Mahadeva." *The History of Religions* 28, 1 (August 1988), 1–37.

———."Wach, Eliade, and the Critique From Totality." *Numen* 35,1 (1988), 108–38.

Aronowicz, Annette. "Musings on Teaching *The Sacred and the Profane*: The Dilemma of the Introductory Course." *Epoche: UCLA Journal for the History of Religions* 15 (1987), 78–91.

Baumann, Gerd. "Anthropologists and Psychology." *Current Anthropology* 30,1 (February 1989), 115–17.

Berger, Adriana. "Cultural Hermeneutics: The Concept of Imagination in the Phenomenological Approaches of Henry Corbin and Mircea Eliade.'' *The Journal of Religion* 2 (April 1986), 141–56.

———. ''Fascism and Religion in Romania,'' *Annals of Scholarship* 6,4 (1989), 455–65.

Brown, Robert F. ''Eliade on Archaic Religion: Some Old and New Criticism.'' *Studies in Religion* 10,4 (Fall, 1981), 429–49.

Calinescu, Matei. ''Between History and Paradise: Initiation Trials.'' *The Journal of Religion* 59,2 (April 1979), 218–23.

———. ''Creation as Duty.'' *The Journal of Religion* 65,2 (April 1985), 250–57.

———. ''Imagination and Meaning: Aesthetic Attitudes and Ideas in Mircea Eliade's Thought.'' *The Journal of Religion* 57,1 (January 1977), 1–15.

———. ''Mircea Eliade's Journals.'' *The Denver Quarterly* 12,1 (1977), 313–15.

Campbell, Joseph. ''Interview with Joseph Campbell.'' *New York Times Book Review* (December 18, 1983), 25.

Carrasco, Davíd. ''Review of *The Conquest of America: The Question of the Other,* by Tzvetan Todorov.'' *The History of Religions* 28,2 (November 1988), 151–60.

Christ, Carol P. ''Mircea Eliade and the Feminist Paradigm Shift: Toward a Feminist Critical Approach to the History of Religion.'' A Paper Presented at the Annual American Academy of Religion. Chicago, Illinois, 1988.

Culianu, Ioan P. ''Mircea Eliade at the Crossroad of Anthropology.'' *Neue Zeitshrift für Systematische Theologie* 27,2 (1985), 123–31.

Dudley, Guilford, III. ''Mircea Eliade as the 'Anti-Historian' of Religions.'' *Journal of the American Academy of Religion* 44,2 (1976), 345–59.

Frazier, Ian. ''A Reporter at Large (The Great Plains—Part III).'' *The New Yorker* (March 6, 1989), 41–68.

Frye, Northrop. ''World Enough Without Time.'' *The Hudson Review* 12 (1959), 423–31.

Gilhus, Inguild Saelid. ''The Tree of Life and the Tree of Death: A Study of Gnostic Symbols.'' *Religion* 17 (1987), 348–49.

Jonsson, John N. ''Retranspositionalization: Missiological Hermeneutics Within the Socio-Human Context.'' *Review and Expositor* 84,1 (Winter 1987), 99–117.

Kim, J. J. ''Hierophany and History.'' *Journal of the American Academy of Religion* 40,3 (1972), 334–48.

Long, Jerome. ''A Letter to Kees W. Bolle.'' *Epoche: UCLA Journal for the History of Religions* 15 (1987), 92–95.

Manea, Norman. ''Happy Guilt: Mircea Eliade, fascism, and the unhappy fate of Romania.'' *The New Republic* (August 5, 1991), 27–36.

Malandra, W. W. ''The Concept of Movement in History of Religions.'' *Numen* 14 (1967), 23–69.

Nemoianu, Virgil. ''Wrestling with Time: Some Tendencies in Nabokov's and Eliade's Later Works.'' *Southeastern Europe* 7,1 (1980), 74–90.

O'Flaherty, Wendy Doniger. "Review of *Historical Atlas of World Mythology* by Joseph Campbell." *The New York Times Book Review* (December 18, 1983), 3–25.

Progroff, Ira. "Culture and Being: Mircea Eliade's Studies in Religion." *International Journal of Parapsychology* 2,3 (1960), 47–60.

Raskind, Lisa Bonoff. "A Thirst for Transcendence: Reflections upon the Influence of Mircea Eliade by the Second Generation." *Epoche: UCLA Journal for the History of Religions* 15 (1987), 6–19.

Rasmussen, David. "Mircea Eliade: Structural Hermeneutics and Philosophy." *Philosophy Today* 12 (1968), 138–46.

Reno, Stephen J. "Eliade's Progressional View of *Hierophanies*." *Religious Studies* 8 (1972), 153–60.

Ricketts, Mac Linscott. "In Defense of Eliade: Bridging the Gap Between Anthropology and the History of Religions." *Religion* 1,3 (Spring 1973), 13–34.

———. "Mircea Eliade and the Death of God." *Religion in Life* (Spring 1967), 40–52.

———. "Mircea Eliade and the Writing of *Noaptea de Sânziene*," *Journal of American Romanian Christian Literary Studies 1* (Spring 1980), 45–56.

———. "The Nature and Extent of Eliade's 'Jungianism'." *Union Seminary Quarterly Review* 25,2 (Winter 1970), 211–34.

Rorty, Richard. "Taking Philosophy Seriously. Review of *Heidegger et le Nazisme*, by Victor Farrias." *The New Republic* (April 11, 1988), 29–34.

Saiving, Valerie. "Androcentrism in Religious Studies." *Journal of Religion* 56 (1976), 177–97.

Segal, Robert A. "Robert Segal's Reply." *Religious Traditions: A Journal in the Study of Religion* 11 (1988), 13–20.

Smart, Ninian. "Beyond Eliade: The Future of Theory in Religion." *Numen* 25 (1978), 171–83.

Smith, Brian K. "Exorcising the Transcendent: Strategies for Defining Hinduism and Religion." *History of Religions* 27,1 (August 1987), 32–55.

Streng, Frederick J. "Three Approaches to Authentic Existence: Christian, Confucian, Buddhist." *Philosophy East and West* 32,2 (1982), 371–90.

Strenski, Ivan. "Love and Anarchy in Romania: A Critical Review of Mircea Eliade's Autobiography, Volume One, 1907–1937." *Religion* 12 (1982), 391–403.

Webster, Alexander F. C. "Orthodox Mystical Tradition and the Comparative Study of Religion: An Experimental Synthesis." *Journal of Ecumenical Studies* 23 (Fall 1986), 621–49.

Werblowsky, R. J. Zwi, "Review of *The History of Religious Ideas: From the Stone Age to the Eleusinian Mysteries,* by Mircea Eliade." *The History of Religions* 23 (November 1983), 181–86.

Yandell, Keith E. "Can There Be a Science of Religion?" *Christian Scholars Review* 15,1 (1986), 28–41.

Reference Articles

Allen, Douglas. "Phenomenology of Religion." *The Encyclopedia of Religion*. Vol. 11. Ed. Mircea Eliade, et al., New York: Macmillan Publishing, 1986, pp. 272–287.

Alles, Gregory. "Homo Religiosus." *The Encyclopedia of Religion*. Vol. 6. Ed. Mircea Eliade, et al., New York: Macmillan Publishing, 1986, pp. 422–445.

Armillas, Pedro. "Urban Revolution: The Concept of Civilization." *International Encyclopedia of the Social Sciences,* 16:218. David L. Sills, Ed. New York: Crowell Collier and Macmillan, Inc., 1968.

Bianchi, Ugo. "The History of Religions." *The Encyclopedia of Religion,* Vol. 6. Ed. Mircea Eliade, et al., New York: Macmillan Publishing, 1986, pp. 399–408.

Eliade, Mircea and Lawrence Sullivan. "The Centre of the World." *The Encyclopedia of Religion*. Vol. 3. Ed. Mircea Eliade, et al. New York: Macmillan Publishing, 1986, pp. 166–171.

Greene, Marjorie. "Martin Heidegger." *The Encyclopedia of Philosophy,* Vol. 3. Paul Edwards, Ed. in Chief. New York: Macmillan Publishing, 1967.

Heisig, James W. "Symbolism." *The Encyclopedia of Religion*. Vol. 14. Ed. Mircea Eliade, et al. New York: Macmillan Publishing, 1986, pp. 198–208.

Henninger, Joseph. "New Year Festivals." *The Encyclopedia of Religion*. Vol. 6. Mircea Eliade, et al. New York: Ed. Macmillan Publishing, 1986.

Singer, Milton. "Culture: The Concept of Culture." *Encyclopedia of Social Sciences,* 3:527. New York: Macmillan Co, 1930–35.

INDEX

Adam, 49
"Against Moldavia" (Eliade), 108
Agriculture, as symbol, 49–50
Al-George, Sergiu, 104–5
Albanese, Catherine, 53
Alchemy, 112, 171
Alexandrescu, Sorin, 177–78
Allah, 61 n.57
Allen, Douglas, 59 n.29, 80
Alles, Gregory, 31 n.55; on Eliade's symbol of the center, 142, 149–51, 153
Altizer, Thomas J. J., 58 n.11
Ames, Roger, 180, 187, 189 n.21
Anamnesis, 65, 81, 82, 84, 86
Anatta, Buddhist principle of "no self," 126, 182, 190 n.39
Anthropic cosmological principle, 191 n.54
Antonescu, Ion, Romanian leader, 158 n.27
Aori, mythical New Guinean hero, 51
Aranda (Australian aborigines), and meaning of term "home," 166 n.145, and symbol of center among, 147. *See also* Tjilpa
Archetypes, 55, 85; in individual and cultural history, 88–90
Aristotle, 42
Arunta (Australian aborigines), and sacred pole of, 117. *See also* Aranda; Tjilpa
Asvattha tree, Indian, 38
Atman, Hindu soul, 126
Auerbach, Eric, 15
Augustine, 124–25
Authenticity, existential concept of, 105–8, 109–10, 117; defined, 104–5
Aztecs, worldview of, 173–74

Baal cult, 38, 39, 167 n.167
Babylonians, 91
Balzac, Honoré de, 7, 87
Baptism, 179
Being, nature of, 74
Berger, Adriana, 18; on Eliade's political life, 13 n.5
Bergson, Henri, 162 n.82
Bhagavad Gita, 108

Bhakti, 108
Bianchi, Ugo, 153
Blaga, Lucian, 163 n.94; on culture and civilization, 131
Bleeker, C. J., 182
Boeckh, August, 16
Bohm, David, 151
Bolle, Kees, 73
"Botanical Knowledge and Ancient India" (Eliade), 9, 185
Brahman, Hindu cosmic spirit, 46
Brancusi, Constantin, 48; and the new humanism, 137
Brauer, Jerald, 30 n.44
Buber, Martin, 52, 99 n.75
Buddhism, 40, 53, 75, 80, 108, 109, 115, 117, 126, 151, 160 n.51, 183, 195
Buonaiuti, Ernesto, as historian who knew mystical experience, 8, 157 n.9
Bynum, Carolyn Walker, 180

Calinescu, Matei, 66, 76–77, 95 nn.15, 21; on Eliade's metaphysics, 18, 30 n.42
Campa (Peruvian Indian tribe), 47
Campbell, Joseph, 69
Capps, Walter, 22
Caputo, John, 160 n.52
Carol, King, Romanian monarch, 10, 11, 133, 138, 158 n.27
Carrasco, David, 173–74
Casas, Bartolomé de las, 174
Cassierer, popularity of, 114
Castaneda, Carlos, 147
Center, symbol of, 33, 50–51, 140–41, 154; definition of, 149; as disjunction, 156; and evil, 156; as many centers, 150–51; in modern consciousness, 116–17; in Near Eastern cosmologies, 142–43, 146, 147–49; and the periphery, 153, 154–56
Certeau, Michel de, 74, 164 n.117
Chagall, Marc, 137
Chagnon, Roland, 53
Changing Woman, Apache spirit, 179
Chaos, order in, 151, 167 n.166